CYCLES

THE SCIENCE OF PREDICTION

CYCLES

THE SCIENCE OF PREDICTION

by EDWARD R. DEWEY

Director, Foundation for the Study of Cycles

and EDWIN F. DAKIN

Associate, Foundation for the Study of Cycles

HENRY HOLT AND COMPANY · NEW YORK

Contents

Charts and Diagrams   vii

Concerning Economic Prediction   An Introduction   xi

I   Why Trends Are Important   1

II   Patterns in Growth of Organisms   10

III   The Growth Trend in Our Basic Industries   22

IV   Trends in Some Other Industries   42

V   Some Rhythmic Cycles in Natural Phenomena   51

VI   The 54-Year Rhythm   69

VII   The 9-Year Rhythm   87

VIII   The 3½-Year Rhythm   102

IX   The 18-Year Rhythm   115

X   Causes, Correlations, Conjectures   135

XI   Analysis and Synthesis   160

XII   Timing a Business   172

XIII   Avoiding Some Economic Illusions   191

XIV   War and Its Dislocations   200

XV   Postwar Trends   215

XVI   Postwar Rhythms   226

APPENDIX I   239

APPENDIX II   246

APPENDIX III   251

Charts and Diagrams

CHAPTER I

FIG.   PAGE

1. *Trend of a Hypothetical Business Organization*   3
2. *The Trend and the Cycle*   6
3. *Growth of Industrial Production in the United States*   7
4. *Index of Spanish Trade*   9

CHAPTER II

1. *Growth in Body Weight of a Male White Rat*   11
2. *Growth in Weight of a Pumpkin*   12
3. *Growth of a Population of Yeast Cells*   13
4. *Growth of a Population of Fruit Flies*   13
5. *Growth of the Population of Sweden*   14
6. *Growth of the Population of the United States*   15
7. *Growth of the Population of France*   16
8. *Growth of the Indigenous Native Population of Algeria*   17
9. *Growth of the Population of Germany*   18

CHAPTER III

1. *Population of Continental U. S., 1830–1940*   24
2. *U. S. Manufactures, 1830–1945*   25
3. *U. S. Merchandise Exports, 1830–1945*   26
4. *U. S. Merchandise Imports, 1830–1945*   27
5. *U. S. Iron and Steel Production*   29
6. *Steam Railways*   31
7. *U. S. Shipbuilding, 1830–1945*   32
8. *U. S. Automobile Production, 1900–1944*   33
9. *Value of U. S. Horse-Drawn Vehicle Production, 1839–1939*   34
10. *Cattle on U. S. Farms, January 1840–1944*   36
11. *U. S. Corn Production, 1839–1945*   36
12. *U. S. Cotton Production, 1830–1945*   37
13. *U. S. Wool Production, 1840–1943*   37
14. *U. S. Wheat Production, 1839–1945*   38
15. *Malt Liquor in the United States*   38

FIG.   PAGE

16. *U. S. Lumber Production, 1839–1945*   39
17. *U. S. Cotton Spindles in Operation, 1839–1945*   39
18. *U. S. Coal Production, 1840–1943*   40
19. *U. S. Smelter Copper Production, 1850–1943*   40
20. *U. S. Refined Primary Lead Production, 1830–1943*   41

CHAPTER IV

1. *U. S. Rayon Yarn Consumption, 1911–1945*   43
2. *U. S. Aircraft Production, 1914–1944*   44
3. *U. S. Electric Energy Production, 1907–1945*   45
4. *Value of U. S. Natural Gas Production, 1882–1943*   45
5. *U. S. Petroleum Production, 1859–1945*   46
6. *U. S. Paper and Wood Pulp Production, 1839–1944*   47
7. *U. S. Tobacco Production, 1839–1945*   48
8. *Trends of Various U. S. Industries*   49

CHAPTER V

1. *Abundance of Atlantic Salmon*   53
2. *Abundance of Lynx*   54
3. *Abundance of Tent Caterpillars*   55
4. *Ozone at London (Kew) and Paris*   56
5. *The 9⅔-Year Rhythm in Insects, Fish, Mammals, Man, and Ozone*   57
6. *Abundance of Mice*   58
7. *Voles and Foxes*   58
8. *Solar and Terrestrial Data*   59
9. *Variation in Human Emotion*   61
10. *Deaths from Pneumonia*   62
11. *Deaths from Influenza*   62
12. *Tree Growth*   63
13. *Flower Growth*   63
14. *Abundance of Sunspots*   64
15. *Variation in Terrestrial Magnetism*   64
16. *Synthesis of Two Cycles*   65
17. *Synthesis of Two Cycles*   65
18. *Synthesis of Four Cycles*   66

CHAPTER VI

1. *U. S. Average Wholesale Prices*   70
2. *U. S. Average Wholesale Prices, Excepting War Peaks*   71
3. *680 Years of Wheat Prices in England*   72
4. *The 54-Year Rhythm in Wheat Prices in England*   72
5. *Long Waves in World Wholesale Prices*   76

CHARTS AND DIAGRAMS

FIG.   PAGE

6. *World Interrelationships: Prices and Exports*   77
7. *Long Waves in Wages*   80
8. *Quotations of Interest-Bearing Securities*   80
9. *The Long Wave in Coal*   81
10. *Pig Iron and Lead Production in England*   81
11. *Long Waves in Prices*   82

CHAPTER VII

1. *The 9-Year Rhythm in Prices*   89
2. *U. S. Common Stock Prices*   90
3. *The 9-Year Rhythm in Common Stock Prices*   91
4. *U. S. Wholesale Prices, 1830–1945*   93
5. *The 9-Year Rhythm in Wholesale Prices*   93
6. *An Individual Business*   94
7. *Recapitulation, the 9-Year Rhythm*   95
8. *Synthesis*   96
9. *U. S. Wholesale Prices*   97
10. *Gold Prices and Currency*   98

CHAPTER VIII

1. *The 3½-Year Rhythm in Industrial Production*   104–105
2. *Rate of Change in Industrial Production*   104–105
3. *The 3½-Year Rhythm in Pig Iron Production*   106–107
4. *Rate of Change in Pig Iron Production*   106–107
5. *The 3½-Year Rhythm in Common Stock Prices*   110–111
6. *Rate of Change in Common Stock Prices*   110–111

CHAPTER IX

1. *The 18⅓-Year Rhythm in Real Estate Activity*   116–117
2. *The 18⅓-Year Rhythm in Building Activity*   118–119
3. *The 18⅓-Year Rhythm in Marriages*   120
4. *The 18⅓-Year Rhythm in Wheat Acreage*   120
5. *Brick Production*   121
6. *Building Construction in Hamburg*   122
7. *New York Skyscrapers*   123
8. *Chicago Skyscrapers*   123
9. *Pig Iron*   129
10. *The 18⅓-Year Rhythm in Loans and Discounts*   130
11. *The 18⅓-Year Rhythm in Railroad Stock Prices*   131
12. *The 18⅓-Year Rhythm in Common Stock Prices*   132
13. *The 18⅓-Year Rhythm in Common Stock Prices*   133
14. *The 18⅓-Year Rhythm in the Sales of an Industrial Company*   133

[viii]

CHARTS AND DIAGRAMS

CHAPTER X

FIG.   PAGE

1. *Residential Building* — 136
2. *Textiles* — 136
3. *Sugar Prices* — 137
4. *Cattle Prices* — 137
5. *Pepper Prices* — 138
6. *Sales of an Industrial Company* — 138–139
7. *Sunspots and Production* — 142
8. *Solar Phenomena and Business Activity* — 143
9. *Solar Radiation and Stock Prices* — 144
10. *Sunspots and Stock Prices* — 145
11. *Wave Spectrum* — 150–151
12. *Sunspot Cycles* — 153
13. *Skeletonized Representation of the 18⅓-Year Rhythm in Sunspot Numbers* — 154
14. *Other Sunspot Cycles and Prices* — 156

CHAPTER XI

1. *Galton's Quincunx* — 162
2. *Frequency Distribution* — 163
3. *Bearing Balls* — 163
4. *Sound Synthesis — Two Components* — 164
5. *Sound Synthesis — Twelve Components* — 165
6. *Tide Prediction* — 167

CHAPTER XII

1. *A Sales Chart* — 173
2. *A Rate of Growth Chart* — 174
3. *Two Regular Cycles* — 175
4. *Synthesis* — 176
5. *The Trend Line* — 176
6. *Trend Line and Cycles* — 177
7. *Projection and Comparison* — 178
8. *An Enlargement* — 179
9. *Sales of an Industrial Company, 1871–1940* — 182
10. *Analysis* — 183
11. *Synthesis* — 183
12. *Sales, 1927–1941, of Another Industrial Company* — 184
13. *Analysis* — 184
14. *Synthesis* — 185
15. *Comparison* — 185

[ix]

CHARTS AND DIAGRAMS

FIG.   PAGE

16. *Projection*   186
17. *Final Synthesis*   187
18. *Diagrammatic Representation of the 54-Year, 18⅓-Year, 9-Year,*
    and 41-Month Rhythms   188–189

CHAPTER XIII

1. *Illusion*   197

CHAPTER XIV

1-A. *First Chinese Epoch (800 years: 221 B.C.–A.D. 588)* .   202
1-B. *Second Chinese Epoch (780 years: 589–A.D. 1367)* .   202
1-C. *Third Chinese Epoch (A.D. 1368 to present)* .   203
2. *War-Time Distortion*   205
3. *Persistence of Wave Influence*   206
4. *Interest-Bearing Debt of the United States*   213

CHAPTER XV

1. *U. S. Patents Issued, 1837–1944*   219

CHAPTER XVI

1. *Profits in the Steel Industry, 1901–1945*   230

APPENDIX I

1. *Equal Rate of Growth — Arithmetic Scale*   242
2. *Equal Rate of Growth — Ratio Scale*   242
3. *Equal Amount of Growth — Ratio Scale*   243
4. *Equal Amounts of Growth — Arithmetic Scale*   244
5. *Trend of a Hypothetical Business Organization*   244
6. *The Trend and The Cycle*   245
7. *Growth of Industrial Production in the United States*   246
8. *Index of Spanish Trade*   247

APPENDIX II

1. *Effect of Moving Average, of Different Lengths upon an Ideal*
   9-Year Rhythm   251
2. *Deviations of an Ideal 9-Year Rhythm from Moving Averages*
   of Different Lengths   252

Concerning Economic Prediction

AN INTRODUCTION

IT IS the business of science to predict. An exact science like
astronomy can usually make very accurate predictions indeed.
A chemist makes a precise prediction every time he writes a
formula. The nuclear physicist advertised to the world, in the
atomic bomb, how man can deal with entities so small that they
are completely beyond the realm of sense perception, yet make
predictions astonishing in their accuracy and significance. Economics is now reaching a point where it can hope also to make
rather accurate predictions, within limits which this study will
explain.

In these pages we shall be primarily concerned with a new approach to economics and the problem of economic forecast, with
the near-term future of the United States particularly in mind.
This approach moves partly through some avenues that in the
past have been the province of other sciences as various as biology, psychology, and mathematics.

The study here falls into two parts. First, it shows that rhythm
and periodicity exist in the natural world, and that our economic
world, analyzed with similar statistical tools, also displays cur-
vilinear forms and distinct rhythms. Second, it deals with some
of the ideas which underlie these facts, suggests implications which
seem safely implicit in them, and indicates some meanings which
such facts hold for all of us.

[xi]

The debt of the authors to those whose names, equations and graphs line the pages of this book — and to many others unnamed — is without end. Theirs is the pioneering that is moving economics out of the blind alley where it stood for many years, so that it can take its rank as a true science.

There are those who, admitting that economics has not been an exact science, also insist that it cannot be, in the sense of predicting outcomes in human affairs. There are even some who consider prediction regarding human life as a kind of impiety — or fakery, at best.

That prediction regarding human affairs so often stands in ill repute with sober men (regardless of whether it " comes true " or not) often stems from techniques used in formulating it. It is less the forecast than the questionable methodology that often lacks scientific credibility.

The reader will be introduced to a method of thinking about the future which — new though it may be to him — seems definitely to have proved of value. It is this method which is of fundamental importance — an importance greater than any specific conclusions to which it may lead. For on its validity depends the whole value of the conclusions.

We shall find, as we go forward, that in this approach to economic phenomena we are abandoning the classical approach based on endless argument over cause and effect. It is hoped that the reader's reward will be the discovery that in economics, as in other sciences, we are apparently dealing with laws regarding rhythmic human response to certain stimuli that give a remarkable working tool to any man who is responsibly concerned with future outcomes — whether he be businessman, community leader, or statesman.

Law in nature, of course, is not the kind of law that is handed down by an authority. It is merely a summary of our observations concerning what has consistently happened, and what we may therefore expect to continue in a consistent universe. Such law permits us, in effect, to assay certain probabilities. The ability to calculate

[xii]

probabilities is a vital part of all our modern scientific progress. As Eddington has pointed out, in speaking of his own field of physics, "The quantum physicist does not fill the atom with gadgets for directing its future behavior, as the classical physicist would have done; he fills it with gadgets determining the odds on its future behavior. He studies the art of the bookmaker, not of the trainer." *

Probabilities have to do with *averages*. When the physicist predicts that a given group of atoms will act in a certain way, he is relying — as physicists now believe — on a knowledge only of what the *average* atom will do. Quite similarly, when an insurance company more or less accurately predicts the number of deaths for next year, it is relying on statistical averages of a like kind.

The discovery that the law of averages applies to humanity — that certain activities of people, viewed en masse, fall into definite patterns, some of which repeat themselves with periodic rhythm — promises to be of great aid in making economics function as a true science.

These patterns will not tell us what any given *individual* will do — any more than laws in physics will tell what a particular atom will do, or life insurance statistics will reveal whether a given individual will die. But the patterns do reveal how masses are likely to act at given times. And to that extent they are a formulation of law.

This discovery has had to wait upon the development of the science of statistics, the invention of index numbers, and the compilation of statistical series over long periods. Today the work is only beginning.

Adequate statistics have not been kept for more than a few generations. Thus we are like doctors following Pasteur, who had incontrovertible evidence that germs exist, but in only a few instances had isolated the germs involved in particular human states.

To assume that from our present limited store of knowledge we

* A. S. Eddington, *The Nature of the Physical World* (p. 301), The Macmillan Company.

can henceforth predict the course of life for humanity would be childish. But we already have discoveries of importance. As the community becomes better informed of their value it will doubtless help us to extend them. Most important, to whatever extent the limited knowledge we do have can be put to practical use, it would seem that now is the time of times to bring it forth.

To be completely exposed to surprise by events — in the complex age we live in — is a fair route to the insane asylum. Experiments at Yale University, on a pig they called " The Broker," have demonstrated that a nervous breakdown can be instituted even in a porker, if he is given shocks of surprise repeated often enough.

A people must plan in order to live. Even an installment purchase assumes a plan for the future. Presidential predictions that " prosperity " was just around the corner in 1930 were well intended, but badly served an entire nation. And esteemed government economists, who predicted unemployment in this country of at least 8,000,000 for the spring of 1946, similarly performed a national disservice. A whole government program was laid out on the basis of a forecast which events proved erroneous.

When a people finds that predictions of many financial advisers, statesmen, historians, and other proclaimed experts are seldom better than the predictions of the astrologers, our social sciences have demonstrably not been earning their way. It is time for action.

This study is an attempt to show that something is indeed being done. The scientists who are busy at the problem seldom report their progress in the language of the average citizen. So their work often escapes his knowledge. The pioneering scientists will hardly be satisfied with this attempt to restate, in a simple way, the outcome of some of their researches. Some average readers, conversely, may feel equally dissatisfied, on the ground that the subject still seems abstruse and the language used is otherworldly, regardless of all efforts to avoid scientific jargon.

To both sources of justified criticism the authors apologize in advance. Every book, like every house plan, represents compromise;

[xiv]

and a completely satisfactory compromise is a contradiction in words.

This book is an attempt to show, in an elementary way for the reader unfamiliar with this form of research, how some of the inept arguments over economic outlooks can be avoided by using a few facts that should now be familiar to all. This application of a new method to a study of economic activity, while relatively young, seems nevertheless more promising, in offering results, than traditional economic theories that fill textbooks with opinions and arguments over whether a given cause is really an effect, and vice versa.

Here are traced trends evidenced in various parts of the American economy — existing trends that can be calculated, measured, and demonstrated beyond reasonable doubt. The overwhelming evidence for distinct rhythm or periodicity in the cycles that accompany these trends is set forth. How such information may be used to assay future probabilities is then suggested.

Before reaching the end of the book, the reader will have attained, it is hoped, some new insight for gauging the probable future that faces America in the years following the most disrupting war in all world history.

The student of periodic rhythms in human affairs has a tool which the law of averages itself puts into his hands. If trends have continued for decades, or if the oscillations of cycles around the trend have repeated themselves so many times and so regularly that the rhythm cannot reasonably be the result of chance, it is unwise to ignore the probability that these behaviors will continue.

The result is not prediction, in the sense in which the word is ordinarily understood. If the reader nevertheless wishes to regard essential parts of this book as prediction, then it should be emphasized that the " forecasts " are written by the data themselves. They emerge as tendencies in the organisms being studied. They do not rest on the opinion of any man, or men. They are, in effect, the *probabilities* of tomorrow.

[xv]

I

Why Trends Are Important

THE FACTS of growth are common knowledge to most mothers, who are encouraged by doctors to keep a weight chart around the nursery, for reference at weighing time. All healthy babies, like other healthy young organisms, show large initial rates of growth — over 100 per cent for babies the first year. As they get older, the rate of growth gradually falls off. At the approach of maturity, the rate of growth finally reaches zero.

Why it is that an organism stops growing we do not really know. We believe that biological organisms — whether dogs or babies or other animals — have their growth controlled by inhibiting secretions of glands. We are not so sure what it is that controls the size of different kinds of trees, or, say, of a Jimson weed.

But knowledge that such an inhibiting factor does exist is important to us, even when we cannot explain it. We find it reasonable that such a factor should be at work in organisms like a baby or a tree, just because we are used to observing it in action. But it also works in other kinds of organisms, such as human institutions and business organizations.

Few executives are used to thinking of a business enterprise as an " organism." But it does have a rate of growth that can be shown by a trend line. For the weight figures, which we might consult in establishing the trend for a baby, we can readily take the business output, as revealed in successive sales figures.

[1]

Suppose we draw such a trend for a hypothetical business organization which shows average annual sales of $20,000 during its first year of business, and proceeds as follows:

		Annual Sales	Five-Year Growth
1905	Company founded	$ 20,000	
1910	Five years after founding	38,000	$ 18,000
1915	Ten years after founding	68,000	30,000
1920	Fifteen years after founding	116,000	48,000
1925	Twenty years after founding	186,000	70,000
1930	Twenty-five years after founding	279,000	93,000
1935	Thirty years after founding	391,000	112,000
1940	Thirty-five years after founding	508,000	117,000
1945	Forty years after founding	609,000	101,000

Offhand this looks like a business that has been expanding rapidly, with a satisfactory forward thrust every five years. But if we analyze the figures, we find them showing signs of what, on the contrary, is a "dying" business. Years may pass before the business really goes under. But it has long been approaching maturity. What the figures show us is a steady decline in the *rate* of growth. The declining rate, by five-year periods, is as follows:

RATE OF GROWTH

1905–1910, 90% of actual sales in 1905
1910–1915, 80% " " " " 1910
1915–1920, 70% " " " " 1915
1920–1925, 60% " " " " 1920
1925–1930, 50% " " " " 1925
1930–1935, 40% " " " " 1930
1935–1940, 30% " " " " 1935
1940–1945, 20% " " " " 1940

It is obvious from the table that during each five-year period the rate of growth of this hypothetical business has decreased 10 per cent and that, if these tendencies continue, the rate of growth in the future will be:

1945–1950, 10% of actual sales in 1945
1950–1955, 0% " " " " 1950

In other words, we see that by 1955 the momentum will cease entirely. By then the organization will become another one of those many which follow a groove in a mature and conservative way — probably entering into a moderate decline until either aggressive competition shoves it aside entirely or " new blood " comes into the picture to give the aging institution a new start-off. A chart showing the sales for this hypothetical business would look like the solid line in Fig. 1.

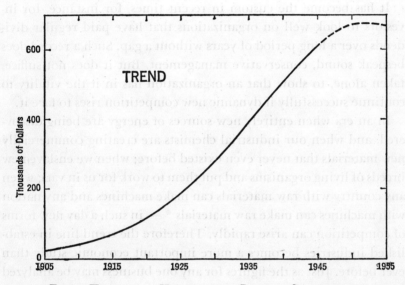

FIG. 1. TREND OF A HYPOTHETICAL BUSINESS ORGANIZATION

Data — 1905–1945, with a projection to 1955. The projection is based on the assumption of a continuation of the constant decline of the rate of growth, as discussed in the text. (For the same data plotted on ratio scale, see Appendix I, Fig. 5.)

This line can easily be projected. We have assumed that sales in 1950 will be 10 per cent greater than 1945. The table shows that sales in 1945 were $609,000. Adding 10 per cent gives $669,900, projected sales for 1950. Assuming that 1955 sales will show no growth over 1950 gives a sales total of $669,900 for this year also. The projected figures are shown by a broken line. Projections of this sort, based on rate of growth pattern and showing the approach to what we may call "maturity," are important tools for all students of practical economics.

In our hypothetical picture here, the design is that of a very regularly declining rate of growth — a regularity which is hardly typical of any of the institutions we shall study. But it is useful for illustrating a fact that both businessmen and investors usually overlook: The rate of growth in an organism is a sound index to its vitality.

It has become the custom in recent times, for instance, for investors to look well on organizations that have paid regular dividends over a long period of years without a gap. Such a record does bespeak sound, conservative management. But it does not suffice, taken alone, to show that an organization has in it the vitality to continue successfully if dynamic new competition rises to face it.

In an era when entirely new sources of energy are being discovered, and when our industrial chemists are creating commercially new materials that never even existed before; when we enslave new breeds of living organisms and put them to work for us in vats; when any country with raw materials can make machines and any nation with machines can make raw materials * — in such a day new forms of competition can arise rapidly. Therefore the trend line in established industries becomes a more important economic study than ever before. Just as the figures for any one business may be analyzed to reveal the trend, so may the figures for a group of businesses, such as those that comprise a manufacturing industry.

In the United States we have a number of great industries — often called "basic" industries — which are fundamental to the support of our established pattern of living. The trends in these industries are of significance to all of our people, and not merely to the executives and workers and stockholders in those particular fields. Such trends do not have isolated meanings. They indicate plainly the state of given organs in the economic body we call the

* See Virgil Jordan's *Manifesto for the Atomic Age* (Rutgers Press, 1946), p. 21 ff.

[4]

nation. If a similar trend shows up simultaneously in a number of the vital organs, we have conclusions that are in many ways applicable to our nation as a whole.

As we shall see shortly, the trends existing in a number of our great industries show definitely that we have been reaching a period of basic " maturity " in our whole economic development. This is a fact of enormous implications that reach in many directions. The implications are so great, indeed, that many people (as usual with humanity) find it easier to deny the fact, in heated argument, than face it honestly and then proceed to deal with it. The argument has reached into the realm of politics — where the only justifiable debate should be concerned not with the reality of the fact, but with what to do about it. It has entered the life of the average man; it has entered the lives of business and social institutions; it is reflected alike in national defense problems and literary patterns.

Here the fact will concern us in just one fundamental way: its effect on business cycles. Business cycles — we shall later define the term more exactly — are not up and down departures from a horizontal line. It is more useful to think of cycles as waves moving around a curved axis, that axis being the trend. (If you like to think in terms of pictures, throw away the one of cycles seen as the jagged peaks of a level picket fence. Visualize instead the peaks of a fence going up and down hill, or a coil-spring which is stretched over a bent poker as the core.)

A more or less typical trend line, around which a simple cycle is moving, looks approximately like Fig. 2. If this trend line represented the growth of your own business, and the cycle represented ups and downs in sales, one thing would be clear: you would not feel dips in the cycle nearly so seriously when you were growing rapidly as you would when the trend had leveled out. For when the trend is shooting up rapidly, the bottom of one cycle is a " depression " only by comparison with its own peak. The bottom may be actually at a *higher* level than the peak of activity in the preceding cycle.

This fact applies to every single business, and it applies to a whole economy. In the years between the Civil War and World War I, when the American economy was expanding at a very rapid rate, the bottom of one depression often represented a level of economic activity not much lower than preceding peaks of prosperity. Hence many a businessman of that extraordinary era knew just two kinds of " times " — times when business was good, and

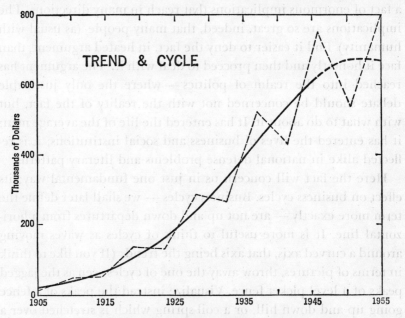

FIG. 2. THE TREND AND THE CYCLE

Trend of a hypothetical business organization as shown in Fig. 1 with a regular 9-Year Cycle of 20 per cent amplitude superimposed. (For the same data plotted on ratio scale, see Appendix I, Fig. 6.)

other times when it was better. Business, even in depressions, was good; although it was under the level of recent peaks, it was still equal or possibly even superior in volume to levels established at other peaks in the fairly recent past.

Figure 3, for instance, is a chart which shows roughly the ups and downs in our industrial production between 1884 and 1937, with a superimposed trend line. The chart has purposely been split into

[6]

two parts. In the first part, up to about 1920, the trend was rising rapidly. In the second part, after 1920, the trend has pretty well leveled out. In the former, the eye can easily note that the depression lows *a*, *b*, and *c* were still practically as high as earlier peaks at *A*, *B*, and *C*. However bad business may have seemed at such lows, it was still at a level that had represented an all-time peak not too long before. Hence it still seemed pretty good.

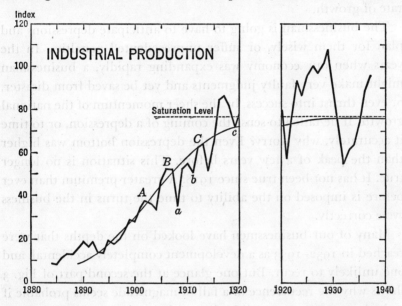

FIG. 3. GROWTH OF INDUSTRIAL PRODUCTION IN THE UNITED STATES
Data — 1854–1937, together with Trend (after Davis). The chart has been split into two parts to emphasize the changing character of the trend. (For the same data plotted on ratio scale, see Appendix I, Fig. 7.)

But now note what happens following 1920, when the growth trend begins to level out. From that point on, depression points really mean something for the economy to experience. They are depression points not merely by comparison with recently experienced peaks. They are depressions that become absolute in character. There is no lift in the trend line to alleviate them.

There are factors present in our economy to indicate that here·

[7]

after our major depressions will have this character. These factors suggest serious future problems for the nation and for the individual businessman. Without enjoying henceforth the advantages of a rapid rate of growth, we may find depression periods harder to bear. Also there is no ground for belief, as we shall note later, that a completely " managed " economy is more likely to avoid wide economic swings than is a free one, granting no difference in the rate of growth.

The businessman is going to have to anticipate depressions and plan for them wisely, or suffer unprecedented penalties. In the years when our economy was expanding rapidly, a businessman might make very faulty judgments and yet be saved from disaster, or even thrust into success, by the sheer momentum of the national growth. If he failed to sense the coming of a depression, or to time it accurately, why worry? Even the depression bottom was higher than the peak of a few years before. This situation is no longer true. It has not been true since 1918. A greater premium than ever before is imposed on the ability to time the turns in the business cycle correctly.

Many of our businessmen have looked on the depths that were reached in 1932–1933 as a development completely accidental, and one unlikely to recur. But one glance at the second part of Fig. 3 shows why the recurrence of a fall of magnitude seems probable if and when our economy slides into a depression again. This chart shows how the trend line in our economy has leveled out, so that no rising trend is present to compensate for a fall in the business cycle.

The phenomenon of increasing intensity of depression — as an economy approaches the upper level, or asymptote, of its trend — is shown suggestively in the history of the Spanish Empire, one of the earliest social organisms for which we have any useful statistical record. E. J. Hamilton, in his study *American Treasure and the Price Revolution in Spain,* has provided us with elaborately detailed estimates of Spain's total imports, valued in standard pesos,

[8]

from 1503 to 1660. On the basis of this data, Harold T. Davis has constructed an index of Spanish trade for this period which is charted in Fig. 4, together with a trend line which has been added by the authors. The period includes most of the great growth and expansion of the Spanish Empire. Of particular interest is the

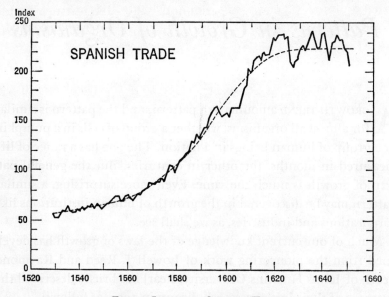

FIG. 4. INDEX OF SPANISH TRADE

Data — 1530–1650 (after Davis and Hamilton) together with Trend. (For the same data plotted on ratio scale, see Appendix I, Fig. 8.)

series of deep depressions that begin to appear after the trend line begins to reach maturity.

In very recent years we have discovered a great deal of new information on this subject, and a new application of scientific methods in its use. But before we reach the problem of the cycle we must know more about trends, and how they are determined and estimated.

[9]

II

Patterns in Growth of Organisms

A GROWTH TREND amounts to a pattern; and the pattern is similar for almost all organisms, whether a group of cells in a pumpkin or a group of human beings in a nation. The one has a range of life measured in months, the other in centuries. But the general pattern of growth is much the same. Even more surprising, a similar pattern may be discovered in the growth of human institutions like corporations and industries, as we shall see.

Much of our current knowledge of the laws of growth has developed from the pioneering work of Lowell J. Reed and Raymond Pearl, of Johns Hopkins University. Pearl has briefly described the outcome of their initial research, begun in 1920, as follows:

As a result of applying certain biological reasoning to the problem, we hit upon an equation to describe the growth of populations, which subsequent work has clearly demonstrated to be a first approximation to the required law. As we were in process of publishing the first discussion of the matter, we found that a Belgian mathematician, P. F. Verhulst, had as early as 1838 used this same curve, which he called the " logistic curve," as the expression of the law of population growth.*

* *The Biology of Population Growth* (p. 3–4), copyright, 1925, Alfred A. Knopf, Inc.

While there are scientists who have shown a disposition to question some of the Pearl methods — on the ground, for instance, that he did not determine the probable errors of constants — and while almost limitless work in this field is still to be done, it remains that Pearl's contribution is of extraordinary usefulness.

[10]

The study which Pearl published in 1925 under the title *The Biology of Population Growth* is still, some twenty years later, a readable, elegantly simple statement of a profound truth which has since been put to work in many fields. The curves Pearl and Reed explored permit city planners to forecast future city populations within a small margin of error; enable great utility companies to weighed a white rat. (Fig. 1) For the growth in weight of a pump-

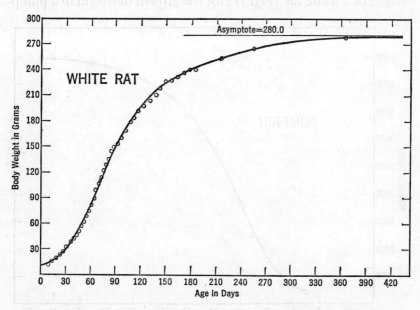

FIG. 1. GROWTH IN BODY WEIGHT OF A MALE WHITE RAT *(After Pearl)*

know with fair accuracy where facilities will be in greatest demand at a given future time. *The Biology of Population Growth* is still required reading for any executive concerned with a scientific approach to the future; a few of its many charts are reproduced here with the publisher's permission.

As Pearl points out, every living being starts as a single cell; the cell divides and is multiplied; the process goes on at different rates but without cessation until complete adult development is reached. Counting the cells is impossible after the very earliest growth

[11]

stages; but periodically repeated weighings give a rough yet sufficiently accurate index of the increase in their number.

" The results of such periodic weighings give rise, when plotted upon co-ordinate paper, to a curve of peculiarly characteristic shape," Pearl showed. It is something like the shape of an elongated italic f. The curve is similar, for instance, for the growth in body weight of a white rat (Fig. 1) ; for the growth in weight of a pump-

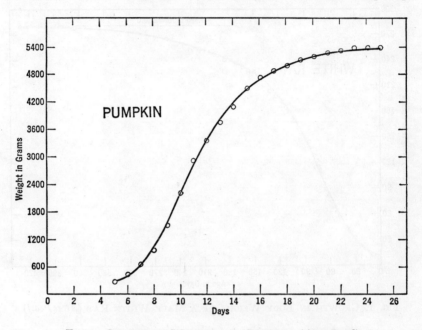

FIG. 2. GROWTH IN WEIGHT OF A PUMPKIN *(After Pearl)*

kin (Fig. 2) ; and for the growth of a population of yeast cells in a test tube (Fig. 3) and of fruit flies, or *Drosophila*, living in a bottle (Fig. 4).

This much seems extremely logical. A population of yeast cells or fruit flies, living in a closed environment, could be expected to reach some upper limit of balance between the number of cells and the living space available. To find a consistent curve in approaching such a balance does not seem surprising. But when Pearl turned to

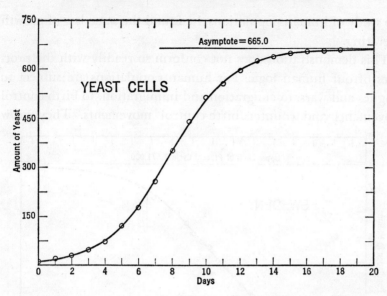

FIG. 3. GROWTH OF A POPULATION OF YEAST CELLS (*After Pearl*)

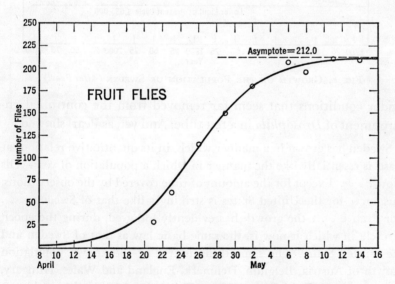

FIG. 4. GROWTH OF A POPULATION OF FRUIT FLIES
IN A BOTTLE (*After Pearl*)

[13]

the study of human populations, he found the same law of growth operating.

This demonstration does not conform so readily with the processes of our human logic. For human populations are subject to plagues and wars, to emigration and immigration, to birth-control movements and counter birth-control movements. They grow

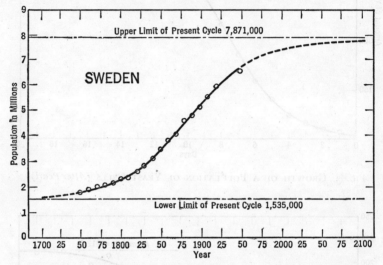

FIG. 5. GROWTH OF THE POPULATION OF SWEDEN (After Pearl)

under conditions that seem far removed from the controlled environment of *Drosophila* in a test tube. And yet, as Pearl showed:

Sweden has grown in a manner which, in its quantitative relations at least, is essentially like the manner in which a population of yeast cells grows. . . . Except for the amount of time covered by the observations, this curve for the United States is strikingly like that of Sweden. . . . For France . . . the growth has evidently followed, during the epoch or cycle in which it now is, the same basic law as that of Sweden and the United States. The same thing is true of the known population growth of Austria, Belgium, Denmark, England and Wales, Hungary, Italy, Scotland, Serbia, Japan, Java, Philippine Islands, the world as a whole, and Baltimore city.*

* *Ibid.,* pp. 13–17.

[14]

The similarities Pearl mentions show up graphically in his charts for Sweden, the United States, and France, reproduced in Figs. 5, 6, and 7.

Now comes a vital and significantly useful fact. *When a consistent pattern of growth exists, we have sound grounds for making predictions.* However qualified those predictions may be, they have the

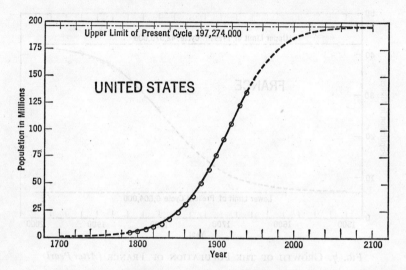

FIG. 6. GROWTH OF THE POPULATION OF THE
UNITED STATES *(After Pearl)*

probabilities on their side. Thus, when we have enough census records — as for the United States — to establish a number of points on the chart of its population growth, we may observe the pattern of growth that exists; and knowing what the pattern is, we may project it into the future for purposes of prediction.

We may similarly project it into the past. France, for example, is an old nation; but we lack reliable census data for France before 1800. Data available since then, however, are sufficient to create the segment of a curve which may be projected backward as well as forward. The curve for France's present cycle of growth had practically reached its upper limit in prewar days, and suggested decline.

[15]

The period of time required by a given nation to go through the familiar pattern of growth varies greatly. With France, the period seems to have been something over four centuries for its current cycle. But records for Algeria convinced Pearl that this one small country had lived through almost a complete cycle of growth, from youth to maturity, in less than a hundred years — that cycle com-

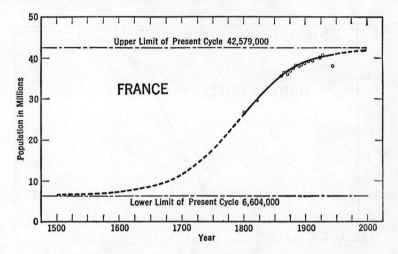

FIG. 7. GROWTH OF THE POPULATION OF FRANCE *(After Pearl)*

prising the period of open French control following conquest, which seems to have been completed around 1850 (see Fig. 8).

This leads to another striking observation. Algeria was an old country, with an indigenous population, before it was brought under French domination. The introduction of French control apparently launched a new cycle in the nation's life. Alterations in the environment were sufficiently radical to permit a new cycle of population growth to superimpose itself on whatever old one had existed — one for which we have no census records. When the new trend began, it followed exactly the pattern of expansion we are now familiar with in other countries.

We may thus reach an interesting observation. New cycles of growth may be superimposed upon old ones. We cannot predict

[16]

when this will happen. Nor can we, as regards humanity, predict the conditions that permit it to happen. But a new cycle can appear when some fundamental change occurs.

If we put our colony of *Drosophila* into a larger bottle, with greater food supplies, a new cycle of growth would begin, but with a pattern quite similar in shape to the old. Similarly, a nation can

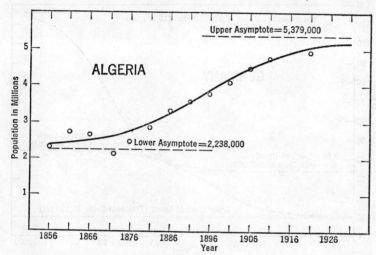

FIG. 8. GROWTH OF THE INDIGENOUS NATIVE POPULATION OF ALGERIA *(After Pearl)*

apparently effect, through a reorganization of its resources, a change in environmental essentials which accomplishes much the same end. It seems to be established, for instance, that the introduction of an industrial economy permits a new rate of population growth substantially in excess of that which was sustained by the community when it was dominantly agricultural.

The world has striking evidence of this in the case of Russia, which following 1917–1918 entered into a new growth cycle. In terms of this new cycle, Russia stands today as the youngest of the great nations in the world. The United States is comparatively an old nation, in the sense of the dynamic forces that are reflected in a rate of growth, biologically and industrially.

[17]

Pearl was convinced that a similar new cycle was once evidenced in Germany, where census records go back far enough to permit him to find a modern cycle of growth superimposed on an old one In the first half of the nineteenth century, Germany's population was reaching the upper level of growth in a cycle that had prevailed

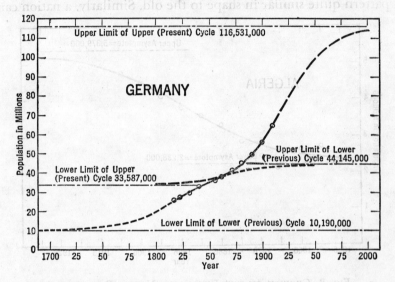

FIG. 9. GROWTH OF THE POPULATION OF GERMANY

This chart (after Pearl) makes apparent two cycles of growth which have overlapped during the period of census history.

since the 1600's. For years the nation had been predominantly agricultural. The abortive democratic revolution of 1848 was coincident with the beginning of a new industrialization, conducted under Prussian leadership, and new political forms. In the twenty years that followed 1850, this industrialization reached a development that permitted the swift defeat of France in 1870. The further unification of Germany that Bismarck then imposed seems merely to have added impetus to the new growth in strength already then established. These events were almost immediately reflected in a rapid increase in the population's rate of growth. The up-

[18]

surge was clearly in evidence by 1870, and subsequent census figures demonstrated that a new cycle of growth had begun, as shown in Fig. 9.

Germany's new pattern of growth, following 1850, demonstrates an interesting and perhaps significant point, when her population chart is compared with those for England, France, and the United States: Germany in 1914 was in one sense the youngest of these four industrialized nations. This may help account for the extraordinary vitality evidenced by the German people in their rapid rise from their 1918 defeat — one which hardly disturbed their social integration. What it may mean hereafter is wholly problematical, since today's Germans, living in the world's greatest mass of ruins, seem only individual remnants or survivors of a population that no longer is a united nation.

For our own purposes here, the past pattern of Germany's population growth is worth noting only because it leads to a conclusion which Pearl phrases succinctly:

When human social evolution does manage to put a kink in the curve of population growth, it has not done it by altering any biological law. It merely shifts, by a greater or smaller amount, the absolute base from which the law operates. Then the process goes on as before.*

It is possible to draw another conclusion from which Pearl abstains, but which seems inherent in the data available to us. The renaissance in the pattern of growth apparently does *not* occur, except concurrently with revolutionary changes in the environment. In viewing the United States, we have no grounds for believing that the prevailing trend in our population growth will undergo any material change, unless we simultaneously have grounds for believing that a great revolution in American affairs is due — and a revolution, at that, complete enough to permeate our political, economic, philosophic, and social institutions.

This is exceedingly important to understand, for it has further

* *Ibid.* p. 29.

implications. We are going to discover that patterns of growth in human organisms — an organism like a group of workers associated in an industry — look and act very much like the patterns or trends in population growth. And, in further similarity — these patterns show what we might call an " urge to fulfillment." That is, they are consistent; they do not change capriciously; and *there seems no reason to expect any change unless we also imply a revolution in the constitution of the organism, or in the environment where the pattern is being worked out.*

It may well be that our discovery of a new source of energy, such as has been revealed to us by nuclear physics, or some of our revolutionary new advances in chemistry, which in effect give us new sources of raw material, do herald a fundamental revolution in our society. For instance, Dr. Hornell Hart, Professor of Sociology at Duke University, who believes many of the activities of the human race can be fitted to the Pearl logistic curves, suggests that harnessing of atomic energy may mean a steep upward swing in some of our familiar graphs.* Others may find themselves inclined to agree with him. Some hope, similarly, that the United Nations is a precursor of a new form of world government that could release wholly new energies in our nation. But it would be some time before we could be statistically sure of any such change. *When a new trend line is superimposed on an old one, the rise will seem to immediate observers like a mere rise in the cycle that rides on the trend.* Some years would have to pass before we could be certain that any such rise is not just cyclic in character, but amounts to a rise in the trend line itself — the imposing of a new, rapidly rising trend line on the old.

This much is worth noting: changes that accompany a new rate of growth in any given society are so profound, and so all-reaching, that old established institutions undergo a severe shake-up. This shake-up will be in evidence long before we get the statistical data to show what is really happening. It is not impossible that the eco-

* *American Journal of Sociology,* June, 1946.

nomic and social upheavals being experienced by our own genera-
tion are the foreshadows, as it were, of revolutionary changes that
ultimately will give us an entirely new curve in our population
growth — to mention just one graph. Simultaneously, many new
industries would be born; some older industries would take on a
new lease of life; some would doubtless die.

For the present, we shall avoid speculation on matters of this
kind, which are still far beyond the realm of statistical projection.
Our concern here is not with guesses concerning possible new
trends in our economy as they might appear in the future, but with
study of the established trends as they can be statistically traced
right now.

III

The Growth Trend
in Our Basic Industries

To DRAW the trend lines that Pearl uses in such population charts as were reproduced in the foregoing pages, we need to deal with equations, of which the smooth curve is the graph.* Such a method is too complicated for the average businessman who wants to explore trends. It is not only that he may lack the training in mathematics. Even more important, he will probably not recognize the fact that he is dealing with a logistic curve when he puts figures down on a chart.

A man who charted the growth of his infant son in pounds, every week from the day the boy was born, would ordinarily know that the rapidly rising line would eventually level out. (He can get weight charts that will tell him just when the " bend-over " in the line is due.) But when he charts his corporate sales he seldom realizes — as he sees the line go steeply up — that something like a logistic curve is being worked out here, too, and that the line will eventually bend over suddenly. Further, when it does eventually bend, he will usually regard this as a temporary slump that will be remedied by a resumption of progress in due course.

* Thus the equation of the logistic curve for France which Pearl employed was

$$y = 6.604 + \frac{35.975}{1 + 0.808e^{-0.0197X}}$$

[22]

It is possible to avoid the dangers leading from such fallacious judgments by charting figures on semilogarithmic, or ratio, scale. That is, instead of using the Pearl type of graph, we can use a ratio scale, then get a curve which, by its changing shape, automatically reveals the falling off in the rate of growth. With such a scale the elongated italic $\int$ of Pearl usually becomes a smooth elongated italic parenthesis $\big($.

Let us turn back for a moment to the Pearl chart showing the population growth of the United States, on page 15. Now if we stood at 1920 on this chart, and no dotted line indicating the future were there to warn us, we might well assume that the upward sweep of the line would continue indefinitely. We might assume this, at least, if our knowledge were limited to that of the average American, and if our emotions were geared to the prevailing American sentiment that progress has always existed in this nation and therefore always must — if not at the same rate as in the past, then at a still better one. Only specialized knowledge and training could warn us that this chart (as of 1920) could not justify such expectation.

Fig. 1 on the next page is a chart of our population's growth on ratio, not arithmetic, scale. Standing at 1920 on *this* chart, we could have looked back and have been readily aware that we were almost at the top of a long slope that was already slowly leveling out. The steady decline in the *rate* of growth at this point is clearly evident, and the approximate point at which growth will peter out entirely is clearly indicated by the nature of this simple curve itself. Taking our place on this curve at 1920, we could have projected it into today without vast margin of error, even if we had merely worked freehand with a pencil. This kind of chart, which shows us the rate of growth at a quick glance, is preferable for our purposes on many grounds.

Pearl has taught us something very valuable — that a *law* of growth exists, and that it operates consistently. In using hereafter a form of chart somewhat different from Pearl's, the authors are

merely charting the operation of that law in a manner they believe
the average reader will find more readily useful and applicable to
his immediate problems.

It is in this form that the growth of America's basic industries will
be graphed. The reader who then wishes to apply the method to

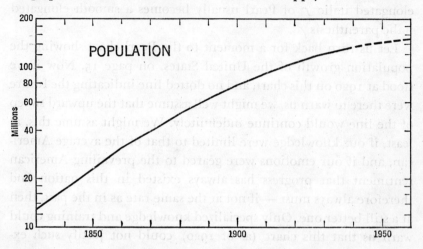

FIG. 1. POPULATION OF CONTINENTAL U. S., 1830–1940

Decennial data. A trend is shown, projected tentatively to 1960. *Ratio scale.*
(For a full explanation of ratio scale, see Appendix I.)

his own business may easily come up with a comparable chart. All
he need do is to chart his own figures on a similar grid. He can then
know immediately where his business stands, in comparison with
other broader national developments, without having recourse to
any special mathematical knowledge.

The charts shown in connection with this chapter are rather
striking in the uniformity of the story they tell. Consider first our
total manufactures, which are shown in Fig. 2 in terms of their
growth since 1830, in dollars compensated for changing purchasing
power.* The rate of growth of our manufactures has been steadily

* All dollar charts in this chapter and the one next following are so compensated. That is, the values for each year have been divided by the index of
the average wholesale prices for that year, 1926 being considered as unity.

declining since around 1900. By 1920, as can be seen from the chart, it had become a fraction of the rate prevailing in the late 1800's. In at least one sense we may completely ignore the peak established during World War II. Notice that it reaches far above the trend line, and surpasses all other peaks attained previously.

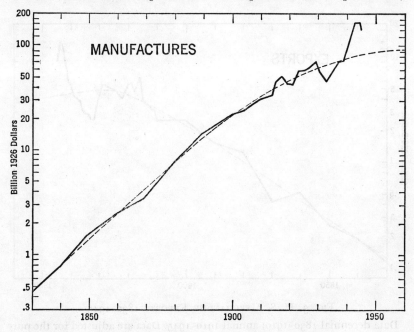

FIG. 2. U. S. MANUFACTURES, 1830–1945

Data decennial 1830–1899; quinquennial 1899–1919 with estimates for war years; biennial 1919–1939; annual estimates thereafter. The data have been adjusted for the purchasing power of the dollar, 1926 = 100.

A trend is shown projected tentatively to 1960. The war years, as the text explains, have been ignored in determining trend in this and in all other charts portraying growth. *Ratio scale.*

Unfortunately — for the purposes of our society — it represents production for purposes of destruction. Being a wartime phenomenon, it tells us nothing beyond the fact that under the centralized compulsion of a war economy we had an enormous capacity to produce.

The underlying trend line tells us much more. What that line says is this: Under the economic system prevailing before the war — to which we are presumably returning — we were closely approaching the upper limit of our ability to *produce and distribute within the frame of that system*. Following its wartime peak, our

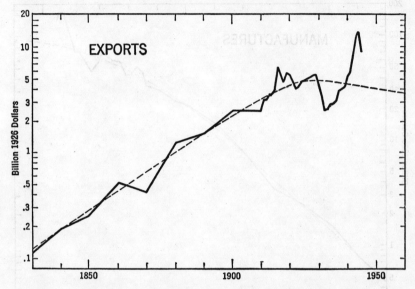

FIG. 3. U. S. MERCHANDISE EXPORTS 1830–1945

Data decennial 1830–1910; annual 1910–1945. Data are adjusted for the purchasing power of the dollar, 1926 = 100. A trend is shown projected tentatively to 1960. *Ratio scale.*

volume of manufactures is bound to fall back toward the trend line, and perhaps well below it, before again stabilizing itself around the trend. Rather than a matter for philosophical argument, this assumption seems supported by the evidence of the pattern that has been established in our economy since the very beginnings of our nation — a pattern that can be approximately determined and, consequently, approximately projected.

When we compare the chart for manufactures with the charts that show rate of growth in our exports and imports (see Figs. 3

and 4), we meet a consistency that we should now be prepared to expect. Both exports and imports are measured here in dollars that are compensated for varying purchasing power, like the value of manufactured goods charted previously. Let us look first at Fig. 3, showing exports. The basic pattern established by the trend is un-

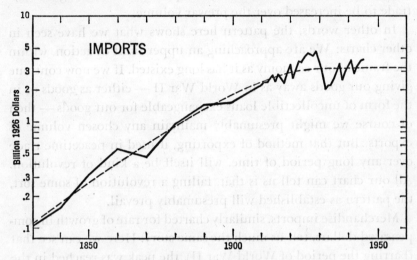

FIG. 4. U. S. MERCHANDISE IMPORTS, 1830–1945

Data decennial 1830–1910; annual 1910–1945. Data are adjusted for the purchasing power of the dollar, 1926 = 100. A trend is shown, projected tentatively to 1960. *Ratio scale.*

deniable, and it tells us something for the future. The export levels we established during World War II, by giving away almost unlimited volumes of goods via lend-lease, mean nothing — *except that we did give these huge volumes of material away.* In peacetime, our export volume should tend to return toward the true trend line — and perhaps sink below it for a while — unless we continue giving goods away in much the same fashion. Or unless a new trend is to be established, one we cannot now calculate.

Devices like the Bretton Woods Economic agreement, or Treasury grants made as political " loans " to foreign nations, may tend for temporary periods to mask this truism — much as the working of the Federal Reserve Act tends to conceal from the general public the fact that we print dollars to meet government deficits. But our chart says forthrightly, in statistical language, that on the basis of the long-established trend, and in terms of foreign trade handled at a real profit, we should not be too optimistic in looking for such trade to be increased over the prewar volume.

In other words, the pattern here shows what we have seen in other charts: We are approaching an upper limit of action, within the frame of our economy as it has long existed. If we now continue giving our goods away as in World War II — either as goods or in the form of uncollectible loans exchangeable for our goods — then of course we might presumably maintain any chosen volume of exports. But that method of exporting, if used in peacetime trade over any long period of time, will itself be a kind of revolution. All our chart can tell us is that, failing a revolution of some sort, the pattern as established will presumably prevail.

Merchandise imports, similarly charted for rate of growth in compensated dollars, tell us much the same story. Here we can see that (barring the period of World War II) the peak was reached in the decade that followed 1920. There seems no evidence to suggest that in our time, or in the frame of our economy as we know it, the peak of the twenties will ever be importantly exceeded. Certainly in a world where economic facilities outside the United States have been so extensively wrecked, and where the United States itself has an unprecedented volume of production facilities of its own, we hardly need a chart to tell us that levels of useful imports in the future will certainly not exceed, for any considerable period, those already established in the past. Not, that is, within the frame of familiar economic relationships.

Probably no industry so accurately mirrors progress in our industrialized economy — and, in turn, is mirrored in that progress — as does our iron and steel industry. Iron and steel are truly basic products in the machine age that has been with us for the last century and a quarter. They are tools in almost every " civilized " activity. That is why iron and steel production reflects both the physical and the psychological drives of a nation like the United States.

Fortunately for statistical purposes, the records for iron and steel production go back further, and are more nearly exact, than those

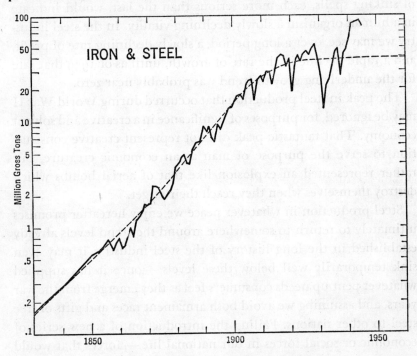

FIG. 5. U. S. IRON AND STEEL PRODUCTION

Shown in gross tons of 2240 lbs. each. Pig iron production 1830–1913 (decennial 1830–1850, annual 1854–1913). Steel ingot production 1914–1945. A trend is shown, projected tentatively to 1960. *Ratio scale.*

for most of the other great American industries. By using pig iron production before 1913, and measuring steel output by steel ingot production after that date, we can trace the history of the industry's activity back almost to its beginning.

The steel industry has been an old industry since 1914. Note the curve showing its growth, in Fig. 5. The relapse it had around

1914 was normal in extent, as compared to all previous depressions that followed peaks in activity. But the next depression that came along, following World War I, carried steel production to lower levels than were reached in the 1914 relapse. The depression of the early thirties carried it to still lower levels. Such a series of sinking spells, each more serious than the last, would indicate in a human organism a slowly declining vitality. In the steel industry we may see, over a long period, a slowly declining rate of profit, and a rapid decline in the rate of growth, until as of 1939 that rate for the underlying growth trend was probably near zero.

The peak in steel production that occurred during World War II may be ignored, for purposes of significance in a creative and solvent economy. That fantastic peak did not represent creative construction to serve the purpose of man as an economic creature, but rather represented an explosion like that of aerial bombs which destroy themselves when they reach their target.

Steel production in whatever peace we enjoy hereafter promises ultimately to return to somewhere around the trend levels already established in the long history of the steel industry; it may even sink temporarily well below these levels — once it has supplied whatever pent-up needs consumers feel as they emerge from the war years, and assuming we avoid both armament races and gifts of free steel to other nations. Failing the introduction of a new series of economic or social forces in our national life — forces that would overturn its old patterns of economic growth — an average annual production of approximately 40 million gross tons is the mean about which future fluctuations will probably oscillate. (A gross ton is 2240 pounds; in terms of net tons of 2000 pounds the figure would be 45 millions.)

Many of our other great industries have also reached their maturity. Note, in Fig. 6, the chart for the growth of steam railroads (miles of road operated). The maximum was reached between 1910 and 1914; since then there has been an actual decline. The railroad industry as such will have no more real expansion under economic conditions as we know them. Just as significant as the maturity reached in mileage operated is the fact that the tons of freight *originated* have actually shown a decline on the per capita of population basis, even during the years of World War II.

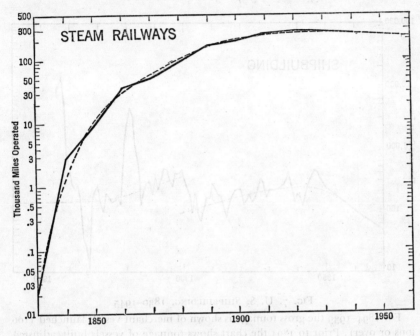

FIG. 6. STEAM RAILWAYS

Miles of road operated (first track) in continental United States, 1830–1940. Decennial data. A trend is shown, projected tentatively to 1960. *Ratio scale.*

Much was made of the unprecedented volume of freight traffic carried by the railroads in the recent wartime period, and of the record of freight-miles built up. Such figures largely reflect long hauls and the fact that the usual unit of measurement is the ton-mile. But by 1943, when our war effort was in full swing, total tonnage originated was still only about 9 per cent more than it had been in 1929. On the per capita basis it was actually less, because the population had increased. General Leonard P. Ayres of the

Cleveland Trust Company, one of the country's foremost statisticians, could only call it " astonishing " that our railroads in 1943 actually originated less freight per capita of the population than they did in most of the years from 1911 through 1929, and far less than in the war years of 1917–1918.

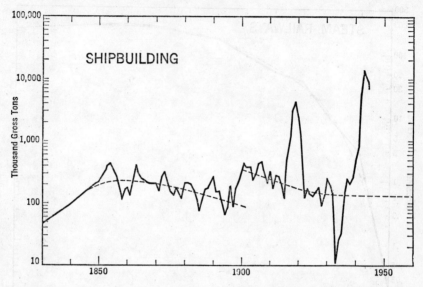

FIG. 7. U. S. SHIPBUILDING, 1830–1945

For 1894–1939 the gross tonnage is shown of merchant vessels launched (100 tons or over). Prior to 1894 the chart shows tonnage of vessels built, adjusted to conform to the average tonnage launched from 1894–1907 and set back one year. From 1939–1945 the gross tonnage is shown of merchant vessels built (1000 tons or over).

Two trends are indicated, the present one projected to 1960. *Ratio scale.*

The shipbuilding industry, which reached fantastic peaks of construction under the war impact, will doubtless go right back to the levels it came from (see Fig. 7). Even continued subsidies to operators can hardly save it from such deflation; these existed, thanks to the Merchant Marine Act, long before the war began. There is nothing in the long-time growth pattern of the shipping industry to suggest that continued subsidies, of whatever probable

[32]

volume, will change the pattern to any appreciable degree. World War I raised shipbuilding twentyfold — from about 200,000 to about 4 million gross tons a year. Thereafter the trend prevailing since around 1907, when a decline had set in, was resumed. This peacetime trend will probably be resumed once more as the axis around which yearly shipbuilding volume will fluctuate.

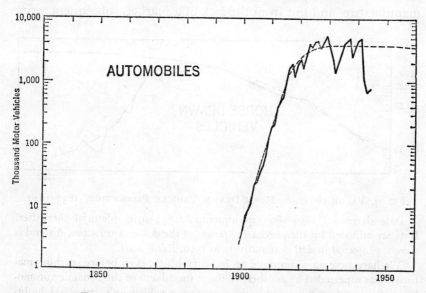

FIG. 8. U. S. AUTOMOBILE PRODUCTION, 1900–1944

Factory sales of motor vehicles, with a trend projected tentatively to 1960. *Ratio scale.*

The automobile industry in early 1946 had a huge volume of new orders, but there was no evidence that these would create a new trend line. The industry's rate of growth was declining sharply well before 1940, and was closely approaching maturity, as shown in Fig. 8. Whatever temporary postwar splurge the industry may enjoy, the trends revealed in the chart suggested it had already attained, prewar, the bulk of the mature maximum of output. A *Fortune* estimate of mid-1944, for instance, concluded that a production of $4\frac{1}{2}$ million cars annually from mid-1945 on would completely saturate the market by 1950; a production of 6½ million cars would saturate it by the end of 1947. Actually, of course, all early forecasts of automobile production for the months immediately following the war were vitiated by the occurrence of a strike wave; even 1946 production fell much below the manufacturers' earlier hopes. While failure to produce more cars in 1946 came from inability to manufacture, and not from the lack of a market, subsequent years

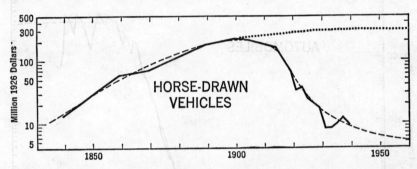

FIG. 9. VALUE OF U. S. HORSE-DRAWN VEHICLE PRODUCTION, 1839–1939

Data decennial 1839–1899, quinquennial 1899–1919, biennial thereafter. Data are adjusted for the purchasing power of the dollar, 1926=100. A trend is shown, projected in dashes tentatively to 1960. *Ratio scale.*

We have here an example of an industry which, even before reaching maturity, was superseded by another. Without the advent of the dynamic automobile industry, which destroyed it, the horse-drawn vehicle industry would doubtless have reached maturity at the levels indicated by the dotted line at the top.

should be watched for an answer to an apposite question: Will even " deferred demand," so called, enable the automobile industry hereafter to get very far above its prewar average production levels?

What happened to the earlier carriage industry is shown in Fig. 9.

Grouped together on pages 36–41 the reader will find charts showing the trend in a number of basic activities as various as cattle on farms, corn production, cotton production, wool production, wheat production, malt liquor consumption, lumber production, cotton spindles in operation, coal production, copper production, and lead production. These are shown not because any one of the series charted is particularly significant in itself, but because as a

[34]

group the charts tell a consistent story, and — most important — because long series of figures are available.

They indicate that maturity has been or is being reached throughout our economic fabric as a whole. In the light of such charts, any talk of the unlimited frontiers that lie before us is a pure expression of faith and hope. The statistical evidence does not support it. Like goldfish nibbling at the glass of their bowl, we have demonstrably been reaching the circumference of our economic *world-as-it-is*.

This is not a tragic fact; it is merely a fact. We may adjust ourselves to it well or badly. Still more, we may decide as a society that we refuse to live in a world of such an established circumference, and try to break whatever bonds have been holding us there (if we can discover what they are, of what they are made, and how to break them), and then create a world with far wider horizons for ourselves. Some may suspect that this course will be the one that Americans will ultimately try to follow.

There are some newer industries in the nation which still have much of their growth ahead of them. We shall survey a few of these briefly in the following chapter. They should be of interest to investors who are concerned with the long-term outlook, and to young people who are intelligently choosing industrial careers.

There is no reason, however, to assume that the activity of any one of them, or of all of them put together, will change the near-term national outlook suggested by the charts discussed in this chapter.

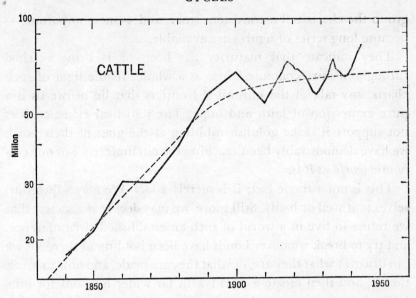

FIG. 10. CATTLE ON U. S. FARMS, JANUARY 1840–1944

Data decennial 1840–1910, annual thereafter. A trend is shown, projected tentatively to 1960. *Ratio scale.*

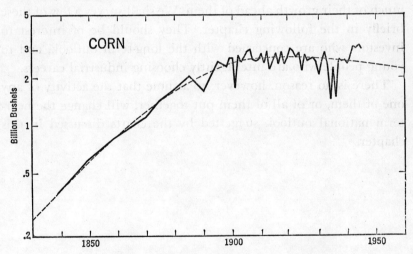

FIG. 11. U. S. CORN PRODUCTION, 1839–1945

Data decennial 1839–1870, quinquennial 1870–1895, annual 1898–1945. A trend is shown, projected tentatively to 1960. *Ratio scale.*

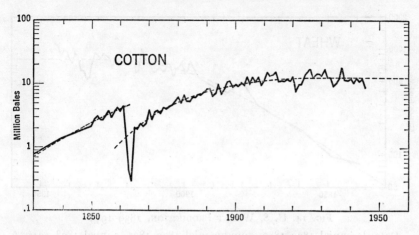

FIG. 12. U. S. COTTON PRODUCTION, 1830–1945

Data decennial 1830–1850, annual thereafter. Two distinct trends are shown, one prior to and the other following the Civil War. The latter has been projected tentatively to 1960. *Ratio scale.*

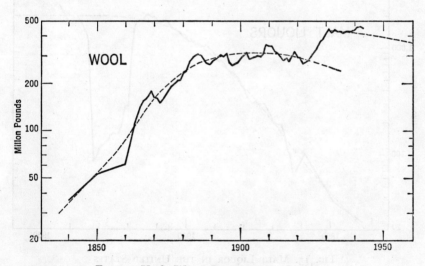

FIG. 13. U. S. WOOL PRODUCTION, 1840–1943

Data decennial 1840–1860, annual thereafter. Two distinct trends are shown, one prior to and one following the Tariff Act of 1924. The latter has been projected tentatively to 1960. *Ratio scale.*

[37]

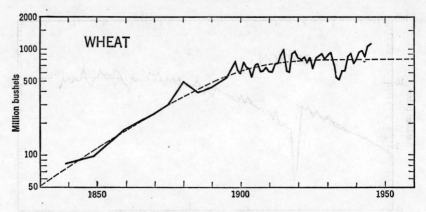

FIG. 14. U. S. WHEAT PRODUCTION, 1839–1945

Data decennial 1839–1870, quinquennial 1870–1895, annual 1898–1945. A trend is shown, projected tentatively to 1960. *Ratio scale*.

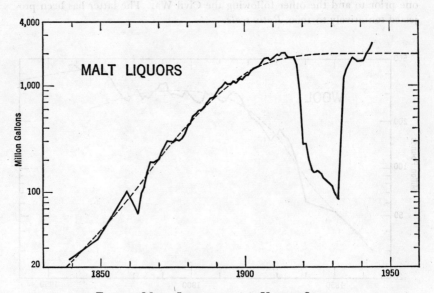

FIG. 15. MALT LIQUOR IN THE UNITED STATES

Consumption 1839–1920. Production 1921–1944. Data decennial 1839–1859, annual 1863–1944. The effect of prohibition is clearly indicated. A trend is shown, projected tentatively to 1960. *Ratio scale*.

[38]

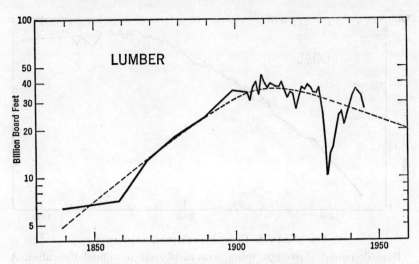

FIG. 16. U. S. LUMBER PRODUCTION, 1839–1945

Data decennial 1839–1899 (1849 missing), annual 1904–1945. First two points are estimated from value data. A trend is shown, projected tentatively to 1960. *Ratio scale.*

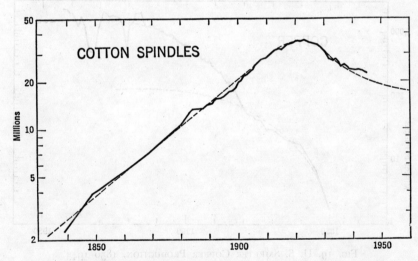

FIG. 17. U. S. COTTON SPINDLES IN OPERATION, 1839–1945

Data decennial 1839–1880, annual 1880–1945. A trend is shown, projected tentatively to 1960. *Ratio scale.*

[39]

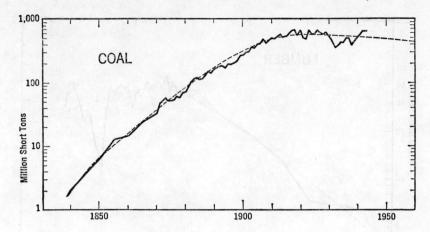

FIG. 18. U. S. COAL PRODUCTION, 1840–1943

Data decennial 1840–1850, quinquennial 1850–1870, annual thereafter. A trend is shown, projected tentatively to 1960. *Ratio scale.*

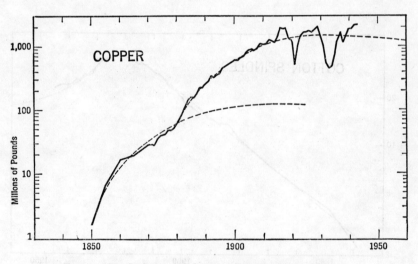

FIG. 19. U. S. SMELTER COPPER PRODUCTION, 1850–1943

Data quinquennial 1850–1870, annual thereafter. A new cycle of growth, coinciding with the birth of the electrical industry, began in 1880. Two trends are shown, the present trend projected tentatively to 1960. *Ratio scale.*

[40]

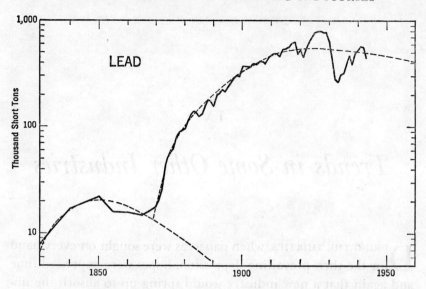

FIG. 20. U. S. REFINED PRIMARY LEAD PRODUCTION, 1830–1943

Data decennial 1830–1850, quinquennial 1850–1870, annual thereafter. Here again two cycles of growth are in evidence. The beginning of the second cycle coincides with the junction of the Union Pacific and Central Pacific tracks at Utah in 1869, when western lead ores were made available to market. Two trends are shown, the present trend projected tentatively to 1960. *Ratio scale.*

I V

Trends in Some Other Industries

DURING THE THIRTIES, when panaceas were sought on every hand for the then prevailing depression, hopes were expressed time and again that a new industry would spring up to absorb the unemployment slack. " Something like automobiles " was the comparison frequently heard. No industry capable of fulfilling the expressed hope appeared. Nor does it seem probable that one will appear on today's postwar scene with enough drive to take up whatever slack in employment may develop in the late forties or early fifties.

It is true that we have a number of relatively new industries. It is equally true that a number of them hold promise of great national service, and eventual large expansion. But from what we know of trends, we are now able to understand that industries follow an orderly pattern of growth, just as do all other organisms. They do not spring full-blown upon the world. Any great industry that can function to create impressive employment in the immediate postwar years is with us right now. It is already on the scene, with an established rate of growth subject to our examination. Furthermore, while these industries offer interesting careers, they are forging ahead with methods that usually produce more material with less human effort than do the processes of older competitors.

What about the various chemical industries, for instance? These

[42]

are a group of industries hailed as the probable savior of the nation's future, a new frontier that will indefinitely extend the nation's progress to ever higher standards of living. Figure 1 provides an answer for one such industry — rayon. Rayon may be viewed as perhaps typical of the young chemical industries. Ignore its wartime distortions, and observe the basic trend. It has a gratifying and in-

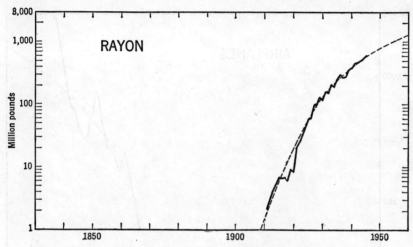

FIG. 1. U. S. RAYON YARN CONSUMPTION, 1911–1945
A trend is shown, projected tentatively to 1960. *Ratio scale.*

teresting course of growth lying ahead of it. Its owners will doubtless make money. But it seems doubtful if they will create any phenomenal amount of extra employment. The fact is that practically none of our chemical industries makes for a volume of direct employment as compared to industries of analogous dollar sales volumes founded in an older era. There are technological reasons involved.

Suppose we consider aircraft. Aircraft was a baby industry before the war; war gave it the status of a munitions industry, and airplanes were turned out as flying platforms for bombs, in numbers limited only by our capacity to build and fly them. To appraise the prospects of the aircraft industry in postwar days we need only glance at the trend line in Fig. 2. Allow for a 100 per cent margin

[43]

of error on the side of underestimate, and we would still have to conclude that following the war the aviation industry would revert to very youthful dimensions. That is just what began happening in late 1945. The two million people it was able to employ in wartime were reduced to a tenth (or less) of their number by the middle of 1946, for the purposes of building peacetime planes.

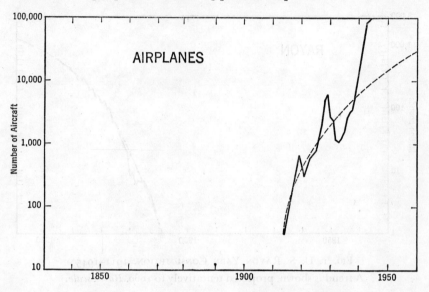

FIG. 2. U. S. AIRCRAFT PRODUCTION, 1914–1944
A trend is shown, projected tentatively to 1960. *Ratio scale.*

Charts showing the trend lines for some of our other younger industries suggest a similarly orderly growth — allowing for due cyclic interruptions of the kind we shall later discuss.

Some industries, like radio manufacturing and electrical refrigeration, are not so young in point of trend as some might suppose. They were already slowing markedly in their rate of growth before the war; replacements had become even then an important factor in maintaining volume; and, after a postwar spurt, the volume of sales will probably not be sufficient to break established growth patterns.

[44]

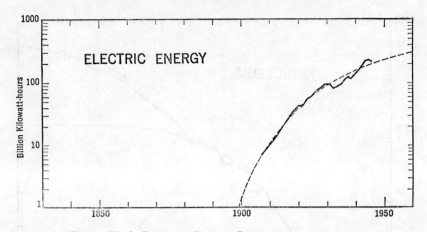

FIG. 3. U. S. ELECTRIC ENERGY PRODUCTION, 1907–1945

Data for 1907, 1912, 1917, 1919; annual thereafter. A trend is shown, projected tentatively to 1960. *Ratio scale.*

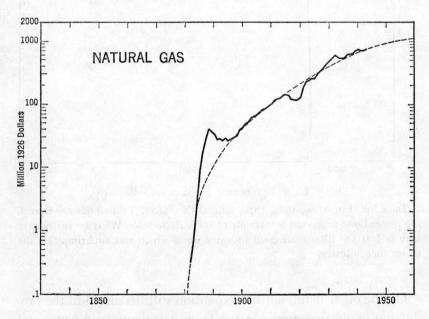

FIG. 4. VALUE OF U. S. NATURAL GAS PRODUCTION, 1882–1943

Data are adjusted for the purchasing power of the dollar, 1926 = 100. A trend is shown, projected tentatively to 1960. *Ratio scale.*

[45]

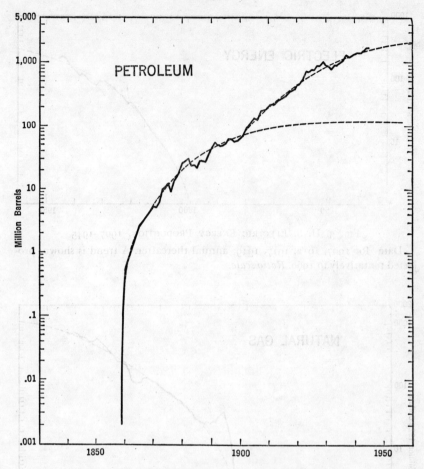

FIG. 5. U. S. PETROLEUM PRODUCTION, 1859–1945

Data for 1859, 1860, 1865, 1870; annual thereafter. Two trends are shown, the present one projected tentatively to 1960. *Ratio scale*. What we really have here is first the illuminating-oil industry upon which was superimposed the motor-fuel industry.

On the other hand, natural expansion still lies ahead in the production of electric energy, natural gas, petroleum, and paper and wood pulp. And industries like electronics and certain branches of chemicals are still almost in their infancy.

[46]

The chart on page 49 is adopted from an idea originally proposed by Roger Babson, to indicate only suggestively — and not with any degree of measured accuracy — the relative positions of a large number of our industries, in terms of their comparable age, or present rate of growth.

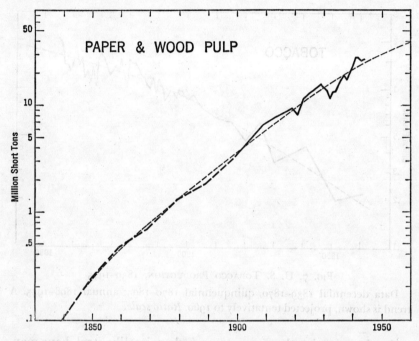

FIG. 6. U. S. PAPER AND WOOD PULP PRODUCTION, 1839–1944

Data decennial 1839–1900, quinquennial 1909–1919, biennial 1919–1929, annual thereafter. Data for 1839–1899 estimated from value figures. A trend is shown, projected tentatively to 1960. *Ratio scale.*

It provides occasion to reiterate that organisms differ greatly in the time they require for reaching maturity. There may be as much variation between two industries, or two corporations in the same industry, in the time span they require for growing from infancy to maturity, as there is between different kinds of animals and different populations.

[47]

The younger industries shown on this composite chart have, in the rapid rate of growth that characterizes youth, a resiliency that may allow them to face the downsweep of postwar cycles with greater aplomb than some of the industries that have reached maturity — for reasons indicated in Chapter I.

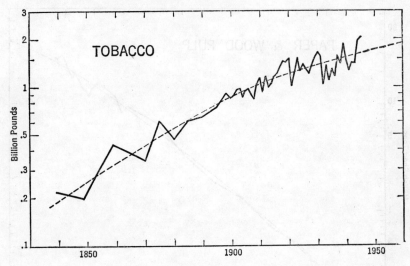

FIG. 7. U. S. TOBACCO PRODUCTION, 1839–1945

Data decennial 1839–1870, quinquennial 1870–1895; annual 1898–1945. A trend is shown, projected tentatively to 1960. *Ratio scale.*

On the other hand, many mature industries, like steel, have managed to build up large financial reserves to carry through lean days, on a scale which young industries have not managed to emulate. Building of comparable reserves has been difficult for today's younger industries like aircraft, which have had their first taste of prosperity in a period of heavy wartime taxation.

Now that we have dealt with trends, we are ready to inquire into the cycles that accompany trends.

To distinguish accurately a trend as it is manifested in the life of the nation's industry, or business, we must first know the cycles.

[48]

Suppose, for instance, that a corporation is enjoying a period of relatively high sales volume, compared to its experience of five years previous. Is this volume the result of its normal rate of growth — a growth proceeding at a relatively rapid rate, because the corpora-

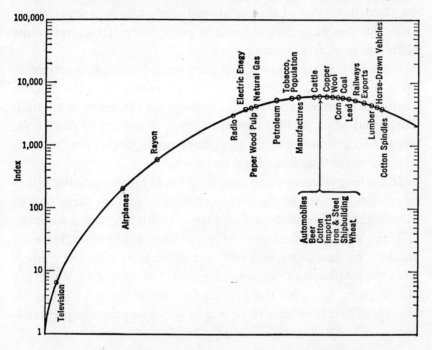

FIG. 8. TRENDS OF VARIOUS U. S. INDUSTRIES

Diagrammatic representation of a growth curve on which there have been located with only approximate accuracy, various American industries, according to their present rate of growth. *Ratio scale.*

When an industry is young and growing fast, it appears here at the left, where the curve is rising rapidly. As it gets older and more mature, it is located near the top of the curve, or even beyond. (Chart after an idea by Roger Babson.)

tion is young? Or is it rather the result of an upsweep that is cyclic — a temporary gain that will be heavily compensated for later? To what extent may the rise be both? So far as the rise is cyclic, when must we be prepared to face a decline? In so far as it is a trend, may it be expected more or less to continue?

[49]

A knowledge of prevailing trends provides us with the first key required for answering such questions — questions that may be applied alike to a whole economy or to an individual corporation. When we know what the cycle is, we are then in a position to isolate its effect from that of the trend, and study trends as separate entities. Studies of the trend without prior study of the cycle must therefore be purely tentative.

We shall quickly discover that the so-called business or economic cycle is in reality a composite of many different cycles. We shall be particularly interested in studying them for evidences of *rhythm*. For if and when we find rhythm we can, *to the extent justifiable*, predict recurrence; and we shall have predictability on the basis of much more than finite logic and guess.

It has long been assumed that if we could only isolate the *causes* of economic cycles we could then effectually prevent them, and so eliminate the downsweeps that plague highly organized societies.

Many volumes have been written to discuss the causes. Here we shall be far less concerned with the cause than with the *timing*. Like the weatherman, we are concerned initially not with altering the weather, but with the problem of predicting it with fair accuracy, so that those due to be out in it can be properly prepared.

V

Some Rhythmic Cycles in Natural Phenomena

CYCLE, as a word from the Greek meaning circle, implies a coming around to the place of beginning. It is used by most people in a very general sense, and we shall employ it here in that same general way. Two other words which hold more exact meaning are "rhythm" and "periodicity."

Cycle does not necessarily imply any regularity in time intervals. Thus one business cycle, as measured from the trough of one depression to the trough of the next, could be four years in length, and the next seven years, and the next thirteen. And one cycle of growth in a human population, as measured from one period of basic stability to another, might be 100 years or a thousand.

Rhythm, or *rhythmic cycle,* will ordinarily be used to denote a cycle which repeats itself at rather uniform time intervals. Rhythm implies a kind of beat. Thus the beating of the heart is rhythmic, though it may be slightly irregular.

Periodicity, periodic cycle, or *regular cycle,* will be used to denote a cycle which repeats itself at mathematically exact intervals. True periodicity, like a true straight line or a true circle, does not exist in nature; but we have close approximations.

[51]

The idea that cycles in human affairs may be rhythmic or periodic has stimulated research for many years.*

Today hundreds of scientists are engaged in some phase of research in the study of cycles. To the man in the street some of their research may seem spent on trivial subjects. Cycles in the incidence of field mice, tent caterpillars, and lynx may appear a far cry from the question of whether or not there are rhythmic cycles in steel production and commodity prices. But just as great advances in medicine, psychology, and other sciences have resulted from the study of lower forms of life, so recent progress in studying rhythms in human affairs owes much to knowledge gained in other fields.

* The list of those to whom the modern student of business cycles must be indebted is long. T. C. L. de Sismondi was among the first pioneers, with his *Nouveaux Principes d'Economic Politique* (1819). Clément Juglar published his *Des Crises Commerciales et de leur retour périodique* in 1860. A. A. Cournot, publishing his *Recherches sur les principes mathématiques de la théorie des richesses* in 1838, is credited with inspiring Jevons, Léon Walrus (1834–1910), F. Y. Edgeworth (1845–1926), V. Pareto (1848–1923), and A. Marshall (1842–1924). W. S. Jevons, who published *On the Study of Periodic Commercial Fluctuations* in 1862, has been called the father of index numbers. Sir Francis Galton (1822–1911) invented correlation analysis, and Karl Pearson (1857–1936) developed it as a tool for statistical analysts. J. H. Poynting in 1884 and R. H. Hooker in 1901 contributed to work on the problem of the secular trend. H. L. Moore in 1914 developed harmonic analysis and correlations in his *Economic Cycles: Their Law and Cause*. Warren M. Persons, who made the first of his business barometers in 1915, began his work on business cycles at Harvard in 1917. Joseph A. Schumpeter, Professor of Economics at Harvard, created a monument with his publication in 1939 of *Business Cycles: A Theoretical, Historical and Statistical Analysis of the Capitalist Process*. The work of George F. Warren and Frank A. Pearson of Cornell is well known. Harold T. Davis, in *The Analysis of Economic Time Series,* published as Monograph No. 6 by the Cowles Commission for Research in Economics, has made an important contribution. Irving Fisher's *The Making of Index Numbers,* published in 1922, was a landmark. N. D. Kondratieff, who published *The Long Waves in Economic Life* in 1926, has thrown much light on the 54-year cycle. Wesley C. Mitchell, who published *Business Cycles, The Problem and its Setting* in 1935, is one to whom every subsequent worker in the field must be indebted. A. F. Burns, in his *Production Curves in the United States since 1870,* is required reading. Such a brief listing can only skirt the fringe of those to whom the authors of this book are deeply obligated. Still others are mentioned in footnotes elsewhere.

Not only is human life complex; it is also evidently subject to a whole complex series of rhythms, as we shall see. And these various rhythms supplement and interfere with each other so that they are often extremely difficult to isolate and trace.

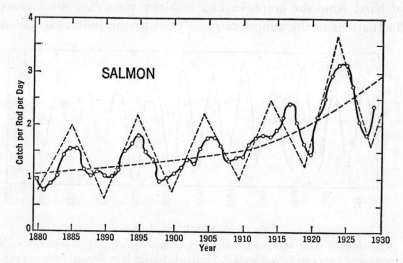

FIG. 1. ABUNDANCE OF ATLANTIC SALMON

Catch per rod per day on the Restigouche River, Canada, 1880–1929, smoothed by a three-year moving average (after Phelps and Belding), together with a regular 9⅔-year cycle. (Appendix II tells about moving averages.)

In the various lower forms of life, which are evidently subject to simpler laws, it is usually possible to find rhythms more clearly revealed than in human affairs. Note, for instance, Fig. 1, which shows the abundance of salmon on the Restigouche River in eastern Canada, from 1880 to 1929. This study was made by Professor Earl B. Phelps of Columbia University, in co-operation with Professor David L. Belding of the Boston University School of Medicine. The statistics were available because an exclusive fishing club along the river had for years insisted on full records regarding the number of fish caught by its members, and the time spent in fishing. The catch of fish per rod per day shows five clear maxima between 1880 and 1930. When a trend and a periodicity

[53]

of 9⅔ years are added to the chart, it is interesting to note that — even though at some points the rhythms are distorted — they later snap back into the pattern.

A rhythm of around 9⅔ years has likewise been found in the lives of lynx. Note the graph in Fig. 2. Many years ago, when great fluctuations in the annual catch of pelts by the Indians troubled

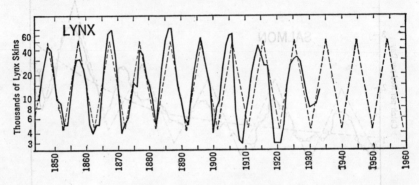

FIG. 2. ABUNDANCE OF LYNX

Offerings of skins to the Hudson's Bay Company, 1844–1933, together with a regular 9⅔-year cycle. *Ratio scale.* Similar behavior is evidenced back to 1735. (Data from Hewett and Hamilton.)

the Hudson's Bay Company, an inquisitive worker in the organization started to plot the annual catch. Since the trappers would work at least as hard in bad years as in times when the catch was good — and probably harder, for a good catch always meant plenty of money for firewater — the plotting may be considered a fair record of the number of animals at large. It apparently varied greatly. The chart shows fluctuations in offerings from as low as 4,000 skins in a poor year to over 70,000 in a really good one. The plotting reveals a distinct 9⅔-year rhythm.

A similar 9–10 year rhythm has been found by other investigators in the abundance of grouse. Curiously enough, it has also been found in the abundance of tent caterpillars. Figure 3 charts the number of letters dispatched in the years 1913–1939 to the New Jersey Experiment Station to complain of the pest. Records of

[54]

three rhythmic cycles are not enough to permit an accurate estimate of the true length; but — so far as the evidence in this particular chart is concerned — the length is clearly in the general neighborhood of 9 to 10 years. A survey of chinch bug incidence covering 120 years, from 1820 to 1940, made by V. E. Shelford and W. P. Flint, also shows some evidence of a rhythm with an average

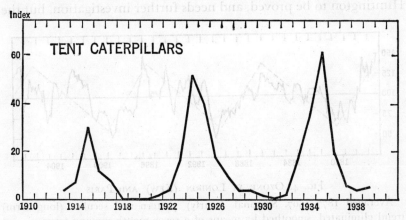

FIG. 3. ABUNDANCE OF TENT CATERPILLARS
Letters of complaint addressed to T. J. Headlee, New Jersey State Entomologist, 1913–1939.

length of about 9.6 years. The last three maxima in Illinois occurred in 1914, 1923, and 1934, these dates being each one year in advance for the maxima in tent caterpillars in New Jersey.

Similar rhythms of a little less than 10 years' average length have been discovered in the lives of such other animals as Canadian marten, fisher, mink, muskrat, and snowshoe rabbit, otherwise known as the " varying hare."

Interestingly enough, a rhythmic cycle of 9 to 10 years — perhaps 9⅔ years — has also been found by Professor Ellsworth Huntington, of Yale, in the rate of death from heart disease in northeastern United States.

Even more curiously, Huntington has traced a rhythm of this same approximate length in the variations in atmospheric ozone.

[55]

The only records for ozone covering an appreciable length of time are those maintained by the Greenwich Observatory in London from 1877 to 1910, and those by the Montsouris Observatory at Paris for about the same period. (See Fig. 4.) The existence of a relationship between the death rate from heart disease and the volume of ozone in the air is of course not claimed by Professor Huntington to be proved, and needs further investigation, but the

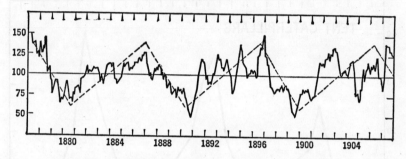

FIG. 4. OZONE AT LONDON (KEW) AND PARIS

Averaged 1877–1907. Seasonal (yearly) pattern and secular (long term) trend eliminated, smoothed by means of a seven-month moving average, and a regular 9⅔-year cycle added. (After Huntington).

coincidence is provocative. Presumably the amount of ozone in the air depends largely on ultraviolet light.

Huntington concludes that the 9⅔-year cycle, whatever its cause or correlations, is basically a biological cycle. It is primarily evidenced both in animals and in men on the "animal," or health, level. (See Fig. 5.) Whatever the conditions giving rise to it, it seems in biological terms to be expressed basically through animal vigor.

There is another rhythm — not to be confused with the rhythm of 9⅔ years — of about 9 years' average length, or a little over, which as a physical rhythm shows up in electrical phenomena in the form of variations in the electric charge in the terrestrial atmosphere. Ellsworth Huntington states that this 9-year rhythm — as we shall call it — is revealed distinctly in the growth of the Sequoias

[56]

in California, as shown by tree rings. We shall note later that a pronounced rhythm of 9 years or so also exists in important economic phenomena.

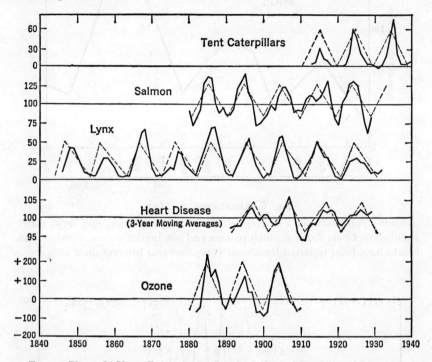

FIG. 5. THE 9⅔-YEAR RHYTHM IN INSECTS, FISH, MAMMALS, MAN, AND OZONE

The ozone curve shows the amount by which the ozone of any given year differs from that of the fifth preceding year, after secular trends have been eliminated (after Huntington).

Many other cycles have been noted at the biological level. One of approximately 4 years shows up in the number, migrations, and epidemics of lemmings, field mice, and the foxes that prey on them in regions as far separated as Norway, Newfoundland, and New York. (See Figs. 6–7.)

Evidence that a rhythm of 41 months exists in the solar constant, as measured by the Smithsonian Institution, has been found by

[57]

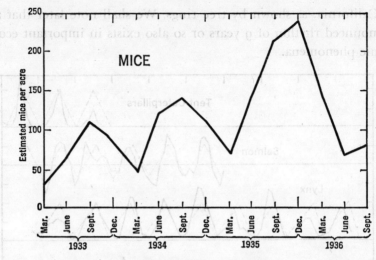

FIG. 6. ABUNDANCE OF MICE

Mouse population in a 20-acre field in central New York, 1933–1936 (after Hamilton). Chart shows seasonal pattern and one rhythmic crest. Previous outbreaks have been reported for almost every four-year interval since 1863.

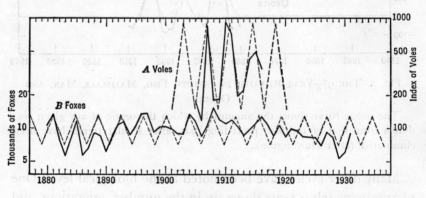

FIG. 7. VOLES AND FOXES

A. Abundance of Voles: Consignments of anti-vole materials sent out in second half of each year by the Agrikultur Botanische Anstalt of Munich, 1905–1916 (after Elton), together with a regular 3 5/6-year cycle. *Ratio scale.*

B. Abundance of Foxes: Number of foxes brought in for bounty in Norway, 1880–1931 (after Elton), together with a regular 3 5/6-year cycle. Note that the fox cycle reaches its crest a year after the crest of the vole cycle. *Ratio scale.*

[58]

T. E. Sterne of Harvard University Observatory. An almost identical rhythm has been shown by Huntington to exist in the daily variability in atmospheric electricity (see Fig. 8).

We shall note later that a rhythm of seemingly identical length is evident in an extraordinary number of economic phenomena.

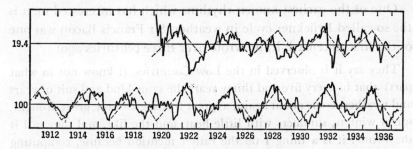

FIG. 8. SOLAR AND TERRESTRIAL DATA

Above, the Solar Constant. Below, Variability of Atmospheric Electricity at London (Kew and Eskdalemuir). Regular forty-one month cycles have been added. The electrical curve is based on percentages of a nine-year moving average with seasonal trends eliminated (after Huntington).

Evidence of the existence of other rhythmic cycles in solar phenomena has likewise been accumulated in recent years. In addition to sunspot rhythms of approximately 11 and 22 years in duration, investigators have isolated other cycles of about 9, 10, and 18 years. The solar constant, or the amount of heat from the sun received on earth, pursues a course different from that of sunspots, but also is subject to rhythmic variations. Our record of solar phenomena, however, is still too short to give us any complete certainty about the exact length of these rhythms.

Some students have laboriously sought to find correlations between such solar rhythms and weather, and also human economic activity. Some interesting evidence of correlation has been adduced.* The reader might here refer again to Fig. 8. But correla-

* See, for instance, the *Quarterly Journal of Economics,* November, 1934: " Solar and Economic Relationships, a Preliminary Report " by Carlos Garcia-Mata and Felix Shaffner; also *Sunspots and their Effects* (Whittlesey House, 1937), by H. T. Stetson.

tion does not prove causality, and data available are still too few to speak of interrelationships in terms of complete scientific certitude. Nor does the problem of interrelationship concern us at this point. One does not need to know the cause of night to know that morning will follow.

One of the earliest known rhythms which has interested men is the so-called Brückner cycle in weather. Sir Francis Bacon was one of the first to remark it; he wrote over three centuries ago:

They say it is observed in the Low Countries (I know not in what part) that in every five and thirty years the same kind and suit of years and weathers come about again; as great frosts, great wet, great drought, warm winters, summers with little heat, and the like, and they call it the prime; it is a thing I do the rather mention because, computing backwards, I have found some concurrence.*

An Austrian, E. Brückner, gave his name to this 35-year cycle in 1891 by writing a book about it, showing clearly that the weather of Europe varies in cycles with an average length of about 35 years. Numerous other weather investigators have found evidence of a rhythmic cycle of the same length. Recent evidence has been accumulated for another weather rhythm of something more than 22 years in average duration.

David Brunt, an Englishman, published in 1927 an exhaustive study tracing some 34 different weather rhythms, with durations of from less than two years up. H. P. Gillette, as a result of a study of droughts, has concluded that one of the basic climatic rhythms is 7.47 years in length — a figure agreeing closely with a climatic rhythm of 7.50 years isolated by Brunt, and of 7.42 years as figured by Beveridge. Gillette multiplies his estimate of 7.47 by three to get a rhythm of 22.4 years, which agrees with a rhythm of that length isolated by Brunt in European weather, and is practically the dominant cycle of 22.3 years, as found by C. N. Anderson in sunspots with alternate cycles reversed.

* As quoted by Ellsworth Huntington in *Mainsprings of Civilization* (John Wiley & Sons, Inc.), p. 455.

H. H. Clayton has found a rhythmic cycle of 7.54 years in baro-
metric pressures prevailing all the way from latitudes above 60° in
Siberia and Iceland to the tropics at Calcutta. Gillette has concluded that other cycles could occur in both an upward and a
downward series where three is either the multiplier or the divisor
of 7.47. The multiple of three applied against 22.4 agrees rather

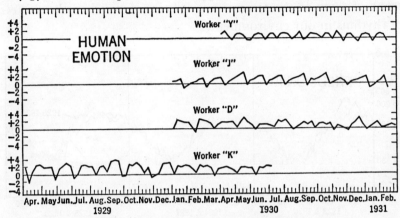

FIG. 9. VARIATION IN HUMAN EMOTION

"Ups" and "downs" in the emotions of four male employees of the Pennsylvania Railroad Company (after Hersey). Reprinted from *Workers' Emotions in Shop and Home,* by Rexford B. Hersey. Copyright, 1932, by the University of Pennsylvania Press.

well with a rhythm of 68 years isolated by Beveridge, and approxi-
mates a rhythm of 66 years which C. E. P. Brooks found evident in
floods of the Nile. But it should be pointed out that it is easy to
romance over interrelationship that ought to exist, and to attach
importance to seeming coincidences that more careful measure-
ments may prove to be entirely disparate phenomena.

Rhythms have even been found in the emotional life of human
beings. Professor Rex B. Hersey of the University of Pennsylvania
found that every individual tends to have his own emotional ups
and downs in rhythmic cycles which may vary in periods, de-
pending on the individual, from $2\frac{1}{2}$ to $9\frac{1}{2}$ weeks. Further studies
conducted in both Europe and America have confirmed Professor

[61]

Hersey's original findings, some of which are charted in Fig. 9. Rhythms have also been found to exist in the incidence of disease (Figs. 10–11). They also exist in growth (Figs. 12–13). They exist in solar phenomena (Fig. 14) and in terrestrial magnetism (Fig. 15). The purpose of a brief summary of this kind can only be to show briefly, for readers unfamiliar with the subject, the scope of some of the research work being devoted to the subject of rhythms in our environment.

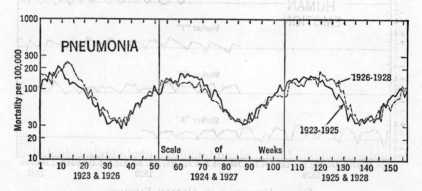

FIG. 10. DEATHS FROM PNEUMONIA

Mortality per 100,000, 1923–1928 (after Metropolitan Life Insurance Company). Chart shows seasonal pattern and three-year rhythm.

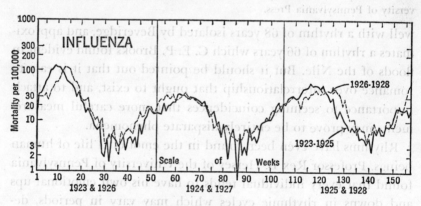

FIG. 11. DEATHS FROM INFLUENZA

Mortality per 100,000, 1923–1928 (after Metropolitan Life Insurance Company). Chart shows seasonal pattern and three-year rhythm.

[62]

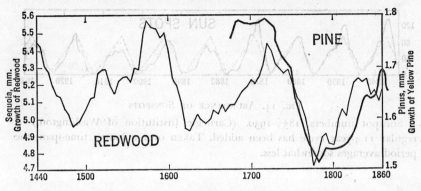

FIG. 12. TREE GROWTH

Long-period fluctuations in growth of Arizona redwood (Sequoia) from 1390 to 1910, and of yellow pine (Pinus) in Calaveras County from 1620 to 1920. One-hundred-year moving averages of tree-ring widths are shown, with the Sequoia curve corrected for trend. A cycle of 150 years, presumably in weather, is disclosed. (After Thompson.)

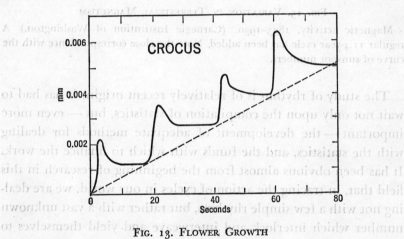

FIG. 13. FLOWER GROWTH

Short-period fluctuations in growth of the crocus. A crocus grows by little jerks, each with an amplitude of about 0.002 mm., every twenty seconds or so, each increment being followed by a partial recoil. (After Bose and Thompson.)

[63]

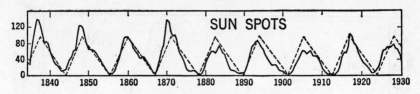

FIG. 14. ABUNDANCE OF SUNSPOTS

Sunspot numbers, 1835–1930. (Carnegie Institution of Washington.) A regular 11.4-year cycle has been added. Taken over a longer time-span, the period averages somewhat less.

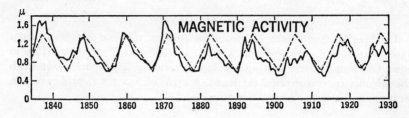

FIG. 15. VARIATION IN TERRESTRIAL MAGNETISM

Magnetic activity, 1835–1930. (Carnegie Institution of Washington.) A regular 11.4-year cycle has been added. Note the close correspondence with the curve of sunspot numbers.

The study of rhythm is of relatively recent origin; it has had to wait not only upon the compilation of statistics, but — even more important — the development of adequate methods for dealing with the statistics, and the funds with which to finance the work. It has been obvious almost from the beginning of research in this field that, in tracing the action of cycles in our world, we are dealing not with a few simple rhythms, but rather with a vast unknown number which interlock and interweave and yield themselves to discovery only through elaborate analysis.

Figures 16 and 17 from Warren and Pearson illustrate the complexity of this problem by showing how two simple rhythms may combine to create a rhythm unlike either of its components. Figure 18, also from Warren and Pearson, shows similarly how several such rhythms may combine into a synthesis. Later on, in Chapter

[64]

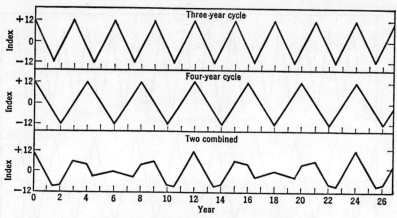

FIG. 16. SYNTHESIS OF TWO CYCLES

Regular 3-year and 4-year cycles, and the two combined. The sum of the two repeats every 12 years. (After Warren and Pearson.)

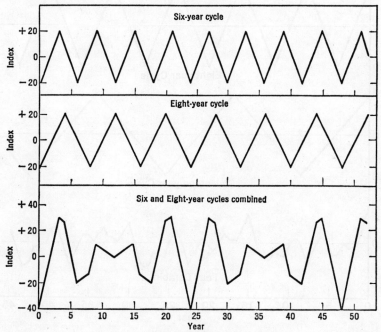

FIG. 17. SYNTHESIS OF TWO CYCLES

Regular 6-year and 8-year cycles, and the two combined. The sum of the two repeats every 24 years. (After Warren and Pearson.)

[65]

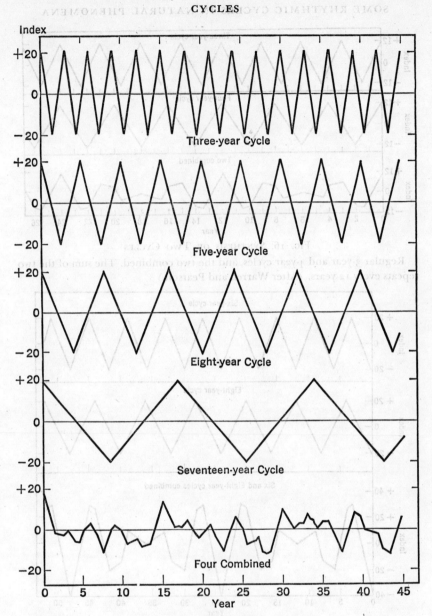

FIG. 18. SYNTHESIS OF FOUR CYCLES

Regular 3-, 5-, 8-, and 17-year cycles and the four combined. The sum of the four repeats every 2040 years. (After Warren and Pearson.)

[66]

XI, more will be said about synthesis and analysis in dealing with rhythmic cycles. Here it is sufficient to note in passing that the cycles with which we must deal in economic life are usually very complex indeed, being seemingly the synthesis of various rhythms of different lengths — together, of course, with numerous accidental variations.

The work of economists in analyzing such complexities is somewhat comparable to that of the astronomers in their task of determining the rhythms in the heavens — with the difference that the astronomers have been dealing with much simpler behavior. As Harold T. Davis has pointed out:

Historically the investigation of time series began with the astronomers. . . . The astronomers, however, were much more fortunate than the economists in one very important matter. The structure of their series as it applied to planetary motion was determined by one or two dominating causes. The motions of the planets were influenced mainly by the excessive mass of the sun and secondarily by the mass of Jupiter. . . . Yet, in spite of this unusual dominance of the sun, one mathematical equation in the set that determines the motion of the moon reaches the incredible length of 170 pages. The economists may learn patience from the astronomers, who have needed three centuries to attain the control which they now have over the elements of their time series. . . .

It is well known that the problem of three bodies — that is to say, the determination of the motions of three bodies — moving under their own gravitational influences has never been completely solved. Hence, the general problem of four, five or more bodies is almost hopelessly difficult. But when one dominating influence exists, such as the dominance of the mass of the sun over the masses of the planets, then the approximation to a complete solution is relatively accurate.*

As we move forward into examining some major rhythms which research has revealed at work in the economic life of our society, we shall do well to remember that we are adventurers in a field of new knowledge. We must be scientifically aware that all our con-

* *The Analysis of Economic Time Series*, pp. 1–2.

clusions are to be qualified by the knowledge that they are tenta
tive. This is still no valid reason why we should not marshal them,
and use them in daily life if they can be made applicable. Had we
waited to apply the tentative findings of any of our major sciences
until they had been proved beyond all possible question, we should
doubtless still have the biological status of cave men. Indeed, all
our sciences have been developed only through having their
hypotheses tested in practical application. When the hypothesis
worked, it was thereafter regarded as proved. Until it was actually
put to work, no amount of argument was adequate to prove it.

As Davis has pointed out, much of our progress in isolating
rhythms depends on the use of elaborate statistical methods which
even yet are in the process of evolution. In the words of Harold
Hotelling: " If only our tyrannical sun were smaller, the family of
planets would enjoy some of the chaos of democratic societies, and
the astronomer would be closer to the statistician. Science would
have arisen later and statistics earlier."

The chaos that seems to prevail in the society we live in is
doubtless one outcome of our own chaotic perceptions. As we have
learned what to look for in nature, we have discovered a remarkable degree of existing order. But we have been pleased to insist
that the activities of man are largely excepted from this rhythmic
order that we note throughout all other manifestations of the universe. Such a credo is as pleasant for our ego as was the long-
enduring geocentric astronomy of our ancestors. But the reader is
invited to suspend it — however tentatively — and to consider with
open mind some data which may lead to other conclusions.

In the pages that immediately follow, we shall consider four
major rhythms that show up prominently in human activity, and
discuss their implications in our economy.

The 54-Year Rhythm

APPARENT in many aspects of the economic life of the United States, since recorded statistics have been available to mark it, is a rhythmic cycle of great importance. Its average length seems to be almost exactly 54 years. That makes it longer than the economic lifetime of most individuals. Thus it readily escapes the notice of the community and of the average businessman whose fortunes, none the less, may in many ways reflect it.

It is a rhythm that is shown statistically, and most clearly, in wholesale price swings. Interestingly enough, there has been in modern times no pronounced long-time *trend* in commodity prices — contrary to general belief. The United States, for instance, is old enough as now organized to have experienced three of these 54-year rhythms; during each one, average commodity prices began at a low level, moved (with interruptions) up to a peak, and moved down again (with interruptions) to approximately the level they had sprung from.

Figure 1 shows the average price level charted for the years 1790–1945, with an ideal 54-year rhythm indicated in dotted lines. One thing is immediately clear. Although the three of the four great wartime price peaks shown on this chart fall fairly well in place, the ideal pattern as it stands could not at any time have foretold, in advance, either the *timing* or the *amplitude* of these war peaks. Wars provide a definite distortion. We shall come back to this matter.

[69]

Meanwhile, look at Fig. 2, which graphs the price average but omits the wartime peaks, leaving merely a gap where they have been eliminated. The actual price wave (ignoring the gaps) now is clearly more in harmony with the ideal wave. It is obvious here,

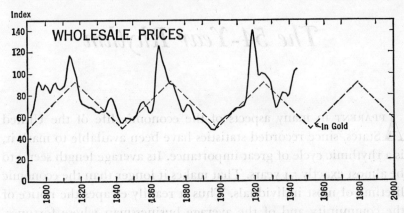

FIG. 1. U. S. AVERAGE WHOLESALE PRICES

Three-year moving average of an index, 1790–1945, 1926 = 100, together with a regular 54-year cycle. The highs of the regular cycle fall in 1817, 1871, 1925, 1979, etc., its lows fall in 1790, 1844, 1898, 1952, 2006, etc. The regular cycle has been extended into the future to indicate approximately what will happen in this series, if the rhythm continues.

however, that some other force or forces are present to distort the actual wave so that it is not in perfect conformity with the ideal pattern. We may correctly suspect that other rhythms should be sought. We shall shortly look for them. Meanwhile, we must first make as sure as we can that the 54-year rhythm is real.

In a remarkably comprehensive study that filled seven volumes, *A History of Agriculture and Prices in England,* J. E. T. Rogers assembled invaluable data on wheat prices over several centuries — data which, however approximate, are useful enough for averages and cover the longest range for any price data we have available. Because wheat in its average value is closely associated with the price of commodities in general, it provides us with a rather useful index.

The Rogers wheat-price data, presented in 10-year averages to smooth out annual fluctuations and converted by N. C. Murray to equivalent cents-per-bushel on the basis of equivalent values of gold and silver, are graphed in Fig. 3. (Shown as percentages of a

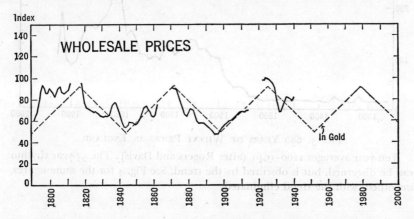

FIG. 2. U. S. AVERAGE WHOLESALE PRICES, EXCEPTING WAR PEAKS

Three-year moving average of index, 1790–1945; omitting periods covering the War of 1812, the Civil War, World War I, and World War II. Conformity to the regular 54-year cycle is more evident with these omissions.

50-year moving average, they are graphed in Fig. 4. Superimposed in dotted lines is an ideal 54-year pattern.) Several facts are striking. Note, first, that from the early part of the thirteenth century until around 1520, there was no important rising "trend" in prices. Then began a long and almost steady upward sweep that was to last through the next three centuries, as world exploration was begun and brought to fruition, and England developed her colonial system and became a great empire.

The first part of the rise, from, say, 1520 to 1576, was rather gradual; from 1576 to a crest around 1660, it was meteoric. Then followed about 80 years of mild decline, to a double bottom around 1740. In the next 70 years there was again a great upsweep, which hardly halted in 1790, and then continued its meteoric flight up to an unprecedented peak coinciding with the Napoleonic Wars.

[71]

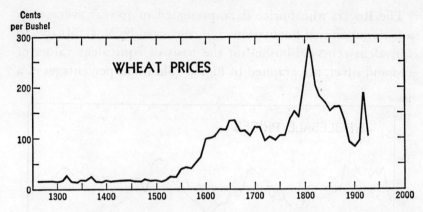

FIG. 3. 680 YEARS OF WHEAT PRICES IN ENGLAND

Ten-year averages 1260–1940 (after Rogers and Davis). The 54-year rhythm can be discerned, but is obscured by the trend. See Fig. 4 for the same figures, smoothed, with the trend eliminated.

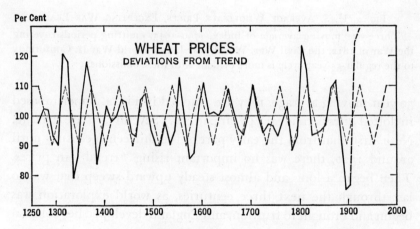

FIG. 4. THE 54-YEAR RHYTHM IN WHEAT PRICES IN ENGLAND

To remove the trend, the prices shown in Fig. 3 have been expressed as percentages of their 50-year moving average; the curve has been smoothed by averaging consecutive percentages. A regular 54-year cycle has been added. A rhythm that has repeated itself as many times (13½) and as regularly as this one cannot easily be the result of pure chance.

[72]

Then followed almost 100 years of decline. In the period from 1845 there was a brief recovery; then decline continued from the war peak to a bottom around 1898–1900. This bottom, reached almost a century after the peak, was lower than any previous level since the late 1500's. The recovery that set in thereafter with 1900, and continued up through World War I, was almost canceled out by the 1930's.

Approximate as the figures on which these averages are based must be, they still furnish us with evidence of a 50–60-year wave in price movements extending well back into history. It becomes immediately apparent if we correct for the trend described above, and then chart the remainder as in Fig. 4. The rhythm, when studied more carefully, proves to have an average length of very close to 54 years.

One of the difficult pieces of work in the history of periodogram analysis was accomplished by Sir William H. Beveridge, to determine whether or not there were permanent cycles in wheat prices in Eastern and Western Europe. In view of the fact that England was for centuries a free-trade country, its wheat prices could be expected to run in consonance with those of the Continent. Sir William used index numbers so constructed that the upward leap in prices during the transition from medieval to modern times was removed, subjecting them to harmonic analysis over a range of approximately 300 years. He found several true periods that gave strong evidence of correlation with known weather rhythms and sunspot phenomena. And at $T = 54.00$ years (which is without such correlation) he also found a relatively significant concentration of energy.

This 54-year wave as we have experienced it in the United States registers itself in commodity price charts rather clearly. The first wave, from low to low, dates itself 1790–1844; the second runs 1844–1898; and the third, in which the United States has experienced two world wars, falls between a low in 1898 and, if the rhythm continues, one around 1952.

[73]

Because of the incidence of three great wars in American history, each of which occurred around the peak of the ideal 54-year wave and coincided roughly with a peak in commodity prices, some observers have called this 54-year rhythm a recurrent " war cycle." Harold T. Davis has gone so far as to suggest that the average interval of about 50 years between conflicts in the Punic Wars of Rome and Carthage might lend force to such a theory, and points out that those wars undoubtedly created in ancient times a degree of inflation in commodity prices such as has attended our modern war periods.

However interesting that thought may be as historical speculation, of more importance to us is a fact which can be ascertained on our patterns by simple observation: in the United States prices have always risen through the upward sweep of the 54-year wave to a major peak, and they have always fallen during its downward turn to a major bottom. Further, as we may observe in the European price patterns, the European prices always tended to make a recovery around the peak of the 54-year wave, even if they were steadily falling in a long-term price trend; and practically always they have tended to halt their rise, even during a steadily rising long-term price trend, when the 54-year wave reached a trough.

Since 1925 the course of the 54-year rhythm in the United States has been generally downward, reaching toward a trough due, as said above, in 1952 (see Fig. 1) . It is significant that — despite the recurrence of war in the 1940's — average retail and wholesale price levels in this country up to mid-1946 did not reach anywhere near the peak of 1919–1920, even though food prices as a group did rise to 1920 levels, as shown in indices like the Dun and Bradstreet index of thirty-one foodstuffs.

We shall learn, when we study the lesser 9-year rhythm which also affects prices, that another rhythmic force was present after 1941 to carry prices upward to moderate degrees. But as a lesser rhythm, it has not served to give prices the enormous rhythmic support they had during the period surrounding World War I, when both the 9-year and 54-year rhythms were moving upward in concert.

Further interpretation of our price data will come more conveniently in the next section, when the reader meets the 9-year cycle in diagram and can see it combined with the 54-year rhythm.

For the present, having seen some evidence for the statistical reality of this 54-year wave, we shall find it useful to consider some challenging ideas regarding its importance in our organized economy. It was N. D. Kondratieff who first succeeded, through his researches, in impressing many economists with evidence that a long wave of approximately this duration characterized the development of our capitalist economy. Joseph A. Schumpeter, Professor of Economics at Harvard University, approaching the problem from various historical angles, has not only confirmed the major conclusions of Kondratieff, but has gone far to provide the basis for a new understanding of the way our economic organism works.

It should be emphasized, in justice to Professor Schumpeter, that he does not accept the need for exact timing or exact estimates of duration for this rhythm, which he regards as the outcome of new efforts in the society toward progress. For the purpose of his researches, which he reported in the two volumes of his *Business Cycles,* he dates the first long cycle in our modern American history — measured from low to low — from the eighties of the eighteenth century to 1842 — noting that " we have seen reasons to believe that this long wave was not the first of its kind." The following long wave as he saw it ran between 1842 and 1897. And the third is our current one, reaching from 1898 on. Perhaps to avoid implying that he considered the datings completely exact, Professor Schumpeter has called these periods " Kondratieff " cycles, rather than cycles of any specific length.

In his admirable study, which surveyed almost two centuries of economic history in England, Germany, and America, he has shown conclusively that every Kondratieff cycle has been uniquely characterized by some particularly important economic or industrial innovation. The first Kondratieff cycle of the last century was the wave in which we moved forward through the process that has been called the industrial revolution, and the absorption of that revolution's effects. The next Kondratieff was the age of steam and steel — and of railroad development. The Kondratieff that is now drawing to a close has been the age of chemistry, electricity, and motors.

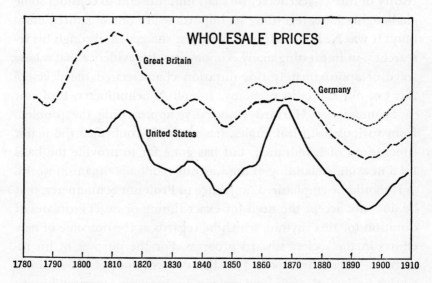

FIG. 5. LONG WAVES IN WORLD WHOLESALE PRICES

Data for Germany, Great Britain, and the United States. Nine-year moving averages of wholesale price indices are plotted on *ratio scale*. (After Schumpeter.)

Figure 5, borrowed from Schumpeter's study, answers the reader's natural question as to how far such a wave may be an exclusively American phenomenon. Here we see traced, in the 9-year moving average of the price indices for the three countries, a correspondence in wave movement that is visible without analysis. As Schumpeter points out:

Not only do cycles in different countries systematically affect each other, so that the history of hardly any one of them can be written

[76]

without reference to simultaneous cyclical phases in other countries; but cycles really are, especially as regards the great innovations that produce the Kondratieffs, international phenomena. That is to say, such a process as the railroadization or the electrification of the world transcends the boundaries of individual countries in such a way as to be more truly described as one world-wide process than as the sum of distinct national ones.*

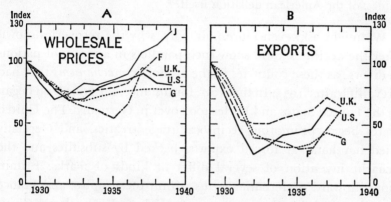

FIG. 6. WORLD INTERRELATIONSHIPS: PRICES AND EXPORTS

A. Indices of wholesale prices, 1929 = 100; B. Indices of total exports, 1929 = 100. (After Davis.)

Davis makes the same point about the unity that prevails in our economic atmosphere:

Was it accidental, for example, that the unrelated inflations of the South Sea Bubble in England and the Mississippi Bubble in France should have developed concurrently and should have collapsed almost within the same month? [1720] And was it a strange coincidence that the collapse of the American securities market in October 1929 should have been accomplished without appreciable lag in the decline of prices and the commerce of all the other nations in the world? †

Davis also shows the two charts which are reproduced in Fig. 6 to illustrate price levels for Germany, France, the United King-

* *Business Cycles* (p. 666), McGraw-Hill Book Co., Inc., 1939.
† *The Analysis of Economic Time Series*, p. 558.

[77]

dom, the United States, and Japan in the decade from 1930 to 1940, together with exports for four of the five nations; and he says:

The astonishing thing to be observed in these figures is that wholesale prices and total exports for all countries follow the same pattern. Could this have been occasioned by the collapse of the American stock market, or is it evidence of something which was the cause, among other things, of the American deflation itself? *

We might ask, even more pointedly, why the recoveries shown after the decline should show such parallels in a group of nations as diverse as these countries in the economic *mechanisms* they had prevailing after 1933. In that year, for instance, the New Deal began in the United States and Hitler took over in Germany. The United States began promoting reciprocal trade treaties, and Germany tried her hand at forced exports, backed by subsidies and the Schacht invention of several different kinds of marks. Britain moved toward preferential tariffs within the Empire, and France moved toward the Blum concepts of socialism. With all such divergencies of mechanism, the nations concerned went through the era with a consistent and continued similarity in economic outcomes.

Even more to the point, the various nations, through all their depressions and ensuing political disturbances and recoveries of the 1930's, displayed in their economies the rhythmic patterns that one could have anticipated from observing their past patterns of response. Says Professor Schumpeter concerning the world-wide depression itself: " We not only know that all the essential features of the post-war period up to the world crisis, but also those of the world crisis itself, answer perfectly to expectation from our model, i.e., past experience." † Of the ensuing economic recovery, he said, after tracing its outcome in England: " Neither new policies nor the numerous disturbances to which England's economy was exposed, effaced the cyclical contour lines which, taking account of specifically English conditions, we should expect from our scheme." ‡

* *Ibid.*　　　　　† *Business Cycles*, p. 984.　　　　　‡ *Ibid.*, p. 966.

As to Germany's burst of activity after 1933, he underlines the fact that in a government-managed economy the rhythms of the previous capitalist economy are still perpetuated, by saying: " This is exactly the kind of performance our model would have led us to expect from unfettered capitalism. Very obviously, however, capitalism was not unfettered." * Of the rise in American prosperity that was attributed after 1933 to the measures of the New Deal — but which arrived strictly as might have been anticipated by anyone projecting the familiar economic waves of the past — Schumpeter declares shortly: " It would be contrary to all experience and common sense, though of course no logical impossibility, that a process which can be strictly proved to have been running its course since at least the sixteenth century and right to the end of 1932, should have come to a stop suddenly on March 4, 1933." †

We shall not labor this point here, noting it chiefly as a matter of background information. Thousands of words could be written in the conventional attempt to trace all the workings of unlike causes which produced such like effects, and in the end no one would be much wiser. For our purposes it is sufficient to note a similarity in the patterns of the phenomena that prevail over such a wide geographic area; those patterns are very closely related, beyond doubt.

Figures 7–11, borrowed from Kondratieff, show some of the workings of the long wave in diverse phenomena.

While the major rhythms we are dealing with seem to prevail more or less universally throughout the world's industrialized economies, some show up more prominently in one nation, others more markedly elsewhere. It is as if different organisms responded with different degrees of receptivity to stimuli in the environment. We shall find this particularly true when we note later how even different industries and different products may be more responsive to one particular rhythm than to another.

Thus we need not find it unusual if the 54-year rhythm usually

* *Ibid.*, p. 972.   † *Ibid.*, p. 985.

shows up in one nation in wider swings, more clearly marked, than in other nations. The 9-year rhythm, which we are shortly to meet, appears more clearly in Germany and America than in England. There is also a 41-month rhythm which similarly stands out more clearly in America than in Europe. On the other hand, there is a rhythm of around $5\frac{1}{2}$ years in the Continental economies which shows up there almost as clearly as the 41-month rhythm in the United States. Here we do find a rhythm of $5\frac{1}{2}$ years in corn and cotton prices, in security prices, and in a number of other series

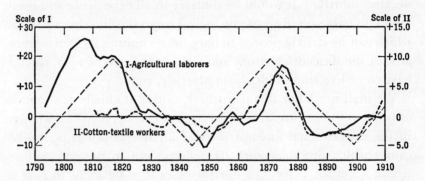

FIG. 7. LONG WAVES IN WAGES

Wages of agricultural laborers and textile workers in England. Deviation from trend on a gold basis, smoothed by means of a 9-year moving average (after Kondratieff). A regular 54-year cycle has been added.

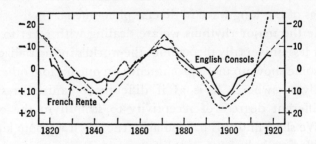

FIG. 8. QUOTATIONS OF INTEREST-BEARING SECURITIES

Deviations from trend of French rente and English consols, smoothed by means of a 9-year moving average (after Kondratieff). The curve has been inverted and a regular 54-year cycle has been added.

[80]

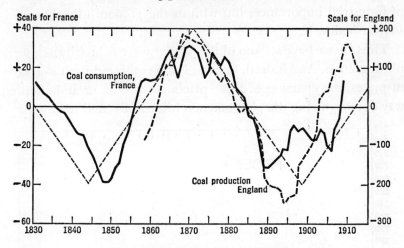

FIG. 9. THE LONG WAVE IN COAL

Coal production in England and coal consumption in France (after Kondratieff). A regular 54-year cycle has been added.

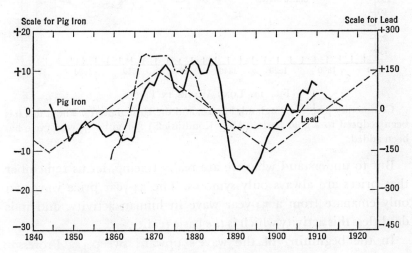

FIG. 10. PIG IRON AND LEAD PRODUCTION IN ENGLAND

Deviation from trend, smoothed by 9-year moving averages (after Kondratieff). A regular 54-year cycle has been added.

[81]

of industrial importance; but with us the 41-month rhythm tends to overshadow it.

Thus far we have spoken of the 54-year wave primarily as a *price* phenomenon. And indeed, because it has registered itself so clearly in prices, the charting of those prices is the clearest and simplest way of recognizing the phenomenon historically, and tracing it.

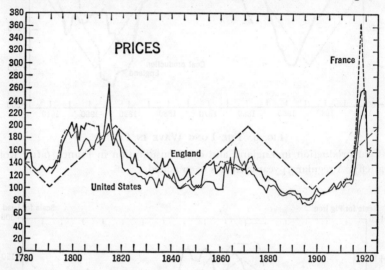

FIG. 11. LONG WAVES IN PRICES

Commodity prices in England, France, and the United States. The index has been reduced to a gold basis. (After Kondratieff.) A regular 54-year cycle has been added.

But to understand what we are really tracing, let us remember that prices are always only symbols. The 54-year price wave can only emanate from a 54-year wave in human activity, and it is doubtless this activity which is *the* basic reality.

In the beginning of the wave's upward sweep, as Professor Schumpeter and others see it, the economy is poised for expansion. The economy is just ending a time of depression when, as in winter, few things grew. Storms have stripped down the decayed trees and weak limbs that could not stand the testing of tempests. In such an economy many debts have been wiped out and others greatly

[82]

reduced; excesses of many sorts have been paid for; surpluses have been largely distributed; people finally begin to sense in the air a kind of burgeoning opportunity, like the faint smell of spring when there is no change yet visible to the eye.

That was the air in our own nation, for instance, around 1790; around 1845; around 1898. It is a time when venture capital starts coming forth — when industries that got started in a small way toward the autumn of the last cycle now begin to find growing opportunities — when even the most casual scatterings of seed may spring up into a lush growth. It is in this early phase of the cycle, as Schumpeter demonstrated, that the innovations which characterize each new cycle of this kind begin to spring up in full force. Just as the railroad was on the scene in primitive form before 1845, but waited until afterward for its real development — just as electricity came into being before 1898, but became a great economic force only in the 1900's — the great industrial innovations that rise in such a springtime were usually planted in the previous cycle. Their really great and characterizing work — a work that is to end in transforming the economic scene — begins in this new spring, as the new industries rise to majestic adult proportions.

A multifarious number of other contributary industries rise simultaneously, some great, some small; and as they thrive, so do older industries that dot the scene. Employment grows; money starts flowing; credit expands. When midsummer has arrived, when the peak of the growing cycle is reached, there seem a million evidences around of a new era, a florid age of growth beyond the memory of living man. Speculation regarding the boundless future is rife. That was 1929, in our own memory.

But now the summer storm gathers; suddenly from nowhere clouds appear, the barometer suddenly falls, and in the quick hail and rains and winds there is a scurrying in from the fields. When the sun comes out again, the humidity is drained from the air, and in its clear light there is already a hint of autumn. That was, say, 1880, and our own 1933.

[83]

This late summer and coming autumn is the period of the great harvest — when the products of industry usually are distributed more widely than ever before. Prices have come down from their peak. And, though they will form occasional tables, they now usually continue to drift generally downward — while wages, on the whole, stay up. This means growing purchasing power for the workers who have jobs. It makes a special kind of proletarian prosperity, where the benefits of the economy are now even more widely shared than in the days when industrial expansion was so rapid.

There is, unfortunately, more unemployment. For, as prices decline, manufacturers naturally look for ways to eliminate extra man-hours, to turn out their product for less. And competition grows among the manufacturers. Newcomers spring up, attracted by the records of lush profits made by those now long in the field. Combinations between manufacturers, sometimes only in the form of silent working agreements, come along naturally, as those most exposed to competition try to protect themselves. And some of these combinations may hang over into the next era — as they did to plague the first Roosevelt — and give him political opportunity.

People begin to try to hold on to what they have. Some of the old enterprise has lost its fervor. There are bursts of speculation and business expansion now and then — we shall see that these come along at fairly regular 9-year intervals, somehow. But the great progress of the era has now been made. As it slowly draws to an end, people look backward to the past midsummer days when great fortunes could sometimes be found almost by turning over a stone, if you were lucky; and jobs were everywhere; and unprecedented industrial and economic achievements were transforming the landscape. And the people begin to wonder if progress has really stopped. Such was the mood in the nineties, for instance, when Bryan was touring the country to tell rapt audiences the nation must not be crucified on the cross of gold. We may see it come again as the mood of the late forties or early fifties.

[84]

This, in very general terms, is the outline of the 54-year rhythm in the economy as it has been outlined by Professor Schumpeter and other observers. Each cycle starts out anew — not where the previous one began, but where the previous one ended. Each leaves the environment vastly different from its state a half century before. The record of the rhythm that appears in the price charts is only a very skeletonized record, but it is at least a record useful for statistical purposes.

Care is needed in interpreting and using the record, just because it is such a skeleton. In viewing the autumn period characterized by price declines, for instance, we must not assume that the declining prices necessarily mean business depression. Under certain conditions, our economy actually works better and smoother when prices are slowly receding. It has been pointed out, a thousand times over, that our chief economic security lies in distributing the output of consumers' goods ever more widely. A slowly falling price level *may* be the sign of such an accomplishment. Such facts serve to warn us that a strong upward sweep in the long-term price chart is not necessarily to be translated as prosperity; and a downward sweep certainly does not necessarily mean depression.

If our 54-year rhythm, which shows up so clearly in the long-term chart of wholesale prices, does not of itself signify times of prosperity and stability and depression, then what does it do? It acts, in effect, as a clock. In association with three other rhythms we are to observe shortly, it gives us a way to know what time it is in our economy.

Suppose a young man has some capital and is going to start a business. Because he is too young to have much personal memory of the great economic tides in the world, and because school education is usually so deficient in such matters, he is like an airplane traveler who travels far around the world without a watch, and then lands in a fog. What time of day is it? How much time has he before evening? Is he sure even of the day of the month? It might be the beginning of a new week, or it might be the end of an old one —

depending on the international date line, and where he is in reference to it. Unless he knows, or can quickly find out, he may manage himself very badly.

Anyone who starts out in business without knowing what time it is on the economic clock will obviously owe much to luck if he succeeds. And many men who have engaged successfully in business for a long time owe much to their sheer good fortune in having started out when the economic sun was rising.

Today the great 54-year rhythm is setting; it has been on the decline since the middle twenties. In the middle 1950's it should be rising again, if the past rhythmic patterns repeat themselves. Unless past precedent fails, we may look forward to that economic time as farmers look forward to spring after a long winter — a spring when seeds long quiet in the ground should be shooting up almost miraculously, with a new spirit of enterprise revealing itself everywhere.

Just as the millions saw electricity and the motor completely transform our environment and ways of living following 1898, those who live into the third quarter of our century may well see the growth of new forces just as dramatic, impelling, and universal in their effect — forces of which atomic energy may be only one.

The start of a new *trend* in our economy cannot be forecast, as we have seen. But even without expecting any lift in the trend lines, this new long-term cycle could be read in advance to provide hope for a coming long-term era of prosperity and progress in our nation, regardless of any depression that may intervene.

VII

The 9-Year Rhythm

IN CHAPTER V we briefly met a rhythm that has been calculated to have a length of very close to 9 years. As previously pointed out, this periodicity should *not* be confused with the $9\frac{2}{3}$-year rhythm, that appears in biological phenomena. We shall now meet this rhythm again in company with our 54-year wave, and shall refer to it hereafter as the 9-year rhythm, for purposes of simplicity. It is the rhythm which Schumpeter, without defining its length too closely, likes to call the Juglar cycle, in honor of that pioneering Frenchman:

His great merit is that he pushed the crisis into the background and that he discovered below it another, much more fundamental, phenomenon. . . . Henceforth, although it took decades for this new view to prevail, the *wave* ousted the *crisis* from the role of protagonist of the play. . . . The problem has again changed its complexion. It is no longer the problem of *the* wave. It is the problem of identifying and, if possible, isolating the many waves and of studying their interference one with each another.*

* *Business Cycles*, p. 163.

Only a few years after Juglar's work appeared in 1860, an American, Samuel Benner, produced a work citing regular cycles in the average yearly price of pig iron — cycles that averaged nine years in length. Benner, who called himself "an Ohio farmer," published in 1875 a curiously interesting book called *Benner's Prophecies of Future Ups and Downs of Prices,* which went through

[87]

Schumpeter finds his "Juglars" clearly indicated in the economic life of Germany, England, and the United States; by charting percentage deviations of price indices from their 9-year moving averages in these three countries, he produces a chart where the Juglars are apparent even to an undiscerning eye (see Fig. 1).

In our stock market, as well as in commodity prices, we find evidence of an approximate 9-year rhythm clearly stated (see Fig. 2). Figure 3 shows the deviations from trend charted with an ideal 9-year pattern.* Rising upon the 54-year rhythm, the shorter wave often serves by its troughs and peaks to mark important events in the economic flow of things. The peak in this 9-year rhythm in 1919, coming at a time when the 54-year rhythm also was reaching toward a crest, coincided with that year's peak in the 3-year moving average of commodity prices, highest in this century (compare Figs. 2 and 3, with 4 and 5).

It was in 1928, again, that this 9-year rhythmic pattern in the stock market once more reached its crest. The top of the 54-year

---

numerous editions. In addition to the 9-year cycle in pig iron prices, he cited cycles averaging 5½ years in corn prices, 11 years in cotton prices, and 18 years between financial panics. He noted that the variations from a standard 9-year pattern in iron prices tended to repeat themselves every third cycle. Time has proved him right to the extent that, if you had purchased and sold pig iron on the basis of his projected 9-year patterns, your gains over a 69-year period would have been twelve times your loss.

There is also clear evidence of the continued existence of the 5½-year rhythm he discovered in corn prices. On the other hand, the 11-year rhythm he found in cotton prices has failed to continue to dominate. His observations as to the existence of an 18-year rhythm — with variations of not more than two years in either direction — fit very well with the facts about the 18⅓-year rhythm we shall discuss in Chapter IX; and the panics of 1893, 1907, and 1929 were all within two years — one way or another — of a rigid 18-year pattern based on 1873.

* Over the period for which we have data 9⅕ years fits stock-market behavior better than a rhythm of exactly 9 years in length. Over the same period, 9⅕ years better fits the swings in wholesale prices, too; but over the longer period for which wholesale price data are available, the length is seen to be more nearly 9 years. See Fig. 5.

[88]

rhythm had already been reached about 1925. In the late twenties, so long as the 9-year rhythm continued rising, the momentum of the market was maintained. But when this rhythm reached its

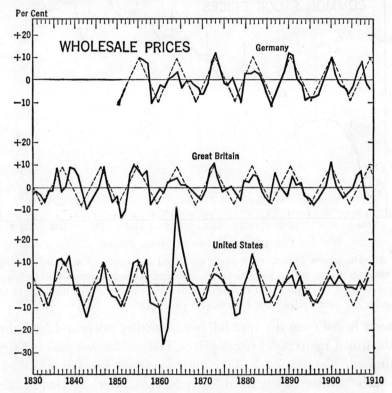

FIG. 1. THE 9-YEAR RHYTHM IN PRICES

Data for Germany, Great Britain, and the United States. Percentage devia‐ tions of price indices from their 9-year moving averages, 1830–1910 (after Schumpeter). Regular 9-year cycles have been added.

crest in 1928 and then turned after the 54-year rhythm, which had already been going down for three years, the beginning of the great fall was close at hand (compare Figs. 2 and 3).

Inversely, it was after this rhythm had reached a trough in 1923–1924 that the economy started rising expansively to the peak reached in 1928. And it was after its trough in 1932–1933 that re‐

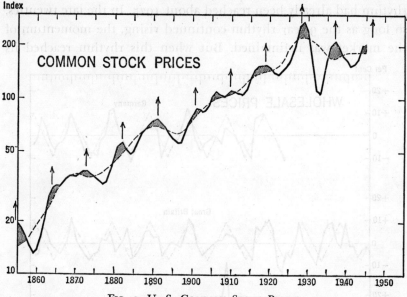

FIG. 2. U. S. COMMON STOCK PRICES

Axe-Houghton Index. 1854–1945, smoothed by means of a 3-year moving average, together with a weighted 9-year moving average, extrapolated to 1944. Shaded areas show time and extent of relative strength. Arrows mark highs of regular 9⅕-year cycles. (See footnote on page 88.)

covery began from the 1928 fall in commodity prices and from the subsequent 1929 crash in stock prices. The well-known peak in 1937 followed. The next peak of the ideal 9-year wave was in mid-1946.

Such " calling of the turns " may be traced to the action of this rhythm, time and again, for scores of years in American economic history. The signal is clearest, as a rule, when near-by turns come also in the other rhythms we are observing. The concurrent movement of two major rhythms may often suffice to indicate such a turn in the symbols graphed on our charts; concurrent movement of three major rhythms indicate it almost unerringly. As Schumpeter has said:

It is clear that the coincidence at any time of corresponding phases of all three cycles will always produce phenomena of unusual intensity, especially if the phases that coincide are those of prosperity or depres-

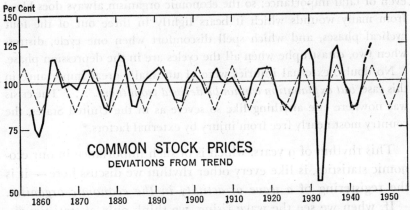

FIG. 3. THE 9-YEAR RHYTHM IN COMMON STOCK PRICES

Percentage deviation of the 3-year moving average shown in Fig. 2 from the 9-year moving average also given in the same chart, together with a regular 9-year cycle.

The highs of the regular cycle fall as follows: 1856.0, 1865.0, 1874.0, 1883.0, 1892.0, 1901.0, 1910.0, 1919.0, 1928.0, 1937.0, 1946.0, 1955.0, 1964.0, 1973.0, 1982.0, etc. The lows fall halfway between these dates. (The exact year indicates the mid-point of that year. Thus " 1928.0 " means June 30, 1928; " 1946.0 " means June 30, 1946.)

A rhythm that has repeated itself as many times (10) and as regularly as this one cannot easily be the result of pure chance.

The regular cycle has been extended into the future to indicate approximately the behavior that may be expected in the deviations of the 3-year moving average from the 9-year moving average, if this rhythm continues.

sion. The three deepest and longest " depressions " within the epoch covered by our material — 1825–1830, 1873–1878, and 1929–1934 — all display that characteristic.*

And further, regarding attempts to look back while the record is still fresh, and find the " causes " of the 1929 collapse:

As a man may suffer from many ills and yet for an indefinite time lead a vigorous life without being inconvenienced by them until, when his general vitality has ebbed away, those ills or any one of them may suddenly acquire what to the specialist's eye will seem paramount or

* *Business Cycles*, p. 173.

[91]

even of fatal importance; so the economic organism always does bleed from many wounds which it bears lightly in three out of the four cyclical phases, and which spell discomfort when one cycle, distress when two, catastrophe when all the cycles are in the depression phase.

No doubt, external injuries were of unusually great importance in this case, *but explanation cannot be derived from them.* . . . The crisis was nowhere else anything like so severe as in the United States, the country most nearly free from injury by external factors.*

This rhythm of 9 years, which is of such importance in our economic statistics, is like every other rhythm we discuss here — it is the registering of *a wave of activity in the economic organism.*

If, when we see the wave rising, we think only of statistics rising, we have a too limited view. For the statistics, of course, are only a reflection of human movement; they are merely *one* way of seeing it, and of measuring it. Schumpeter has shown, for instance, that what this 9-year wave really reflects is this: Repeatedly — at something like the 9-year interval — the industries creating the great economic thrusts-forward in the 54-year cycle have new surges of activity. There are new bursts of enthusiasm, of energy, of speculation, of production, of progress. The rise of this rhythm registers this almost unerringly. It is not surprising that the rise in such activity is accompanied by a rise or a " recovery " in wholesale prices.

If the reader will glance again at the chart for wholesale prices in the previous chapter, on page 70, he will be better prepared to look at Fig. 4, which is the latter part of this same chart with a 9-year moving average trend added. Figure 5 shows the deviations from trend charted with an ideal 9-year pattern. It is clear at first glance that they fit with astonishing regularity. The 9-year wave here is extremely evident. It shows up strikingly in many individual businesses (see Fig. 6) as well as in wholesale prices and prices of common stocks. (See Fig. 7 for a summary of the wave.)

Now we are ready for another step: in Fig. 8 see the experiment

* *Ibid.,* p. 911. Italics supplied.

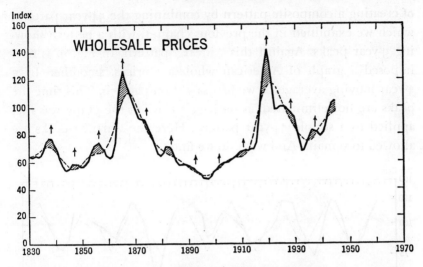

FIG. 4. U. S. WHOLESALE PRICES, 1830–1945

(1926 = 100. A 3-year moving average, together with a weighted 9-year moving average, extrapolated to 1944.) Shaded areas show time and extent of relative strength. Arrows mark highs of regular 9-year cycles.

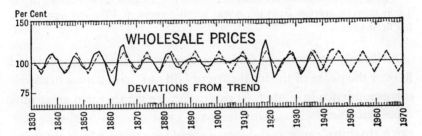

FIG. 5. THE 9-YEAR RHYTHM IN WHOLESALE PRICES

Percentage deviations of the 3-year moving average from the 9-year moving average, 1830–1944, together with a regular 9-year cycle.

A regular 9-year cycle has been added and projected into the future to show what will happen if this rhythm continues.

The dates of the turning points of the regular cycle are the same as those given for the regular cycle of common stocks in Fig. 3.

[93]

of creating a composite pattern by combining the 54-year pattern, which we examined in the previous chapter, with a pattern showing 9-year peaks. Against this " ideal " pattern, in Fig. 9, is now imposed a graph of American wholesale prices, smoothed by a 3-year moving average, as we first saw it on page 70. This time the peaks are not eliminated, as on page 71, when the graph was first applied to a simple 54-year pattern. Here the wartime peaks are allowed to remain. And what do we find?

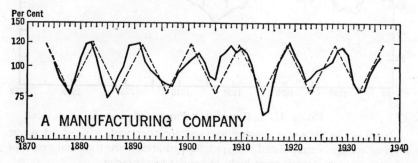

FIG. 6. An Individual Business

The 9-year rhythm in the sales of company A. Percentage deviations of the 3-year moving average from the 9-year moving average. A regular 9-year cycle has been added.

Strikingly enough, we find that the peaks in the actual record fit over the peaks of the ideal pattern laid out, with a most dramatic correspondence in timing. In particular, we see that two great wartime price peaks, occurring near the crest of each of the 54-year price rhythms, came at the top of the 9-year wave which rides the longer rhythm. Further, it was a 9-year peak occurring on the *up*-side of the 54-year wave. The combination of three forces — the upsweep in the 54-year wave, the upsweep in the 9-year wave, and the incalculable force of war — provided together a leverage of great intensity. The height of the two great inflation peaks here reflects that.

Now compare these two price peaks, as shown on the chart, with the third and smaller peak toward which our price line was reach-

[94]

ing in 1945. From 1939 on into 1945 there was also a war to act as an inflationary force on the price level. But — in this 1939–1945 period, the 54-year wave was declining. Would the reader have said

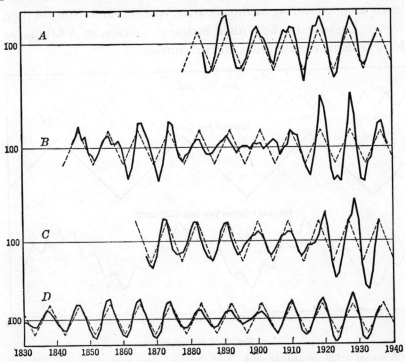

FIG. 7. RECAPITULATION, THE 9-YEAR RHYTHM

Percentage deviations of the 3-year moving averages from the 9-year moving averages in (A) Sales of Company A; (B) Sales of Company B (another company in a totally different industry); (C) Prices of Common Stocks; and (D) Wholesale Prices.

Regular 9-year cycles have been added to all curves. The first, third, and fourth have been smoothed by a 3 nine-year-section moving average.

in advance that prices during World War II would rise as high as in World War I — knowing that the 54-year rhythm was no longer moving up, and that only the rising 9-year wave was there, working in conjunction with wartime forces, to hold up prices?

On the basis of these patterns, he could have guessed, when the

[95]

war commenced — and before he knew anything about the government price controls that would be imposed — that wholesale price levels during World War II would probably *not* reach the levels attained during or shortly after World War I. Nor did they. Not in England, or the United States, or Canada, or Australia, or New Zealand, or numerous other countries.

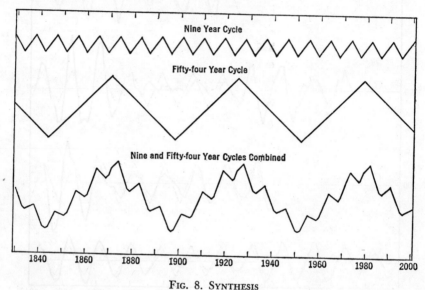

FIG. 8. SYNTHESIS

A 9-year cycle, a 54-year cycle, and the two combined. (See also Figs. 16, 17 and 18 on pages 65 and 66 in Chapter 5.)

The real price inflation that occurred in connection with World War I reached its maximum not with the end of the war, but about a year and a half later. There have been indications in the rhythms of the American economy that prices might similarly mount for a year or so following World War II — say, into 1947. But whether all average wholesale prices would reach the high levels of 1919 and 1920, before recession, could be doubted by those aware of the timing of the 54-year and 9-year cycles.

The man in the street could have told you that government " control " was the " reason " why World War II prices stayed below

World War I levels. But our charts are not concerned with " reasons why " — they reflect rhythms.

Look at the chart again, *circa* 1933. Do you see the 9-year wave rising there? That is the year in which American commodity prices started to rise again from depression bottoms of the 1930's. It is

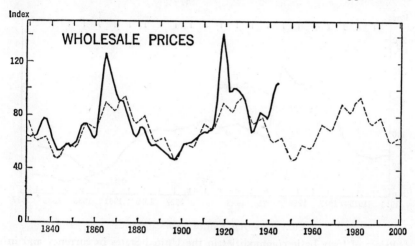

FIG. 9. U. S. WHOLESALE PRICES

Three-year moving average, 1926 = 100, together with the 9-year and 54-year cycles in combination (see Fig. 7 above). The projection should be thought of in terms of gold, 1937. It shows approximately what will happen (of course barring war distortions) if these two rhythms continue.

also the year in which the United States abandoned the gold standard. Many reasons have been cited for the economic upturn which began at that time. But if we record the facts only as seen in our rhythms, we may note that when the long-prevailing 9-year rhythm signaled for a rise, the rise came. After the country went off gold, prices in terms of gold still kept on going down. But prices in terms of the dollar — " real " prices so far as the American public was concerned — now went up, just as a projection of the 9-year rhythm could have forecast (see Fig. 10, borrowed from Warren and Pearson).

It has of course been argued that the rise in prices was " caused "

[97]

by the departure from gold; and in so far as our price level is influenced by the price of *imported* commodities, that thesis is defensible. But whether departure from the gold standard then acted causally for the whole subsequent uptrend in prices is exceedingly problematical.

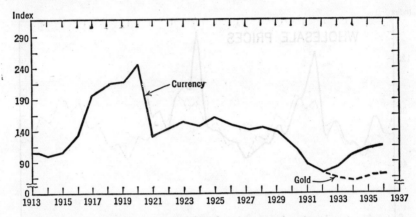

FIG. 10. GOLD PRICES AND CURRENCY

Prices of forty basic commodities in the United States in currency and in gold, 1913–1936 (after Warren and Pearson). 1910–1914 = 100.

This rise of prices from 1933 on, in harmony with the indicated 9-year pattern (the rise can possibly be dated from an earlier turn in 1932), was doubtless the event that inspired Professor Schumpeter's observation that a process running its course since at least the sixteenth century could hardly have come to a stop on March 4, 1933.

If this veers on a determinism disturbing to some readers, it is worth recalling — parenthetically — that all of us are born into a highly determined form of society in which everyone adjusts himself constantly to prevailing social patterns or goes down trying. (The greatest ability is adaptability, as Samuel Crothers once said.) Further, it is clear that there is room in these charts for all the freedom and accident of choice any reader would like to have implied. Consider, for instance, the wartime peaks in commodity prices. So far as our pattern is concerned, there is nothing there that calls for a *war*time peak at any time, or anywhere. Nor is there anything that tells us if and when war will break out. Nor, when it breaks, have we any way of measuring in advance the intensity of the leverage which this force will exert on the price level, once the force has been introduced into the pattern.

Davis, by measuring the intensity of war's effect on commodity prices, has worked out an interesting equation for comparing such a skirmish as our Spanish-American War with our effort in World War I. By comparison with 1917–1918, the affair of 1898 was no war at all.* But these are matters which may be seen only after the event, by noting the deviations of actual commodity prices from levels called for by long-term patterns. As previously noted, we have no way of knowing in advance when war is going to break. And we can only reason by analogy in judging what final effect a war might have.

There is nothing in the first two 54-year rhythms in our nation's history, for instance, to suggest that the third one would see two wartime peaks in commodity price levels. There does not seem to have been any pattern demanding even one war inflation. If our peak of 1919 did have two earlier precedents in the peaks of 1814 and 1865, occurring at nearly corresponding points on the cycle, there appears nothing to suggest that a wartime peak was bound to come then. All one could have done in 1914, when world war did break, was to have reasoned by analogy to the conclusion that world war at that point of the cycle, where two major rhythms were moving up together, would result in a very large leverage on prices. It did.

Quite similarly, and again only by analogy, it was possible to reason in 1939 that at this point of time — when the 54-year rhythm was moving downward — the advent of war would not have the price leverage of years such as 1914–1919, when war and two up-sweeping cycles accompanied each other.

* *Analysis of Economic Time Series,* p. 554.

[99]

It would seem that such an interpretation, viewed from the vantage point of 1946, had justified itself. It must of course be stated flatly that analogy can always be dangerous. It must always be used warily, with full knowledge of the dangers.

Before we leave this subject of wartime commodity prices for a while, another warning, by way of qualification of the analysis, is worth registering. Please note, on Fig. 9, the last 9-year rhythm which starts rising on the declining 54-year rhythm in 1941 or 1942. This shorter rhythm, due to reach a peak in mid-1946, represented a strong rhythmic force. Though it was not reinforced by a rising 54-year cycle, to act in conjunction with it, it was given incalculable war leverage as a partner in its 1942–1946 rise. The combined result — as our 9-year rhythm reached for its peak — was a very heady inflation.

By analogy we could have reasoned in advance that the 1946 inflation would not reach 1919 heights, because of its position on the 54-year wave. But we had no ready way of estimating accurately *in advance* whether the inflationary leverage of World War II would be greater than in World War I, or by how much.

In the forties, of course, there were vastly greater quantities of money in circulation, stemming from wartime government deficits that far exceeded those connected with World War I. But statistical comparisons of this kind threw small advance light on comparable leverage, in view of such factors as the greater will-to-save on the part of the people, the tendency of many to hoard money and credits as a store of value, and the abolition of the free market effected under OPA and other government controls. Such variables made difficult any prediction based on estimates of the comparable war leverage factors during the two periods.*

But granting the hypothesis of much greater war leverage behind prices in the larger war of the forties, one could still ask in 1946 whether or not it would prove great enough to compensate for the

* For further discussion of ways to measure the distortions of war, see Chapter XIV.

lack of any price leverage in the declining 54-year rhythm. If so, then one might expect prices rising on the 9-year rhythm to reach a peak matching or exceeding that of 1919. If not, then the price level could still be expected to reach a substantial 1946–1947 peak, at the crest of the 9-year wave pattern — though probably well under the peak of 1919 when the 9-year and 54-year rhythms had both been rising in conjunction.

Our patterns could give us no definitive advance answer concerning the height of the peak to be reached. They could only indicate the approximate timing. But it seemed safe, even from the early vantage point of 1941, to assume that a very substantial 4- to 5-year rise in commodity prices and stock market levels lay ahead. The course of the 9-year rhythm made that forecast clearly possible. Those who made their plans accordingly, on the basis of the 9-year rhythm's projection, profited well.

In making judgments as to timing, one fact always must be underscored. The 9-year rhythm, and also the other economic rhythms we are to consider, manifest themselves *progressively* in various sorts of business activity and prices. For example, note Fig. 7 in this Chapter again. And compare, in Chapter VIII, Figs. 3 and 5.

From 1946–1947 onward, the 9-year rhythm, as well as the 54-year pattern, is due to be reaching for a bottom around 1951–1952. Whether, in declining after their excess wartime inflation, wholesale prices and stock market values may temporarily fall below the trend line is another question the patterns do not answer. But, past observations tend to show that wartime distortion in prices *above* the trend suggests some compensation below it that can be expected ultimately — if precedent prevails.

VIII

The 3½-Year Rhythm

CLEARLY INDICATED in the Federal Reserve Index of Industrial Production, in pig iron production, in common stock prices, in scores of other production and price series, runs a rhythm that has been variously estimated at from 39 or 40 to 42 months in length.* It would seem that 40.8 months is the length that provides the closest fit for many series from 1900 to date, but the true length has as yet not been determined for certain. There may be two rhythmic tendencies, for instance — one slightly over 42 months, perhaps, and one slightly less than 40 months — that combine to produce a fluctuation with a seeming length of almost 41. This 41-month rhythm has continued true from its discovery back in 1923.

It is comparatively easy to find rhythms in anything — even ran-

---

* Professor W. L. Crum, in 1923, showed a rhythm of approximately 40 months in monthly commercial paper rates in New York from 1866 to 1922. Joseph Kitchin around the same time found the same rhythm in bank clearings, wholesale prices and interest rates, both in the United States and in Great Britain. Chapin Hoskins in early 1935, as a result of a time-chart analysis of pig iron production and many other economic series, concluded the cycle had an approximate 40.5-month periodicity. Later he came to believe the length to be 41.0 months.

Professor Schumpeter's analysis of five American systematic series gave a mean duration of 42.05 months. Armstrong of the Bell Telephone Company determined the length, in general business conditions in the United States since 1885, to be 40.78 months.

[102]

dom numbers — although, of course, such rhythms do not occur with enough regularity or with enough repetition to justify belief in their reality. Nevertheless, it is true that rhythms in almost anything can be found after the event. If, however, the numbers are random and the rhythms are merely read into them, they will not continue as the series continues to unfold. For example, in dealing cards face up, one might get a black and a red, a black and a red, a black and a red, ten times in a row. This is a rhythm of unusual regularity, but conceivably the result of chance. If, however, having made this observation, we find that the next ten cards also come up black and red, we can begin to suspect that the cards have been stacked, and that there is a real rhythm, somehow incorporated in the arrangement.

With the rhythm that concerns us here, as with many other rhythms, thousands of hours of labor must doubtless still be spent before we can maintain more than tentative conclusions regarding periods. If now we call this rhythm one of $3\frac{1}{2}$ years, it is primarily for convenience of reference. Professor Schumpeter likes to call it the Kitchin cycle, in recognition of one of the first discoverers, and observes that " the Kitchins can be best observed, for all countries, on the chart of rates of changes."

A charting of the Federal Reserve Index of Industrial Production, given in Fig. 1 with a 41-month pattern added, shows how, on an actual *production* chart, the rhythm concealed in the figures may elude the average businessman. True, there is much evidence of rhythm here, but the existence of the pattern is not obvious until it is revealed by the rate of change technique. To see this, look at Fig. 2, where these same production figures are graphed for the *rate of change*. For an example of the same kind of analysis applied to pig iron production, see Figs. 3–4.

A rate-of-change graph is based on a simple calculation. Here, instead of plotting the actual tonnage figures, the tonnage for each month is plotted in terms of its *percentage* of the figure for a previous fixed interval. For instance, on the basis of a one-year

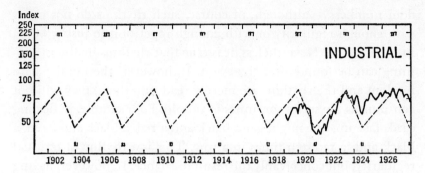

FIG. 1. THE 3½-YEAR RHYTHM

The 3½-year rhythm in the Federal Reserve Index of Industrial Production, January 1919 — December 1945. A regular 41-month cycle has been added and projected through 1954, to indicate approximately what will happen if the rhythm continues.   (After Chapin Hoskins.)   *Ratio scale.*

interval we would compare January with the previous January, February with the previous February, etc. This method eliminates many of the short-term variations, minimizes long-term swings, and enables us to see more clearly the variation of medium length. Percentage relationships of this kind are familiar enough. If we say that business this month is 10 per cent above business a year ago, we are using the same sort of comparison.

In Fig. 4 the agreement of the actual pattern with the ideal wave is rather astonishing, with the majority of the highs and lows com-

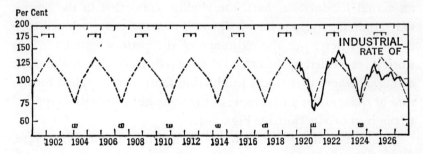

FIG. 2. RATE OF CHANGE

The 3½-year rhythm in the rate of change of U. S. industrial production, January 1920 — December 1945. Here, are charted moving percentages of the

[104]

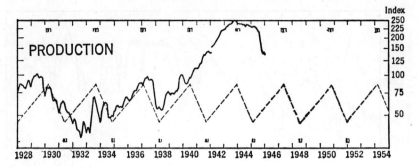

PRODUCTION

IN INDUSTRIAL PRODUCTION

The regular 41-month cycle was determined and projected by Mr. Hoskins early in 1938. The dates for the three next ensuing highs of the projected 41-month cycle would be April 1947, September 1950, and February 1954. The two next lows of the same cycle would be June 1948 and November 1951.

ing pretty closely within the frames at top and bottom that indicate majority performance. And the points where complete agreement is lacking are as significant for our purpose as the others. Notice, for instance, the trough reached in 1908. It is delayed; it falls outside the pattern. Some force has entered the picture here which our $3\frac{1}{2}$-year pattern does not account for, and the unknown force is distorting the wave. But now notice the next trough, at the end of 1910. Here our figures have snapped right back into the pattern, just as if no previous distortion had taken place. Whatever

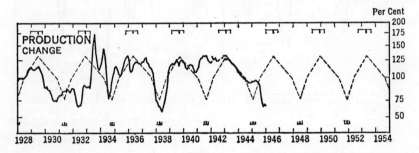

PRODUCTION
CHANGE

IN INDUSTRIAL PRODUCTION

Federal Reserve Index of Production Figures shown in Fig. 1. A regular 41-month cycle has been added. (After Chapin Hoskins.) *Ratio scale.*

[105]

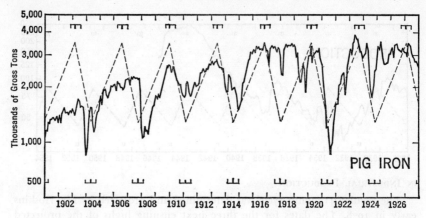

FIG. 3. THE 3½-YEAR RHYTHM

Pig-iron production in the United States, January 1901–February 1946. A regular 41-month cycle has been added and projected through 1954, to indicate in general terms what will happen if the rhythm continues.

The regular 41-month cycle was determined and projected by Mr. Hoskins

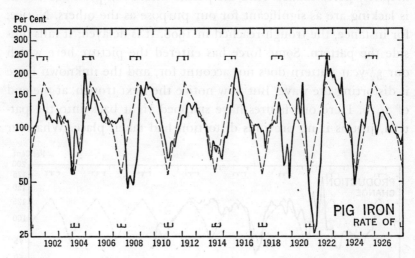

FIG. 4. RATE OF CHANGE

Moving percentages (rate of change) of pig-iron production, January 1901–February 1945, showing the 3½-year rhythm.

The chart shows the percentage that the actual production for each month is of the corresponding month one year before. A regular 41-month cycle has been added and projected through 1954, to indicate in general terms how the

[106]

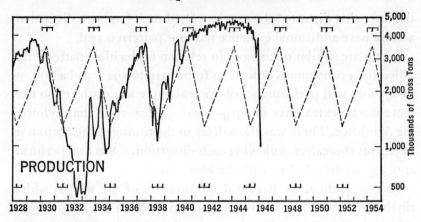

IN PIG IRON PRODUCTION

early in 1938. The dates of the three next ensuing highs of the regular 41-month ideal wave are July 1947, December 1950, and May 1954. Ensuing lows in the regular 41-month ideal wave are September 1948, and February 1952. (After Chapin Hoskins.) *Ratio scale.*

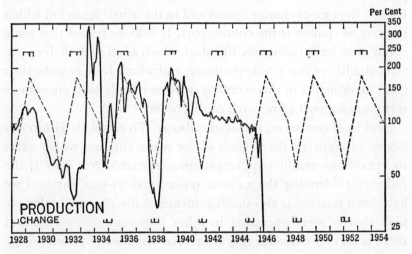

IN PIG IRON PRODUCTION

moving percentage will behave if the rhythm continues acting as in the past.

It will be noted that the high points in the regular 41-month cycle, fitted to the rate-of-change data, are reached 14 months prior to the high in the regular 41-month cycle fitted to the actual data. The lows lead by two months. (After Chapin Hoskins.) *Ratio scale.*

[107]

the force that distorted the previous rhythm, it has been dissipated, and we have additional evidence that our pattern is real.

There are similar distortions in relation to the ideal pattern that called for a continuous downturn from 1919 to 1921, and a bottom in 1931. Actual performance of the real curve was distorted so that there was an extra wave in 1919–1920 — a distortion that followed the Armistice. There was also a delay in the timing of the bottom in 1932. But thereafter, following each distortion, the actual performance again falls into line with the ideal wave.

In Fig. 4, then, we have a demonstration of the way in which rhythms act, which is even more important than if Fig. 4 showed us a perfectly patterned performance. For — as we shall see — the performance on this chart shows us rhythms interacting, with, of course, chance distortions as well. Study of such interaction is the fundamental task of those today who are analyzing the rhythmic patterns in our social and economic organism. They can be studied both in the rate-of-change figures and in the actual figures of which the rate of change is the counterpart. It is to be hoped that some of our great basic industries, like steel, which affect with their operations the life of our whole economy, and which have at stake such great investments in this economy, will eventually lend encouragement and support to research of this order.

Steel is, of course, an involved industry. To establish within any degree of accuracy the periods of the many rhythms which affect its operations would require extensive research. Not only is the industry evidencing the 54-year, 9-year, and $3\frac{1}{2}$-year rhythms we have been tracing; it also shows evidence of the 18-year rhythm we shall shortly meet operating in other important industries; and there is further evidence that it involves rhythms of around 6, $7\frac{1}{2}$, and 15 years, along with shorter rhythms of 6, 9, 24, and 33 months.

Regardless of the amount of work yet to be done on the problem, the cursory data we already have in hand are useful enough to suggest that a search for more would be well warranted. As late as midsummer of 1944, for instance, an iron and steel trade journal was debating whether the industry's capacity would be sufficient to meet the postwar demand for steel. No one familiar with the postwar implications of the various cycles, in combination with the industrial trend lines we have explored, could be seriously concerned with such a question until after the half-century mark, at the earliest.

Interestingly enough, the 3½-year rhythm which we see in pig iron production is also duplicated in scores if not hundreds of other economic phenomena, including stock prices, where peaks tend to come about five months earlier, and valleys one month earlier, than in pig iron production.

The existence of this same rhythm in stock prices is provocative. (See Figs. 5–6.) Iron is a tangible commodity, a thing, a visible reality that would exist in some form or other if no man had ever been on earth, or if all men disappeared. But stocks and prices have a different sort of reality. A stock certificate is a slip of paper which depends for its being on states of mind; whatever the assets behind it, only the mind can provide a link between them and the paper. Further, prices also have a basic reality that is purely mental, for — regardless of what the figures be that prices are quoted in — the figures can only be an index to a mental attitude focused as desire. Stock prices reflect, far more than some commentators ever pause to realize, the psychological states prevailing in a community.

The stock market which has rhythms is not located in Wall Street. It is only an expression of ideas, and ideas are expressions of people. If there is rhythm in the action of the market, it obviously must spring from the fact that the rhythm is flowing in the human organism. In studying the market we are studying men, and studying them in one of the fundamental aspects of their nature.

As a study for exploration, the questions regarding the nature of reality and its relation to the mind have been left by the economists largely to the philosophers, and perhaps to the psychologists. But, in an era where all the sciences are drawing closer together, the

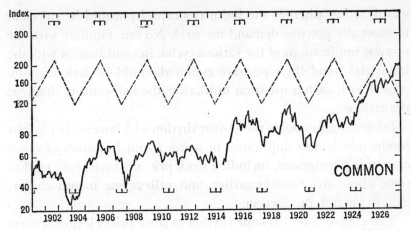

FIG. 5. THE 3½-YEAR RHYTHM

Dow-Jones industrial common stock prices, January 1901–March 1946. (Scale prior to 1914 adjusted to conform to subsequent basis.) A regular 41-month cycle has been added and projected through 1954, to indicate approximately what will happen if the rhythm continues.

This regular 41-month cycle, like the cycle in Pig Iron Production and the

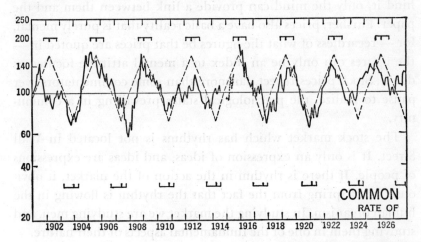

FIG. 6. RATE OF CHANGE

The 3½-year rhythm in the rate of change of common stock prices, in terms of moving percentages of the Dow-Jones Industrial Averages shown in Chart 5.

Like Charts 2 and 4, this chart shows the percentage that the actual prices of each month are of the corresponding month one year before.

[110]

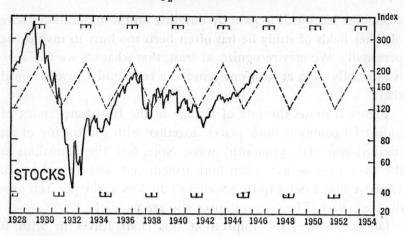

IN COMMON STOCK PRICES

cycle in the Federal Reserve Index for Industrial Production, was determined and projected by Mr. Hoskins early in 1938.

The dates projected for the three next ensuing highs in the regular 41-month cycle are February 1947, July 1950, and December 1953. The two next lows are August 1948 and January 1952. (After Chapin Hoskins.) *Ratio Scale.*

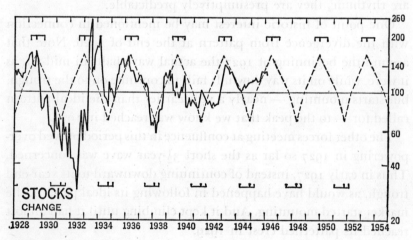

IN COMMON STOCK PRICES

A regular 41-month cycle has been added and projected through 1954 to indicate approximately how the moving percentages will behave if the rhythm continues.

(After Chapin Hoskins.) *Ratio scale.*

[111]

economist has much to gain by building on the accumulated lore of other fields of study he has often been too busy to investigate personally. We may recognize, at least, that what we see in Fig. 5 is primarily — in at least one sense — a community psychological chart.

Figure 6 shows the rate of change in the Dow-Jones index of industrial common stock prices, together with the tracing of an ideal $3\frac{1}{2}$-year (i.e., 41-month) wave. Note, first, the distortions in the 1932–1933 period, when both trough and crest were delayed. Here we find a delay quite parallel to the lags in the pig iron production chart. The circumstances also are parallel.

On the whole, the impression this chart leaves us with is one of amazing regularity, with the majority of troughs and crests alike closely associated with the ideal pattern as shown by the dotted lines. Where the departures from the pattern do show up, we have other data that go far to explain the deviations in terms of interacting waves of other periodicities. And insofar as these other waves are rhythmic, they are presumptively predictable.

One point of historic interest may be mentioned in connection with the divergence from pattern at the end of 1926. Note that around the beginning of 1927 the actual wave halts in mid-air, as it were, while on its way down. It fails to continue on to the trough, but starts mounting — nearly a year earlier than the ideal pattern called for — to the peak that we know was reached in 1929.

The other forces meeting at confluence in this period proved overpowering in 1927 so far as the short $3\frac{1}{2}$-year wave was concerned. Thus in early 1927, instead of continuing downward to its year-end trough, as would have happened in following its ideal pattern, the market started mounting. And it kept climbing until it had almost reached its patterned crest in 1929.

A rather similar divergence in market action from the pattern called for by the $3\frac{1}{2}$-year wave occurred in 1944. At that time, instead of falling into a trough, as the projected pattern would have forecast, stock market averages showed buoyancy. We may postulate that in 1944, as in 1927, it was an extraordinary inflationary force that kept the market steady when the pattern called for decline. In 1945, as in 1928, when the pattern again called for a rise, the inflationary forces still present made that rise almost meteoric.

This rise continued in the stock market, with few interruptions, until the turn-down in the ideal 9-year wave came in mid-1946. The ensuing break in the market in August-September is history. The 1946 break came just after the 9-year wave started receding, although the shorter 3½-year wave was still mounting.

When the time comes in early 1947, as then indicated by the projected pattern, for the 3½-year wave to turn down again, and add its down-thrust to that of the 9-year rhythm, observers will be interested in watching to see whether post-1929 history is approximately paralleled.

It has already been stated that in the early forties our charts enabled one to foresee a very substantial and heady rise in stocks and commodities into 1946. Those who look back from the vantage point of subsequent history may have occasion to note that the inflation of the forties only added to the tolling of the bell when 1950 came. For — to repeat — with the 9-year rhythm turning down in 1946, and the 3½-year rhythm scheduled to turn down in 1947, the market will then be left with no dominant rhythm to support it — at least, none that we have traced.

Whatever the war leverage amounts to up to 1947, we may postulate tentatively that its inflationary force can hardly act after that year, when there will be no major market rhythm to act through.

Many volumes have, and will be, written on the subject of interpreting stock market patterns. Here only the most cursory illustrations can be given of the way in which the major economic rhythms may be seen at work in the market's operation. Our patterns show up clearly here, as elsewhere; the 3½-year wave is one of the most important among them; and the incidence of such events as wars and war inflation, though it may distort the wave, does not fundamentally change the pattern.

[113]

Out of more than 500 different kinds of economic series that have been analyzed by various research workers, something more than half show fluctuations which are of the $3\frac{1}{2}$-year interval type. Many of these can serve as extremely useful barometers, not only in the stock market but in many other economic organizations — particularly when the shorter waves are viewed in connection with the longer rhythms, and what we have learned about their working is applied to the interpretation.

One danger should be emphasized. This, strangely enough, is the danger of traditional "thought." The average businessman who uses rhythmic patterns to guide his planning is using an instrument so foreign to his ways of *thinking* about his work that he may let faulty judgments interfere with accurate reading. Most of us, taught to think in conventional terms of cause and effect, and trained in a system where the educational wares are often cut to the lowest common denominator of mass intelligence, find it hard to remember that the human mind is very finite. It can never hope to grasp in any situation all the causes that may work together to produce any given result. That is why judgments are so faulty when we reason solely on the ordinary cause-and-effect basis. Some if not most of the actual causes will escape our knowledge, and those we do take into calculation may be pure assumption. If despite this we reach a correct conclusion, it is a triumph of accident — or of intuition.

Awareness of economic patterns, and such knowledge as we can gain of their operation, helps avoid some of the pitfalls inherent in the limitations of our ability to think accurately about the infinite world that surrounds us.

Readers willing to pursue further some of the problems inherent in cause-and-effect thinking will find Chapter XIII devoted to the subject.

[114]

I X

The 18-Year Rhythm

THE 18–YEAR rhythmic cycle has been calculated to have an average length of around $18\frac{1}{3}$ years. It is hardly to be regarded as a doubling of the 9-year rhythm we have already seen in action. It shows up for the most part in an entirely different series of categories. Figure 1 shows it in the index for real estate activity in the United States, after adjustment for trend, as compiled by Roy Wenzlick. Figure 2 shows it in building activity, according to the Warren and Pearson composite index. All building activity timing mentioned hereafter in this Chapter refers to this particular index. Choice of another index might slightly advance or retard the timing. However, no matter what index be used, this 18-year rhythm seems one of the clearest, most regular patterns revealed in our economic life.*

* Clarence D. Long, Jr., who has made one of the most extensive studies of this rhythm, declares: "At first consideration, it may seem that considerable variation exists even in the United States between the duration estimates of various writers. Actually, the cycles themselves vary over time, and the variations (in estimates) are due to differences in the period of time studied. The closest approximation is probably the one-hundred-year study of John Riggleman, which places the average duration for the entire six cycles at seventeen years and for the last three cycles at slightly more than eighteen years. . . . It might be supposed that the industry in each locality would have great individuality. . . . Actually, although such individuality exists, long cycles do appear in all cities and the agreement of the turning points of these cycles is surprisingly high, especially with respect to the troughs." (*Building Cycles and the Theory of Investment,* Princeton University Press, pp. 145, 159.)

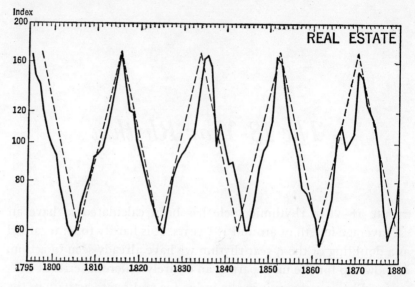

FIG. 1. THE 18⅓-YEAR RHYTHM

Real estate activity in the United States, 1796–1946 (after Roy Wenzlick in the *Real Estate Analyst*). Data are for January of each year. A regular 18⅓-year cycle has been added and projected to 1970, to show in a general way what will

The existence of a similar rhythm in the marriage rate (see Fig. 3) could readily lead to some false assumptions. It would be simple enough to reason that people who get married start to think about house hunting and home building, and that this results in building projects. Or one could start his reasoning in reverse, and end in the same place, by saying that building stimulates prosperity, and when people feel prosperous they get married, and when married they buy the homes that contractors have previously erected to attract customers who feel prosperous because money is being spent to erect buildings for people who will get married.

Such reason-why arguments chase their tails. Nor is this statement of them unusual, except in brevity. Whole books have been written that incorporate such " reasoning " into learned syllables. We should be prepared to ignore reasoning of that kind, but we are justified in asking *why* our building statistics should formulate

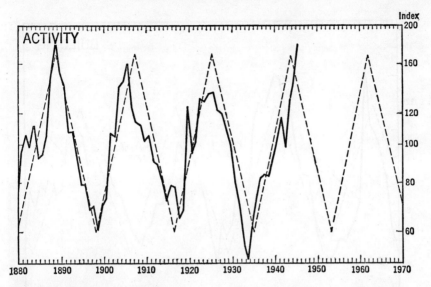

IN REAL ESTATE ACTIVITY

happen if this rhythm continues. *Ratio scale.* Ideal tops fall 1888.6, 1907.0 (i.e. June 30, 1907), 1925.3, 1943.6, and 1962.0; lows 1897.8, 1916.2, 1934.5, 1952.8, 1971.2.

themselves in such exceedingly regular rhythms. Before research of the future supplies us with a definitive answer to this particular query, we may hazard a postulate that man's mating instinct and man's building instinct may be aboriginally associated in his being, just as they extend down the biological scale to the birds. If both instincts proved to flow in the race in a common rhythm, it should not seem too surprising. Perhaps economists could well join forces with biologists in the new kind of research such a problem suggests.

The 18-year rhythm is evident not only in real estate activity, new building, and the marriage rate, but has even shown up in acreage planted to wheat (see Fig. 4.)

As far back as the eighteenth century, which is about as far as available statistics on the subject go, we can see traces of this 18-year rhythm at work. H. A. Shannon, for instance, published in 1934 the results of research on the number of bricks produced in England

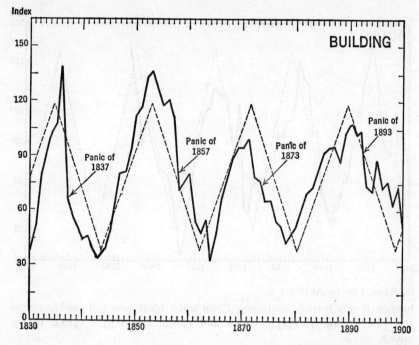

FIG. 2. THE 18⅓-YEAR RHYTHM

Building activity in the United States, 1830–1936. The Composite —
Riggleman, Wenzlick, and 120-City-Index of building activity. (After Warren
and Pearson.) Value of construction contracts awarded in thirty-seven states,
F. W. Dodge Corporation, 1925–1945. A regular 18⅓-year cycle has been added,

and Wales from 1785 to 1849; since bricks were then taxed, records
were kept. Warren and Pearson, interpolating population data,
drew the chart shown in Fig. 5 to illustrate the production pattern.
A distinct 16- to 18-year rhythm is shown. Building statistics for a
given circumscribed area, such as a particular city, do not always
reveal the same rhythm. Glasgow, Scotland, for instance, has had a
building cycle of around 30 years in length since the middle of the
last century. London's cycle in recent times seems to have been
around 25 years. In Hamburg, on the other hand, the rhythm for-
merly proximated the length of that in the United States (see
Fig. 6).

[118]

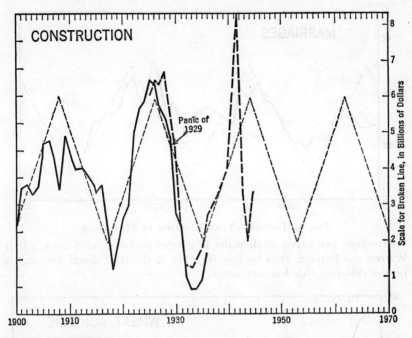

CONSTRUCTION

Scale for Broken Line, in Billions of Dollars

Panic of 1929

IN BUILDING ACTIVITY

and projected to 1970 to show approximately what will happen if this rhythm continues. Pattern has tops 1834.3, 1852.6, 1871.0 (i.e. June 30, 1871), 1889.3, 1907.6, 1926.0, 1944.3, 1962.6; lows halfway between at 1843.5, 1861.8, 1880.2, 1898.5, 1916.8, 1935.2, 1953.5.

American cities vary as between themselves; in some the 18-year rhythm is not so evident as in others. Further, areas where the rhythm is pronounced may show a difference in timing of peaks and valleys. In Florida, for instance, peaks have tended to precede New York peaks in recent times. But on the whole, as Long pointed out, there has been remarkable agreement. Here we shall be concerned only with national averages.

The length of time between peaks in over-all building activity in the United States has varied from 16 to 19 years; the 18-year span is an average. The peak of the twenties was reached in 1925; that of the forties seems to have come in late 1942, in which wartime

[119]

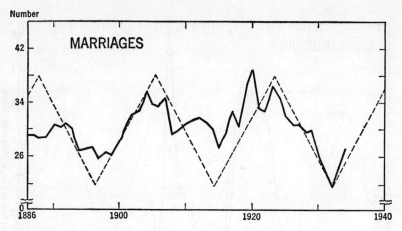

FIG. 3. THE 18⅓-YEAR RHYTHM IN MARRIAGES

Marriages per 10,000 adult males in greater St. Louis, 1886–1934. (After Warren and Pearson. Data by Roy Wenzlick in the *Real Estate Analyst*.) A regular 18⅓-year cycle has been added.

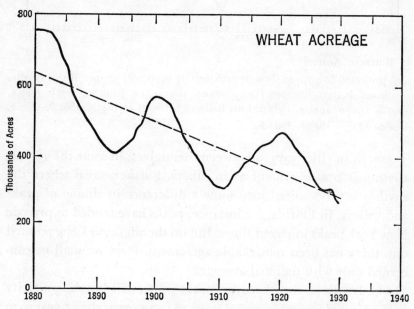

FIG. 4. THE 18⅓-YEAR RHYTHM IN WHEAT ACREAGE

Acreage planted to wheat in New York, 1880–1930. (After Warren and Pearson and King.)

[120]

year total new construction, public and private, amounted to some 13.5 billion dollars. Building costs and rentals, incidentally, tend to stay up for periods well after building activity has started to decline.

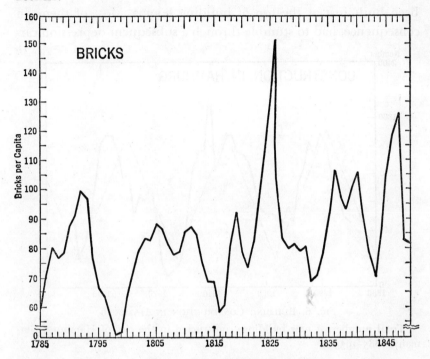

FIG. 5. BRICK PRODUCTION

Bricks produced per capita in England and Wales, 1785–1849 (after Warren and Pearson).

Strangely enough, in the face of a cycle that is so regular, so clear to the eye on any chart, and so often repeated that there can be no reasonable doubt of its reality, few businessmen refer to it in their operations, and neither does the home-buying public. Thus many of the foreclosures of the depression in the thirties were the aftermath of properties bought at top prices between 1925 and 1929. We shall perhaps see similar foreclosures in the fifties on realty bought at inflationary prices in the forties.

The small operators are not the only ones readily caught in the snares of the nest-building urge when the rhythm rises to its peak. Warren and Pearson have compiled records to show that, in large cities like Chicago and New York, most of the skyscrapers have been built just at the top of building booms. Most of them, in consequence, had to stumble through a subsequent depression car-

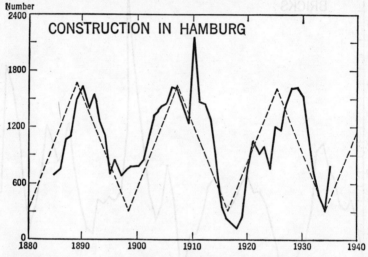

FIG. 6. BUILDING CONSTRUCTION IN HAMBURG

Total number of new buildings constructed in the city of Hamburg, Germany, 1885–1935.

rying vacant offices that were never occupied until the next cycle came along to produce the necessary tenants. Meanwhile many of the buildings went through what specialists call the "wringer." The findings are illustrated in Figs. 7 and 8.

From these two charts, one might conclude that in the twenties Wrigley was one of the shrewdest operators in Chicago. In New York, one of the best judges of the market in the early thirties seems to have been Rockefeller, who built Rockefeller Center almost at the bottom of the building cycle, and then cashed in as the rising demand for space took every square inch available in the Center during the recovery period in the late thirties and the forties.

[122]

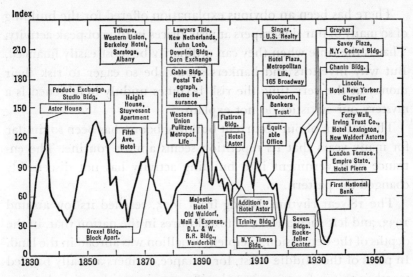

FIG. 7. NEW YORK SKYSCRAPERS

Dates when certain large buildings were constructed in New York City and the Composite – Riggleman, Wenzlick, and 120-City-Index of building activity 1830–1936. (After Warren and Pearson.)

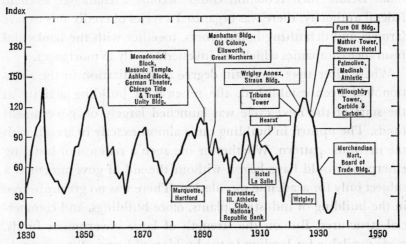

FIG. 8. CHICAGO SKYSCRAPERS

Dates when certain large buildings were constructed in Chicago and the Composite – Riggleman, Wenzlick, and 120-City-Index of building activity, 1830–1936 (after Warren and Pearson).

[123]

There has been an obvious explanation offered for the building of so many of our skyscrapers at peak prices in time of peak activity. That is the time when they can ordinarily be most easily financed. But why investors and bankers should be so eager to risk their money at the very time the risk becomes unduly heightened is a mystery our statistics do not explain.

The pattern of our recurrent building booms has been so similar for many years that its repetition seems almost routine. The entrance of government into building activity has not discernibly changed the pattern.

The 18-year rhythm, falling from 1925, reached its low around 1933, and left such a wake of foreclosures in the nation that, in the depths of the depression, incipient rebellion was abroad in the land. In parts of the Middle West, for instance, farmers actually banded together to use force against sheriffs entering with writs. Auction sales of foreclosed properties had their purpose defeated by the refusal of attending visitors to bid. Refusals to pay taxes were common. Before such rebellion could become a challenge even to federal authority, there was organized a series of credit aids to save farmers and defaulting homeowners, together with the banks and insurance companies which had invested heavily in mortgages.

When, after 1933, a certain degree of stabilization in the situation had been established, the renewal of building activity at the start of the next cycle was launched largely on government funds. The upturn in building came almost exactly in accord with the rhythmic pattern. Whether or not such a renewal of building enterprise would have begun without the aid of government is a subject only for academic speculation. There was no great upsurge in the building of industrial plants, office buildings, and commercial structures. But on the strength of large government funds, made available for lending to the builders of homes, the new cycle got under way, and the home-building activity conducted in it was largely under government control.

The government continued control of the financing — even

after the time when the banks would have been glad to enter the mortgage market again — by offering terms more favorable than the banks had traditionally extended. By controlling the financing, it was simple for the government also to maintain control of the cost, the planning, and even the architectural design of the houses built with Washington aid. Additional public funds invested throughout the country, in public works like new government buildings and gigantic enterprises such as great dams and power plants, carried the total volume of building steadily forward from its previous depression lows.

This was the situation as building activity mounted toward new peaks until approximately 1940, after the outbreak of the war in Europe. At this time there was still an abundance of commercial building space available in most parts of the country.

The American government then decided that vast expansion in American manufacturing facilities must be rushed. But industrial leaders in general hesitated to invest large funds in expanding plants for war purposes, only to be left in postwar days with an investment on their hands that might then be worthless. The government, on the theory that national defense needs were vital, promptly devised measures that would permit industrial plant expansion with a minimum of private investment. If an efficient industrial operator showed willingness to borrow or invest funds for construction purposes, he was permitted to amortize his investment out of profits at a rate far more rapid than previously permitted under income tax laws. Where industries showed reluctance to borrow even under these terms, the government itself built vast industrial plants which were leased to operators, with or without option to buy.

As a result of such measures, government funds invested in industrial plant facilities from 1940 through 1943 amounted to a total of some 25 billion dollars. When the United States actually became involved in war at the end of 1941, building of homes and farm structures had to cease almost entirely, under government decree

— the famous L–41 regulation of the War Production Board. The chief exception to cessation of home-building was the hastily built housing erected for war workers in plant communities. But the continuing boom in industrial construction carried total American building activity steadily forward into new highs.

The peak of this activity seems to have been reached in the third quarter of 1942 — about two years ahead of the " ideal " peak in the 18-year pattern. Total new construction, public and private, declined from 13.5 billion dollars in 1942 to 7.7 billions in 1943, 3.9 billions in 1944, and around 4.7 billions in 1945.

As the nation was drawn into its economic organization for war, the needs of government for land were intensified also, and great areas were taken over for purposes connected with wartime production and military training. The outcome was that in July of 1944 a Public Lands Subcommittee of the House of Representatives could announce that 24 per cent, or almost one-fourth, of all the land in continental United States was owned by the government. The figures of course include national park areas, as well as mountain and desert wasteland.

We may expect continued efforts, in postwar years ahead, to return to private ownership some part of these landholdings and also a good part of the wartime industrial facilities which the government acquired. But whether this happens or not, it is worth repeating that government operations apparently do not alter the rhythms prevailing in a nation's economic life. Government undertakings seem rather to follow the rhythms. The fact that government, by the sheer weight of its holdings, may now be said to control a good part of the American real estate market and the activities of the building industry does not necessarily indicate any change in the 18-year real estate cycle.

This has important implications for those who have advanced the theory that government planning, and timely government action, may be used to overcome cyclic depressions. In view of such a hope, the course of real estate activity in the United States during the immediate postwar years becomes a matter of challenging interest to all concerned with theory in national planning projects.

As already stated, statistical downturn in building in late 1942 came some two years prior to the turn called for in the established pattern. A prior judgment based only on the projected pattern would have declared that, from 1944 on into the fifties, building activity would do exactly this, gradually declining toward a bottom due around 1953.

On the other hand, by the end of World War II swollen mass incomes had created the same enormous demand for new housing, and for office and loft space, that had been experienced following World War I. By 1946 the nation was conscious of an overwhelming housing problem that seemed quite comparable to the one it had experienced in 1919 and the early twenties. Those who based their 1946 judgments on events following World War I, when a building boom promptly got under way and lasted for years, would naturally assume the inevitability of a similar great expansion in American building activity in the years following, and a boom in the building industry that would last — once under way — almost indefinitely.

Will government attempts to use all possible measures in promoting new housing succeed in duplicating, after World War II, the building boom that followed World War I? Those who look back from the fifties will know the final answer. For the present, we must content ourselves with noting that the 18-year rhythm was just near the beginning of its cyclic rise when World War I ended. The rise in the pattern extended through 1925. The building boom which rode this rising rhythm with increasing momentum lasted well through 1929, when the total of new construction, public and private, amounted to some 10.7 billion dollars.

To have told the average man in early 1946 that no similar boom was probable following World War II would have seemed fantastic prophecy. The need of housing seemed enormous all over the country. Economists talked about millions of purchasing power available. The fact remains that projections of the 18-year rhythm seemed to say, long before the war, that the over-all real estate market in the United States after World War II would find itself in a situation hardly comparable to that which it knew after 1918.

We can of course expect a large amount of building in this country in the late forties — this country engages in vast building operations in " abnormal " as well as in " normal " times.* There is a minor rhythm in residential building of 33 months (see Fig. 1, next chapter) which suggests that home building will rise to another peak around 1948. Projections of our 18-year rhythm merely suggest the probability that over-all building operations will not reach the scale some observers have forecast; that they will in general be declining, irregularly, from the 1942 peak; that they will reach a postwar low in the early fifties.

The 18-year rhythm is found not only in our building and real estate activity. It evidences itself in the activities of many industries whose operations are allied to those of the building industry. The construction industry, using the products of heavy industry, follows a pattern related to all enterprise, and full employment in production and distribution in other industries usually occurs only when building activity is at high levels.

Not only is building activity reflected in the volume of carloadings, for instance; it is also interesting to note that railroads have done most of their construction work at times when other building was active.

Figure 9, adopted from Warren and Pearson, indicates a close association between building activity and deviations from the normal trend in pig iron production. That this 18-year rhythm should show up in pig iron, on top of the 9-year and $3\frac{1}{2}$-year rhythms, can hardly surprise us.

The volume of lumber production and of furniture produced moves with, and lags slightly after, the index for building activity

* Even in the war years, for instance, private construction totaled some 2.8 billions in 1942, 1.6 billions in 1943, 1.6 billions in 1944, 2.7 billions in 1945.

— an association we should find natural. In the past, total loans and discounts of American banks have also tended, with variations in volume, to move with the 18-year rhythm in building, with a lag of around three years (see Fig. 10).

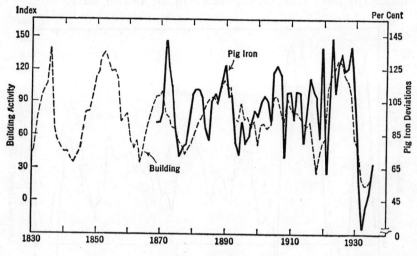

FIG. 9. PIG IRON

The 18⅓-year rhythm in pig iron production, 1870–1936. Data expressed as deviations from normal trend. The Composite — Riggleman, Wenzlick, and 120-City-Index of building activity, 1830–1936 has been added. (After Warren and Pearson.)

Similarly, prices of common stocks have tended in their major swings to move with the building rhythm (see Figs. 11–12–13).

The 18⅓-year rhythm, as it shows itself in the sales of a large industrial company, is charted in Figure 14.

The building cycle movement, as compared to that of industrial stock averages, has been interpreted by Warren and Pearson as follows:

Prices of industrial stocks appear to rise in the early part of the building cycle, then fall and rise again. This may be because recovery in clothing, automobiles and other things with a short cycle combine in

[129]

such a way as to form a minor peak before building is proceeding actively, and then reach another peak about the same time as building.*

Further research in this field seems to indicate that the phenomena referred to here by Warren and Pearson appear as the 9-year rhythm " rides on the back " of the 18-year wave.

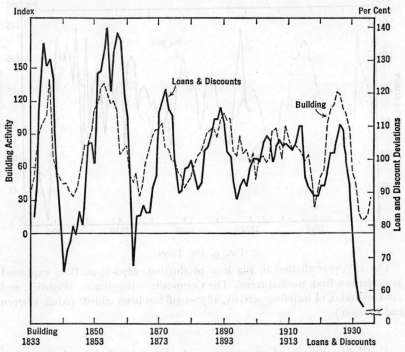

FIG. 10. THE 18⅓-YEAR RHYTHM IN LOANS AND DISCOUNTS

Variations in the volume of loans and discounts, 1833–1936, expressed as a percentage of normal, and set back three years to correspond with the Composite — Riggleman, Wenzlick, and 120-City-Index of building activity, 1830–1936 (after Warren and Pearson).

Most important, we find a tendency in major panics to date themselves by turns in the rhythms of building activity. Usually the panics have come within two to four years after the building activity

* Reprinted by permission from *World Prices and the Building Industry* (p. 145), George F. Warren and Frank A. Pearson. Published by John Wiley & Sons, Inc.

peak. The 1836 peak was followed by panic in 1837. The 1853 peak was followed by panic in 1857. The peak around 1871 was followed by panic in 1873. The 1890 peak was followed by panic in 1893. The 1906 peak was followed by panic in 1907, albeit a brief credit panic of no great length or severity. The peak of 1925, on the other

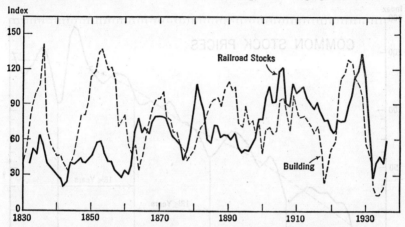

FIG. 11. THE 18⅓-YEAR RHYTHM IN RAILROAD STOCK PRICES

The Cleveland Trust Company index of price of railroad stocks and the Composite — Riggleman, Wenzlick, and 120-City-Index of building activity, 1831–1936 (after Warren and Pearson).

hand, was followed in 1929 by the most severe panic in our history, and long depression afterward. It will be interesting to observe whether the precedent holds, and whether the peak in building activity reached in late 1942 will ultimately be followed by comparable events. As Warren and Pearson have pointed out:

When it is apparent that a building peak has been reached, it is a warning of the danger of a serious reaction. If there is also an impending rise in the value of gold, the danger is accentuated.*

And they continue, in an analysis which makes it clear that the 18-year rhythm is one of the most important economic clocks we have:

* *Ibid.,* p. 150.

[131]

The building cycle is so long that few people experience two complete cycles in their business life. Education, to be effective, must therefore be " book knowledge " rather than experience. . . .

For many individuals, an unfavorable first experience means a lifetime tragedy. The experiences of the last fifty years have emphasized

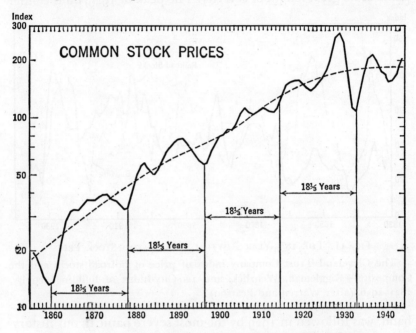

FIG. 12. THE 18⅓-YEAR RHYTHM IN COMMON STOCK PRICES

Three-year moving average of the Axe-Houghton index of common stock prices in the United States 1854–1945, together with an 18-year moving average trend extrapolated. The 18⅓-year lows are clearly in evidence.

the dependence of the individual and the nation on price movements . . . price movements are important to the individual regardless of his monetary theories. The next most important factor is the building cycle. These two forces are the major factors in business.

The welfare of an individual is often determined by the time in which he was born. If he is old enough to start business at the low of a building cycle, which is accompanied by a falling value of gold and rising prices, his chances for success are very good. Conversely, if he is

[132]

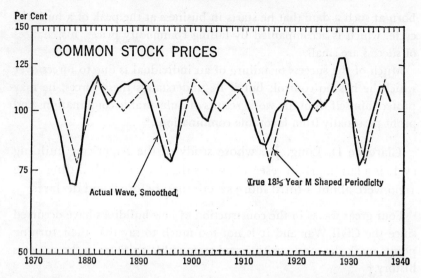

FIG. 13. THE 18⅓-YEAR RHYTHM IN COMMON STOCK PRICES

Percentage deviations of the 3-year moving average, Axe-Houghton index 1854–1939, from the 18-year moving average trend (extrapolated) and smoothed by a two 18-year section moving average plotted to the second section, together with a regular M-shaped 18⅓-year cycle.

The irregularities of the highs are to be explained by the concurrent presence of a 9-year rhythm. (See Chapter VII.)

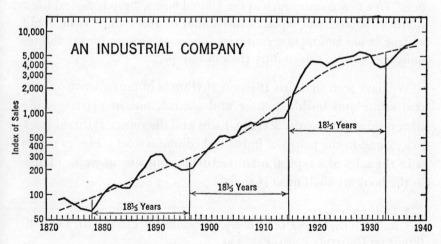

FIG. 14. THE 18⅓-YEAR RHYTHM IN THE SALES OF AN INDUSTRIAL COMPANY

born at such a date that he starts in business at the peak of a building cycle, which is accompanied by falling commodity prices, his chances of success are small.

Much of the success or failure of an individual is due to forces over which he has no control; but if he understands these forces, he may protect himself from the worst results of unfavorable combinations and profit personally from favorable combinations.*

Clarence D. Long, Jr., whose study of the American building cycle is a landmark in research, notes that " cycles in building since 1900 were about a third more severe than before," and declares:

Four great waves in the construction of new buildings have occurred since the Civil War and it is not too much to say that their turning points mark the most exciting and memorable episodes in the nation's history.†

Professor Long, as part of his research, examined all possible explanations for the consistent rhythm and characteristic length of the cycle, and ended with the conclusion:

We are left, therefore, with only the psychological feeling on the part of business men concerning the life of assets in a " progressive business." In a new country such as the United States, " psychological life " would be shorter and replacements would recover sooner, than would be true in old and mature countries. This may account for the shorter building cycles in this country than in Europe.‡

We have seen that this $18\frac{1}{3}$-year rhythm is important not only in real estate and building, here and abroad, but in marriage, pig iron production, wheat acreage, loans and discounts, railroad stock prices, and in the prices of industrial common stocks. Fig. 14 shows it in the sales of a typical manufacturing company as well. Later in the book we shall meet it again.

* *Ibid.*, pp. 174–177.
† *Building Cycles and the Theory of Investment,* Clarence D. Long, Jr. (Princeton University Press) . Page 150.
‡ *Ibid.*, p. 165.

Causes, Correlations, Conjectures

IN THE FOREGOING ANALYSIS of rhythms in our economy we have confined our description to the four which may be regarded as the most important of the many that have been isolated. These four are, to summarize:

A. The 54-year rhythm in wholesale prices and industrial innovations.
B. The 9-year rhythm in wholesale prices, security prices, pig iron production, and industrial activity.
C. The 3½-year rhythm in security prices and in business activity, wholesale and retail.
D. The 18-year rhythm in real estate activity, and in related industrial enterprise.

Various other economic rhythms have been observed. Figure 1, for instance, shows a 33-month rhythm in residential building activity. A rhythm of this length is also important in many lines of retail trade, and in consumers' goods production. A 23-month rhythm in textile production is illustrated in Fig. 2. This length is also found frequently. Figure 3 shows a 34-day (i.e., market day) rhythm in the rate of change of prices of raw sugar. Figure 4 shows Professor Pearson's index of the purchasing power of beef cattle prices,* together with a true 14.8-year periodicity added. Similar

* Dividing the price of a given commodity, X, by an index of prices of other commodities, eliminates the effects of all the factors common to both X and the other commodities. It gives a quotient, the purchasing power of X, which provides some indication of the factors peculiar to that particular commodity.

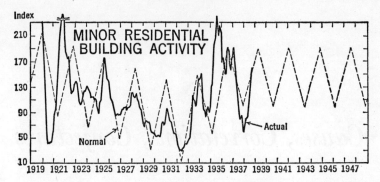

FIG. 1. RESIDENTIAL BUILDING

The 33-month rhythm in residential building activity, 1919–1939. Rate of change. A 12-month moving percentage of actual data, together with a regular 33-month cycle (after Pearson). The regular cycle has been extended to show approximately what will happen if the rhythm continues.

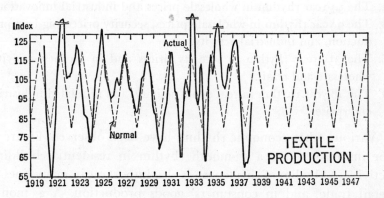

FIG. 2. TEXTILES

The 23-month rhythm in textile production, 1919–1939. Rate of change. A 12-month moving percentage of actual data, together with a regular 23-month cycle (after Pearson). The regular cycle has been extended to indicate approximately what will happen if the rhythm continues.

[136]

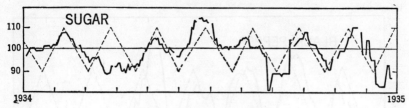

FIG. 3. SUGAR PRICES

The 34-market-day rhythm in raw sugar prices, 1934. Rate of change. A 16-day moving percentage of actual data, together with a regular 34-market-day cycle. This tendency persists before and after 1934, as does the tendency for every third wave to be greater.

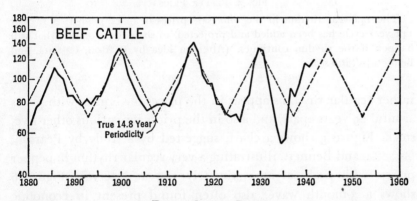

FIG. 4. CATTLE PRICES

The 14.8-year rhythm in the purchasing power of beef cattle prices. Professor Pearson's index is charted here, and a regular 14.8-year cycle has been added. The cycle has been projected to show more or less what will happen if the rhythm continues. *Ratio scale.*

[137]

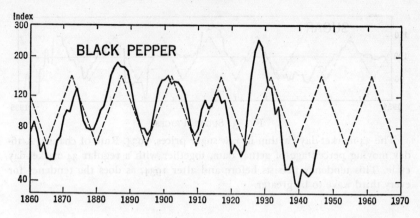

FIG. 5. PEPPER PRICES

The 14.8-year rhythm in the wholesale prices of black pepper. A regular 14.8-year cycle has been added and projected, to show more or less what will happen if the rhythm continues. (After an idea by Pearson, Cassetta, and Bennett.) *Ratio scale.*

rather regular rhythms appear in the prices for horses, with peaks around 25 years apart, and also in the prices for various other livestock. Figure 5 shows a chart, suggested by a study by Pearson, Cassetta, and Bennett, illustrating a very regular rhythm in pepper prices, with peaks at approximately 15-year intervals. Figure 6 shows a 3-month wave, also often found present in economic phenomena.

These rhythms are introduced here merely to illustrate the diversity of the forces with which we must deal; there are many

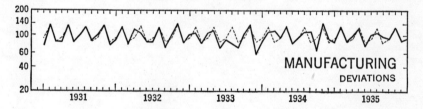

FIG. 6. SALES OF AN

The three-month rhythm in the sales of a large industrial company. Curve

[138]

others. But to explore any of them exhaustively, after four have been analyzed, could involve us — as Professor Schumpeter has remarked in a similar connection — in the law of diminishing returns.

In the rhythms of 54, 9, $3\frac{1}{2}$, and $18\frac{1}{3}$ years, we have measuring scales which provide, when the average businessman asks what time of life it is by the economic clock, as accurate a guide to timing as we may hope to establish, for the purpose of general economic procedure. In Chapter XII we shall show how it is possible to go further for an individual business, and isolate the rhythms peculiar to its own operation.

These economic rhythms, as we have already noted, need to be read — like the hands of a clock — in conjunction with each other. And because they are repetitive they may be combined, together with a trend, to obtain a great deal of light on the near future of the economy.

But before reaching that problem in synthesis, it seems well to pause here briefly to answer the reader who is curious about causes. What is the cause of these rhythms? Can we really accept anything as true until we know the cause of it? If we judge by the progress made in other sciences, we can well understand that ultimate cause is an extremely difficult factor to discover. It is more a problem for philosophy than for science. Nor is it even admitted, in some fields of thought, that we shall ever discover ultimate cause at all — on the theory that finite mind is by its very nature unable to understand the ultimate working of an infinite universe. But in the study

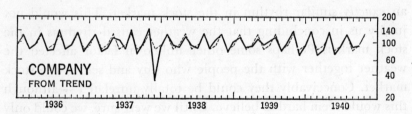

INDUSTRIAL COMPANY
shows deviation from 3-month moving average. A 3-month cycle is added.

[139]

of various rhythms in our environment and in ourselves, research workers have at least made great progress in isolating some significant data.

In the various categories of rhythms we know, some are as familiar to the man in the street as day and night and the tides; others are relatively unknown to him. Analytical work on these rhythms has been developing in what might be called the interstices of the sciences. We have as yet only the beginnings of a science of rhythms *per se*. But in each field of science some group of workers becomes especially concerned with the subject of rhythms in the special field of phenomena he is observing; such a group eventually compares notes with a corresponding group engaged in some other scientific field; and slowly all concerned begin to suspect that they are dealing, however diverse the fields, with phenomena somehow related.

The object of all true scientific inquiry is to find the simplest possible explanation to cover the greatest possible number of diverse phenomena. The further we go in science, the more we become convinced that the universe is a unity, that its laws of action are relatively few and simple, and that they apply to all things. We thus have a right to suspect, when we find rhythms present in so many kinds of phenomena which our sciences study, that we may be dealing with related parts of a whole.

We must guard, of course, against confusing *relationships* with *causes*. Suppose, for instance, that a meteorologist found a rhythm of exactly 41 months in the weather, and that we already knew of an *exactly* similar rhythm in the stock market. This would not justify us in concluding that the weather caused rhythms in the stock market. Perhaps some other unknown factor affected the weather together with the people who buy and sell in the stock market. Conceivably they could be totally unrelated — although this would seem hard to believe. Until we were sure, we could only speak of relationships, or of *correlations* — this last being a technical term for a particular measure of relatedness.

[140]

The study of rhythms has not yet proceeded beyond problems in correlation. Even to this point our progress has been wavering and uncertain. The greatest single piece of progress to date, in the study of economic phenomena, has undoubtedly been the recognition that we are in fact often dealing with *rhythms* rather than mere oscillations. This recognition has recently changed the whole focus of economic inquiry. Until it was reached, millions of words had been written in the quest for *reasons* for economic changes. Pursuing such a method of inquiry the old economics had made little progress toward becoming a true science. Rather, it became a larger and larger debating society, devoted to examining reasons why a given event should cause some particular result.

The mere abundance of such reason-why material — so great that no student could ever master it, reconcile it, and put it to practical use — was itself evidence that the method was fruitless. True scientific progress is measured in the growing ability to reduce the essential laws and relationships in a given field of inquiry into small compass, and to predict. In fact, it is possible to assert that the ability to predict measures the status of a science.

With the discovery of rhythm in economic phenomena, some economic inquiry immediately changed direction. The question was no longer *why* we have business cycles, and *why* we meet recurrent economic slumps. Now the fundamental question was simply: Are the cycles really rhythmic? And if so, does the rhythm spring from within or without the economy?

To the first part of the query continued research has been able to give an affirmative answer almost beyond doubt. Some of the evidence is in the foregoing pages. In concentrating on the second part of the question, economic inquiry has produced theories that fall into two classes. Hotelling has referred to them as theories of " free and forced oscillations." Both terms are borrowed from mechanics.

" Forced oscillations " means rhythms caused by forces entering from outside the economic environment. Jevons, for instance, en-

[141]

tertained a forced oscillation theory. He believed it possible to show that changes in the sun affected agricultural production, and the resulting changes in agricultural production eventually caused changes throughout the economy that registered themselves in factory production, prices, and even stock market values.

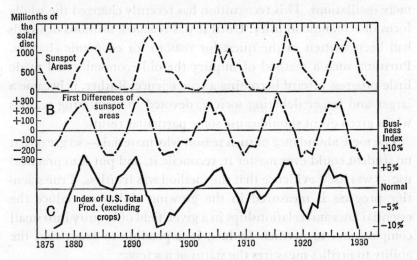

FIG. 7. SUNSPOTS AND PRODUCTION

A. Sunspot Areas, B. First Differences of Sunspot Areas, and C. an Index of U. S. Total Production Excluding Crops. B and C 4-year moving averages. (After Garcia-Mata and Shaffner.)

Many years later, in 1934, two Harvard research workers, Carlos Garcia-Mata and Felix Shaffner, re-examined the Jevons studies and checked them; they ended with the conclusion that sunspot phenomena showed no correlation with agricultural production, but — that solar phenomena showed a remarkable correlation with industrial production (see Fig. 7), business activity (Fig. 8), and with stock market prices (see Figs. 9 and 10). Since this particular outcome of their studies apparently left them a little surprised and aghast, the two students threw up their hands and passed the problem over to the biologists and the psychologists.

It may be observed that — even though they had discovered an

[142]

approach to the problem different from Jevons's — they were still dealing with " forced oscillation " data. Some of their data has since been confirmed by no less an astronomer than Dr. H. T. Stetson,* together with others, and it may be considered that Garcia-Mata and Shaffner made a real contribution to modern research. Fur-

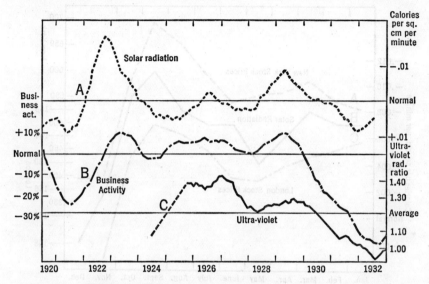

FIG. 8. SOLAR PHENOMENA AND BUSINESS ACTIVITY

A. Solar radiation — that is, variation of the solar constant — June 1920–June 1932, inverted. B. Col. L. P. Ayres Index of American Business Activity, June 1920–December 1932. C. Ultra-violet solar radiation, June 1924–December 1932 (after Garcia-Mata and Shaffner).

Although the period is too short for statistical deduction, the comparison is interesting.

ther, in recognizing the psyscholgical implications of their work, they have done much to enhance its scientific usefulness.

The other theory of economic rhythms — that referred to as " free oscillations " — has also been called the " random shock "

* Research associate, Massachusetts Institute of Technology, and director, Laboratory of Cosmic and Terrestrial Research. See his *Sunspots and Their Effects* (Whittlesey House, 1937).

theory. If, for instance, you take a pendulum and subject it to one or more random blows, it will start swinging in regular rhythm, as it is the nature of the pendulum to do. Exhaustive mathematical studies have been made with the purpose of demonstrating that our economy acts in the same manner, in response to events which come

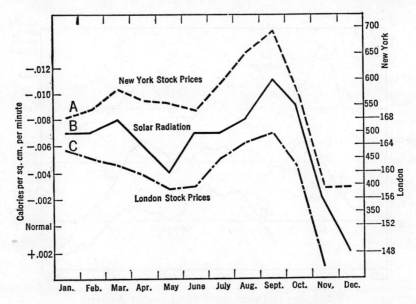

FIG. 9. SOLAR RADIATION AND STOCK PRICES

A. New York stock prices (Barron's average). B. Solar Radiation, inverted, and C. London stock prices, all by months, 1929 (after Garcia-Mata and Shaffner).

Correspondence between curves over a short period of time may be provocative, but by itself proves nothing except that for the period shown the curves do somewhat correspond.

as erratic shocks, but set up rhythmical responses. E. Slutsky has explained this point of view cogently in an essay, first published in 1927 in Russian, called, *The Summation of Random Causes as the Source of Cyclic Processes,* in which he said:

The summation of random causes generates a cyclical series which tends to imitate for a number of cycles a harmonic series of a relatively small number of sine curves. After a more or less considerable number of periods every regime becomes disarranged, the transition to another regime occurring sometimes rather gradually, sometimes more or less abruptly, around certain critical points.

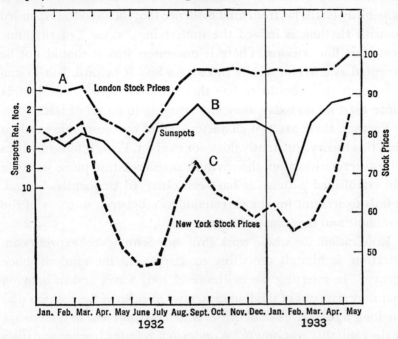

FIG. 10. SUNSPOTS AND STOCK PRICES

A. London stock prices (Banker's Magazine Index). B. Sunspots in the Sun's Central Zone, inverted, and C. New York stock prices (Dow-Jones Industrial averages), all from January 1932 through May 1933 (after Garcia-Mata and Shaffner).

Here again, the curves are much too short to warrant any deductions whatsoever. For an example, of two series that are presumably related see the curves of sunspots and terrestrial magnetism shown on page 64.

The "random shock" is the theory that Professor Schumpeter apparently prefers in accounting for the rhythms in the capitalist economy which he analyzes in his monumental *Business Cycles*. He finds it easy to believe that innovations, acting as such shocks, account for the cyclic movement.

[145]

This much deserves to be said: The resources of modern mathematics in the hands of our eminent mathematicians today are quite ample to demonstrate the *possibility* that random shock does account for our economic rhythms. But such a demonstration as to possibility is still far from final evidence that such shock, responded to with rhythm, is indeed the underlying "cause" of rhythmic economic fluctuations. There is no reason why it should not be accepted as a hypothesis by those who find it helpful. But in embracing it they should realize that, until we know considerably more than we do today, they are engaging in an act of faith.

Further, there are two characteristics of our economic rhythms that this theory apparently does not explain. First, it fails to tell us why, after a distortion, the rhythms snap back into phase with the old established pattern, as has been observed frequently. Second, it fails to account for the correspondence between so many of the economic and the "natural" rhythms.

Kondratieff, for whose work Professor Schumpeter expresses admiration, is himself unwilling to agree with the random shock theory: "In asserting the existence of long waves and in denying that they arise out of random causes, we are also of the opinion that the long waves arise out of causes which are *inherent in the essence* of the capitalist economy." * Kondratieff refrains from speculating on the problem of what this essence might be. Nor does he speculate on the obvious comparisons with biological organisms, where rhythm as an essence of the organism itself can actually determine whether the organism will respond to external stimuli or be unmoved by them. The rhythm in the sex life of women is an almost perfect parallel.

Kondratieff makes bold to assert, however, that causes usually assumed for our rhythms "reverse the causal connections, and take the consequence to be the cause, or see an accident where we really have to deal with a law governing the events." Sometimes

* Italics supplied. This and the following quotations are from the *Review of Economic Statistics,* November, 1935, pp. 105–115.

improvements in technique have been alleged as a cause. But, says Kondratieff, it would be a great error " if one believed that the direction and intensity of those discoveries and inventions were entirely accidental. . . . The development of technique itself is part of the long waves." Similarly, it is a mistake to regard wars as causal: " Wars and revolutions can also be fitted into the rhythm of the long waves and do not prove to be the forces from which these movements originate, but rather one of their symptoms."

As for the results of exploration: " The opening up of new countries does not provoke the upsweep of a long wave. On the contrary, a new upsweep makes the exploitation of new countries, new markets, and new sources of raw materials necessary and possible." Nor does gold production play a causal part, as Kondratieff views it: " Gold production, even though its increase can be a condition for an advance in commodity prices and for a general upswing in economic activity, is yet subordinate to the rhythm of the long waves and consequently cannot be regarded as a causal and random factor."

Many other research workers who are working on evidence of "forced oscillation" have produced data of interest and significance. Dr. Huntington of Yale is a distinguished representative of these.

In his monumental work that shows the influence of climate on history, *Mainsprings of Civilization,* Dr. Huntington states his belief that we are dealing in our studies not with one force, but with three, which create three different kinds of rhythmic responses; he has summarized his conclusions as follows:

Our most important finding is that human life and the progress of civilization are influenced by three distinct but closely interlocking types of cycles in addition to the more obvious cycles of the day and year.

The most familiar of these is cycles of ordinary weather. No one doubts the existence of these, for everyone sees the effect of unusual heat or cold, rain or drought, sunshine or fog. Variations in the growth of plants, including all kinds of crops, are directly dependent on such

[147]

cycles, and are influenced by them far more than any other factor. Weather also influences reproduction and growth of animals, both directly and through plants and the food supply. The indirect effect of the weather on man, however, is for this very reason greater than upon animals and far greater than upon plants. Cycles of weather have been and still are among the chief stimulants to invention, thrift and foresight.

The next great type of cycles is especially evident in animals. It shows itself primarily in physiological processes, especially reproduction. . . . The only known factor which shows the required periodicity and seems competent to produce the observed results is atmospheric ozone. . . . Thus the most tenable working hypothesis seems to be that, in addition to cycles of temperature and moisture, there are cycles of ozone which are especially associated with the reproduction of animals. Man also appears to be influenced, but not so much as animals.

The third cyclic type is primarily human and psychological. At any rate it is only in human beings that we have as yet found clear signs of it. It displays itself in business and prices in a most interesting way. Similar rhythms are found in atmospheric electricity. The evidence is sufficient to warrant the working hypothesis that atmospheric electricity, due presumably to the sun, but perhaps also to the whole solar system, is a cyclic factor closely associated with psychological reactions.

The three types of cycles, due supposedly to heat, ultra-violet radiation and electrical radiation, appear to be so intimately connected that it is often difficult to separate them. . . .*

These three types of cycles, as Huntington observes them, are associated with *solar* phenomena. Variations in heat received from the sun are primarily responsible for weather variations that act directly on plants. Variations in ultraviolet radiation create variations in ozone content of the earth's atmosphere, with a direct effect on biological processes in animals. Variations in radiated electricity seem directly to affect the psychological processes of man — or, as Huntington also suggests, " the nerves."

Edgar Lawrence Smith has suggested that such an electrical radi-

* *Mainsprings of Civilization* (John Wiley & Sons, Inc.) , pp. 526–527.

ation may react directly on the blood, and affect its acid-alkaline balance.

Reproducing a pH curve showing 1938 changes in the ratio of acidity to alkalinity in the blood stream of numerous persons tested by Dr. William F. Petersen, of the University of Illinois, Smith compared it with the 1938 course of the stock market variations, found it closely similar. He then sought the doctor's opinion. Dr. Petersen, who is author of *The Patient and the Weather,* confirmed Smith's own impression:

Offhand, I should say that the pH curve certainly coincided with your stock market variations for 1938. . . . In general, the population is apt to be depressed and blue when the pH is low, and buoyant and energetic and optimistic when the pH curve is higher. There are, of course, many exceptions, but in general I would say that this would be the effect. This quite coincides, as you will notice, with your stock market.*

The work of two Germans, Bernhard and Traute Düll, has produced some important data bearing on Huntington's hypothesis as to a relation between changes in atmospheric electricity on the psychological states of men. First, the Dülls showed synchronization between solar eruptions of incandescent gas and curves in the instrumental records of atmospheric electricity at Saint-Cyr in France and at Tunis in North Africa. Their work seems to have made it clear that *variability* in solar activity, more than the area and number of sunspots, is the solar factor we should consider in seeking to establish solar-terrestrial relationships; and that *variability* in the average potential gradient on earth, instead of its average intensity, is the factor that shows most promise of yielding a correlation.

Having established a relationship between solar activity and atmospheric electricity, the Dülls then plotted for three months the daily deaths in Copenhagen, Frankfurt am Main, and Zurich.

* *Tides in the Affairs of Men* (The Macmillan Company), p. 82.

The curves for the days when most deaths occurred from suicide, mental disorders, and diseases of the nerves, sensory organs, and nervous system, ran almost parallel with the curve for magnetic disturbance on these same days. A similar plotting of suicides in Denmark, Germany, and Switzerland showed an apparent close relationship between the course of the curve on 735 days when suicides

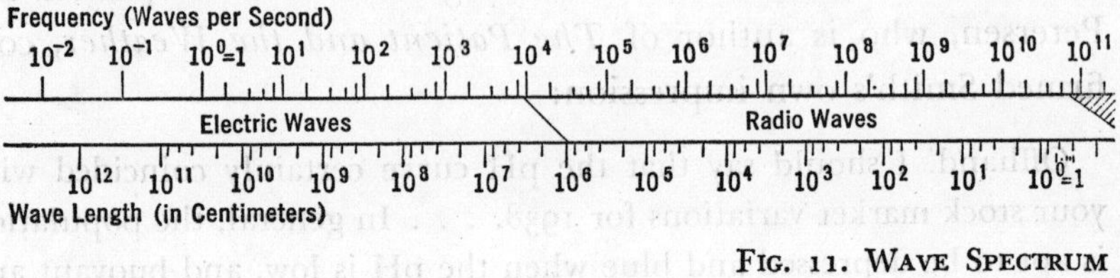

Frequency (Waves per Second)

10^{-2} 10^{-1} 10^{0}=1 10^{1} 10^{2} 10^{3} 10^{4} 10^{5} 10^{6} 10^{7} 10^{8} 10^{9} 10^{10} 10^{11}

Electric Waves   Radio Waves

10^{12} 10^{11} 10^{10} 10^{9} 10^{8} 10^{7} 10^{6} 10^{5} 10^{4} 10^{3} 10^{2} 10^{1} 10^{0}=1

Wave Length (in Centimeters)

FIG. 11. WAVE SPECTRUM

A Spectrum of Electromagnetic Waves with Lengths from 10^{12} to 10^{-14}

were especially numerous, and a similar rise in the curve for calcium flocculi on the sun's surface.

Increases in the number of sunspots or in solar eruptions are ordinarily accompanied by increases in solar radiation. Solar radiation consists not only of heat waves and ultraviolet rays — which affect us as sunburn — but of many other forms of waves which do not register on our senses at all. Our increasing knowledge gives us ground to suspect that many of these unsensed waves affect us as vitally (perhaps even more vitally) as those we know about through our sense organs.

The earth circling through space is a target for wave lengths of enormous range. We know, for instance, that electromagnetic waves alone cover a range of at least 25 " octaves " — an octave here meaning the interval from one wave length to another ten times as great.

Some waves have a length of 5,000 miles or more — we use similar waves on high-tension power lines. Some have a length of only a trillionth part of a millimeter — these being the waves that help ionize the air at high levels, permitting it to reflect radio waves and so making radio communication possible.

Figure 11 is a chart which shows some of the characteristics of this enormous electro-magnetic wave band, and serves also to indicate how few of the radiations register on our senses. We have discovered the others only as we developed instruments which served — as a supplement to our five senses — to detect them. Visible light, it will be noted, occupies only about a single octave of the radiation.

Frequency (Waves per Second)

| 10^{12} | 10^{13} | 10^{14} | V10^{15} | 10^{16} | 10^{17} | 10^{18} | 10^{19} | 10^{20} | 10^{21} | 10^{22} | 10^{23} | 10^{24} | 10^{25} |

Infrared   Ultraviolet   X-Rays   Gamma Rays | Secondary Cosmic Rays

| 10^{-1} | 10^{-2} | 10^{-3} | 10^{-4} e | 10^{-5} | 10^{-6} | 10^{-7} | 10^{-8} | 10^{-9} | 10^{-10} | 10^{-11} | 10^{-12} | 10^{-13} | 10^{-14} |

Wave Length (in Centimeters)

(AFTER COMPTON AND CALDWELL)

Centimeters; that is, with Frequencies from 10^{-2} to 10^{25} Waves per Second

Our social sciences have tended to forget, in the bravura of modern times, one fact which to many of the ancients was clear: Man is a child of the earth, and by that same token a part of it, and for this reason he must also be a child of the sun. If our modern research should find clear evidence that the rhythms of the sun dominate in man's life, as they dominate in many of the other phenomena our sciences study, only men too proud to remember their paternity should be surprised.

But before such a hypothesis can be more than a mere hint to guide the direction of our research we need a great many more data than we have yet amassed. Data we do possess would indicate we are on a track well worth following.

We already have good evidence that one of the major rhythms felt by our economic system — the $3\frac{1}{2}$-year rhythm — has a parallel in solar activity. It will be remembered that this rhythm runs from 40 to 42 months. T. E. Sterne, of the Harvard University Observatory, has determined that the solar constant, as measured by the Smithsonian Institution, fluctuates in a compound rhythm, one part of which averages almost exactly 40.8 months in length. The wave is quite clear. It will be further remembered, in this connection, that Huntington has also shown a 41-month rhythm in the variation of atmospheric electricity — the potential gradient — over a longer period of time than Sterne's study covers.

As for the other three rhythms to which the major portion of our study has been directed, the evidence as to closely corresponding rhythms in the sun is worth analyzing. Not all students have found satisfying parallels.

Here is a table compiled by H. H. Clayton, which shows the calculations made by various workers of certain major sunspot rhythms, in intervals of years: *

Periods in Years

A. Schuster	4.8	...	...	...	8.4	....	11.13	13.5	....
K. Stumpff	...	5.6	7.3	...	8.8	10.0	11.13	12.9	14.3
A. E. Douglass	...	...	...	...	8.5	10.0	11.4	13.5	14.3
D. Alter	...	...	7.6	8.1	8.7	10.0	11.37	....	14.0
H. H. Clayton	...	5.6	...	8.1	8.94	9.9	11.17	....	14.9

Clayton's 8.94-year period shown here might seem suggestive of our 9-year economic cycle, but no more. On the whole, there is nothing here to throw light on our four major economic rhythms.

Great efforts have been made to show that there is a business cycle corresponding to the obvious sunspot cycle of around 11 years. But evidence of a direct relationship between business and the 11-year sunspot rhythm seems open to some criticism. For, while a parallelism has been shown, for short spans, between the 11-year cycle and business activity (see the work of H. T. Stetson, and of Garcia-Mata and Shaffner), these spans are not long enough to give us conclusive evidence. On the contrary, we have better evidence that other rhythms are far more important in our economy. Certainly none of the periods listed by Clayton corresponds to the rhythms we have been noting in the economy.

C. N. Anderson, of the American Telephone and Telegraph Company, has originated a different technique in research on the same subject, with far more interesting results. Figure 12 shows his

* From "The Sun Spot Period," *Smithsonian Miscellaneous Collection*, Vol. 98, No. 2.

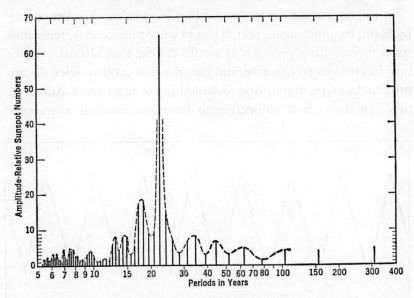

FIG. 12. SUNSPOT CYCLES

Relative Importance of Various Components of a Harmonic Analysis of Sunspots, with alternate cycles reversed. Fundamental 312 years. (After C. N. Anderson.)

A list of some of the more important lengths follows:

Fundamental	312	years	9th Harmonic	34.6 years	17th Harmonic	18.35 years
2nd Harmonic	156	"	10th "	31.2 "	18th "	17.33 "
3rd "	104	"	11th "	28.40 "	19th "	16.42 "
4th "	78	"	12th "	26.00 "	20th "	15.60 "
5th "	62.4	"	13th "	24.00 "	21st "	14.85 "
6th "	52.0	"	14th "	22.28 "	22nd "	14.18 "
7th "	44.6	"	15th "	20.80 "	23rd "	13.56 "
8th "	39.0	"	16th "	19.50 "	24th "	13.00 "

analysis of components of the sunspot cycle. Using sunspot data that goes back to 1749, he found a long-term cycle of 312 years, with a rhythm of 22.28 years as the chief component. In Fig. 12 * the component rhythms of the cycle are shown by lines which indicate — in their relative length — their relative importance as components. Their position on the scale indicates the length of each component rhythm in years.

* Reproduced from the *Bell System Technical Journal*, April, 1939, p. 298.

[153]

In the beginning Anderson used an interesting discovery made by Hale. In alternate 11-year cycles in solar phenomena, most sunspots reverse their polarity. It would appear that alternate cycles may be considered negative, and that the true cycle is twice the approximate 11.13, amounting to something over 22 years. Adopting this hypothesis, and subjecting to harmonic analysis a 300-year

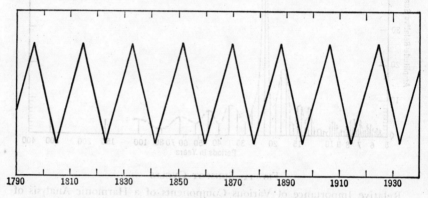

FIG. 13. SKELETONIZED REPRESENTATION OF THE 18⅓-YEAR RHYTHM IN SUNSPOT NUMBERS

Diagram of the 17th harmonic of C. N. Anderson's Harmonic Analysis of Sunspot Numbers with alternate cycles reversed. The diagram is correct for amplitude and dates, and approximately correct for average shape. (Compare with the 18⅓-year rhythm discussed in Chapter IX.)

series of sunspot numbers with alternate cycles reversed, Anderson found rhythms that closely correspond — both in time span and in timing — with our economic data. Inspection of this chart in Fig. 12 shows immediately that the 22.28-year rhythm is of dominant importance. This is very close to rhythms we find in many meteorological phenomena.

Next in importance in Anderson's chart are the two adjacent rhythms of 17.33 and 18.35 years. The rhythm at 18.35 years is an almost perfect match for our 18⅓-year economic rhythm that we see evidenced so clearly in real estate — and it reaches its crest at the same time. (See Fig. 13.)

The 17.3-year rhythm shows up in epidemics of disease, in cotton prices, and in a number of other economic series.

It will be noted that the component at 14.8 years also is very strong. Seemingly the same rhythm shows up in the purchasing power of beef cattle prices (see page 137), of pepper prices (see page 138), and in bond prices.

Clustered around the 9- to 10-year period the reader will note rhythms at 8.91, 9.17, 9.45, 9.8, and 10.1 years. This diagram does not mean — either at this point or elsewhere — that rhythms with exactly these periodicities have been isolated. It does indicate that either at or between these points there are waves of at least the importance indicated. The fact that five such waves show up in the 8.91- to 10.1-year period suggests that further research may disclose counterparts of the 9-year rhythms we have encountered in economic phenomena. As a suggestion of possibilities, see Fig. 14.

Anderson's data should also be examined to see if the wave indicated around 52 years may not — when isolated — correspond to the 54-year economic cycle already discussed. Some observers, like Gillette, have suggested that the 54 may be viewed as a multiple of the 9 or the 18. We may well view the use of such multiples with reserve, until we have more evidence warranting such an approach to the use of the data. They are interesting, but hardly conclusive.

A number of other research workers have made extensive computations on the solar rhythms, and have traced various other correspondences between solar periods and rhythms in terrestrial phenomena.* Unfortunately, the research is still in its infancy. In view of the great possibilities glimpsed in the short period of study described here, one would presuppose that many resources had immediately been put behind the work. On the contrary. To date the work has been conducted with extremely limited funds. This is one of the gaps in our knowledge that needs filling promptly. In

* See H. W. Clough, *Monthly Weather Review*, April, 1933, U.S. Department of Agriculture, pp. 99–108.

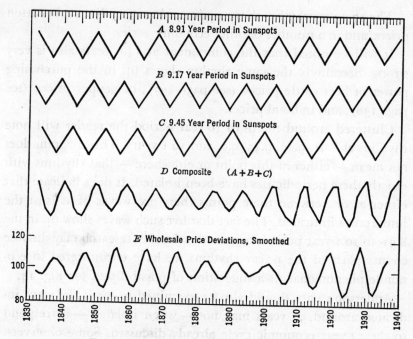

FIG. 14. OTHER SUNSPOT CYCLES AND PRICES

Skeletonized Representation, 1832–1939, of (A) the 8.91-year, (B) the 9.17-year and (C) the 9.45-year Components, as used by C. N. Anderson in his Harmonic Analysis of Sunspot Numbers. Alternate Cycles Reversed.

Also included are (D) the Combination of A, B and C, and (E) the 9-year Wave in Wholesale Prices, 1832–1939.

It will be noted that turning points in prices generally *precede* the corresponding turning points in the combined solar series. Prices are smoothed by a three 9-year section moving average. (For an explanation of the section moving average, see Appendix III.)

particular, as Huntington has suggested, we need to analyze the solar cycles not only in terms of the *number* and *area* of sunspots, flocculi, etc., but in terms of the rate of change, or variability. When this has been done, it is to be hoped that both biologists and psychologists will extend the research to determine just how far solar rhythms are related to human rhythms — including those in economic life — and what the relationship may be.

[156]

Tchijewski, a Russian, has conducted a series of studies which shortly before World War II were gaining wide attention in Europe, but have had small audience in English-speaking countries. It is his conclusion that increased electrical activity in the sun, especially around sunspot maxima, increases ionization of the air. He believes this in turn stimulates mankind both physiologically and psychologically, with effects that can be traced throughout all social relationships.

Dr. Raymond Holder Wheeler, of the Psychology Department at the University of Kansas, has developed a theory of the effect of changes in heat radiation on society and civilization, which as a study is related to this same type of inquiry. His exhaustive accumulation of historical data tends, just as does Tchijewski's, to support the postulate that solar rhythms of many lengths and amplitudes are connected with human rhythms that show up regularly through history.

One important finding results from Anderson's studies. In a number of the solar rhythms, the peaks usually come at the time of, or after, the crest of the rhythm in economic affairs. This suggests that the solar rhythm is itself not causal — that the sun is itself responding to some rhythm which also affects men.

None of the data we have to date regarding the ultimate origin of these rhythms is satisfying proof of anything. But they do suggest that we are just at the gate of a new field of exciting knowledge.

And they suggest a possible postulate:

We know that our space is permeated by radiation from the sun — there are light waves, for instance, of a wide band of differing wave lengths. We know that here on earth some objects, such as a red pencil, respond to waves of the " red lengths "; that other objects, such as a blue pencil, respond to waves of the " blue lengths "; and that a third object, such as a woman's dress, responds to both " red and blue waves " and reflects a combination of these which we regard as purple. Light of all wave lengths, including yellow, is falling on these three objects; but they are " blind " and unresponsive to any waves except those of a length which "fit" their respective natures.

We also know that there are, in the universe, waves longer than light waves, with a longer time interval from crest to crest, which are used for radio transmission. Here, similarly, certain waves may be affecting one radio, whereas another radio, in the next room, may be totally unaffected by them, but is being affected by other waves of different frequencies.

Now, let us suppose that there are still longer waves in the universe — "Y" waves we may call them. Imagine some of the waves with peaks which come $3\frac{1}{2}$ years apart, others with peaks 9 years apart, $18\frac{1}{3}$ years apart, 54 years apart, and perhaps much farther spaced. It is not inconceivable that these longer waves could directly or indirectly affect the sun, the weather, animals, and human beings, and that just as a red pencil may respond to light waves of only one length, so a particular kind of organism might respond only to Y waves of one particular length.

Such a state of affairs is wholly imaginary. But the idea might serve to explain how so many different phenomena could oscillate with rhythms of identical length, and how one set of phenomena could fluctuate in waves with lengths entirely different from those of rhythms in adjacent phenomena. But such conjectures completely outrun the facts in hand.

That we have discovered solar rhythms only in the past few years, and are only learning about human rhythms now, may be put down to the same sort of slow human development which kept us from knowledge of such vital matters as electromagnetic radiation until the nineteenth century of our era.

There is, of course, an excuse. For these rhythms are extremely complex. How long, for instance, might it have taken men to discover the rhythm of the tides, if the earth — like Jupiter — had nine moons instead of one? Suppose, in addition, that our earth were so surrounded by fog we could not see the moons. How complex the tides would be, and how mysterious! We might even yet have failed to discover that the tidal sweeps of our oceans were gravitational rhythms united in a complex synthesis.

The work ahead of us stretches far and long. Fortunately that knowledge of ultimate cause, though it may be an ultimate goal, is not immediately vital to the conduct of our study, any more than to that of other sciences. As the great Eddington has declared: " In spite of popular opinions to the contrary, scientific investigation does not lead to the knowledge of the intrinsic nature of things. Whenever we state the properties of a body in terms of physical quantities, we are imparting knowledge of the response of various metrical indicators to its presence, *and nothing more*. To go further is the task of philosophy."

Whatever working hypothesis concerning the cause of human rhythms the reader may prefer to adopt for purposes of study — whether he looks more favorably on the theory of free or forced oscillations, or prefers some other one — he can still find the analysis of the rhythms full of reward. For, as Dr. Willford I. King, professor of economics at New York University, has said so well:

If the oscillations in business are dominated by forces following some mathematical formula, whether that formula be one representing a composite of sine curves or otherwise, the pattern of business must to a considerable extent be repetitive in nature and hence predictable. For any curve, or combination of curves, represented by mathematical formulae, can be reproduced indefinitely into the future.*

* *The Causes of Economic Fluctuations* (The Ronald Press), p. 244.

XI

Analysis and Synthesis

To TAKE a complex wave and analyze it into its simple components involves certain technical knowledge, and so does the task of synthesizing simple rhythms into a totality. It is not necessary that the reader of this study understand the techniques involved, and anyone desiring to avoid even the semblance of a mention of methods may prefer to skip this chapter. But the principles are simple, and he may find this understanding helpful before approaching — in the next chapter — a practical application of the knowledge to a specific business.

It should be made clear that in speaking of waves the word is used to describe what may be seen on the charts, and not to describe exactly what happens in society. As Sir James Jeans has said:

" A mathematical formula can never tell us what a thing is, but only how it behaves. . . . This point of view brings us relief from many of the difficulties and apparent inconsistencies of present day physics. We need no longer discuss whether light consists of particles or waves; we know all there is to be known about it if we have found a mathematical formula which accurately describes its behavior, and we can think of it as either particles or waves according to our mood and the convenience of the moment." *

* *The Mysterious Universe* (The Macmillan Company and Cambridge University Press) , pp. 951–2.

Jeans tentatively identifies the *wave* with *probability,* in a beautifully clear passage. He says:

Most physicists would, I think, agree that the seven-dimensional space in which the wave-mechanics pictures the meeting of two electrons is purely fictitious, in which case the waves which accompany the electrons must also be regarded as fictitious. . . . Yet . . . the waves of a single electron are real enough to record themselves on a photographic plate. . . .

Some physicists meet this situation by regarding the electron-waves as waves of probability. When we speak of a tidal-wave we mean a material wave of water which wets everything in its path. When we speak of a heat-wave we mean something which, although not material, warms up everything in its path. But when the evening papers speak of a suicide-wave, they do not mean that each person in the path of the wave will commit suicide; they merely mean that the likelihood of his doing so is increased. If a suicide wave passes over London, the death-rate from suicide goes up; if it passes over Robinson Crusoe's island, the probability that the sole inhabitant will kill himself goes up. The waves which represent an electron in the wave-mechanics may, it is suggested, be probability-waves, whose intensity at any point measures the probability of the electron being at that point.*

Just as our reference to waves of light is a mathematical reference, not a sensory one, so is our reference to waves in the economy. The waves we talk about are a mathematical record of energies which — so far as people are concerned — appear in their lives as pay cuts or raises, or the courage to buy a new automobile, or the self-denial involved in making the old hat do, or the determination to see that the family moves into another neighborhood before Nellie becomes of school age. Trillions of such daily events, built up from people's decisions and impulses, are the energies that distribute themselves through society.

Now, distributions of energy are easily recorded as curves. Fig-

* *Ibid.,* p. 130.

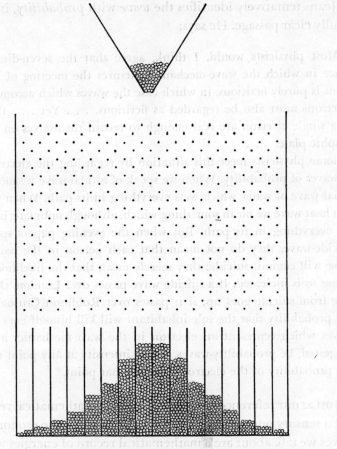

FIG. 1. GALTON'S QUINCUNX

A device for illustrating the physical basis of the normal frequency law (after Worthing and Geffner).

ure 1 shows a device called Galton's Quincunx, which puts small shot into the hopper at the top and lets them fall through a small hole, past interfering pegs, into bins at the bottom. They fall in a way that illustrates the physical basis of the normal frequency distribution law.

Figure 2 shows a graph of this same law of normal frequency distribution, in which you can recognize the wave form apparent in

[162]

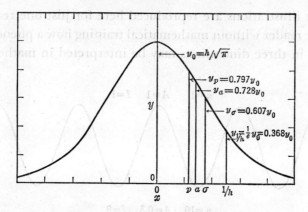

FIG. 2. FREQUENCY DISTRIBUTION

A graph of the law of normal frequency distribution, showing the Precision Indices (after Worthing and Geffner).

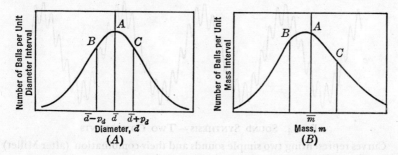

FIG. 3. BEARING BALLS

Distribution of (A) the diameters and (B) the masses of a group of bearing balls. If A is assumed normal B is necessarily skewed. (After Worthing and Geffner.)

the Quincunx, the purpose of which is to show a wave form by mechanical means.

Figure 3 shows how the mass distribution may be " skewed," and hence nonnormal, when a group of bearing balls of equal density and sphericity, but of varying diameter, follow the law of normal frequency distribution. Were this an ordinary wave, one would say it is distorted. But even the " distortion " follows law.

[163]

These illustrations are reproduced here for just one reason: to show the reader without mathematical training how a phenomenon familiar in three dimensions may be interpreted in mathematical forms.

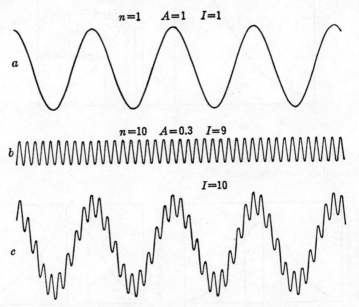

FIG. 4. SOUND SYNTHESIS — TWO COMPONENTS
Curves representing two simple sounds and their combination (after Miller).

Something quite similar happens when pig iron production, say, becomes a chart on a piece of paper.

The vibrations caused by sounds may similarly be made into a chart. Probably most readers are familiar, from their school days, with the diagram of a simple sound wave as shown at the top of Fig. 4. The middle figure in this diagram shows a second sound wave. The bottom figure shows the two combined in what we call a synthesis.

Synthesis is, of course, the reverse of analysis. Figure 5 shows, at the top, the curve made by the tone of an organ pipe. The sine curves shown below are the harmonic components of this curve,

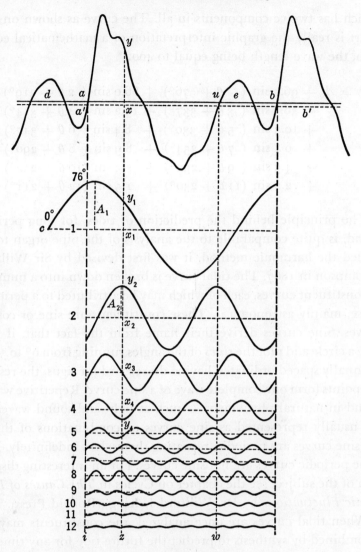

FIG. 5. SOUND SYNTHESIS — TWELVE COMPONENTS

An organ pipe curve (top) and its first twelve harmonic components (after Miller).

which has twelve components in all. The curve as shown on this chart is really the graphic interpretation of a mathematical equation, the wave length being equal to 400: *

$$
\begin{aligned}
y = A_0 &+ 96.5 \sin (\;\;\theta + \;\;76°) + 66.0 \sin (\;2\,\theta + 319°) \\
&+ 36.5 \sin (\;3\,\theta + 337°) + 19.2 \sin (\;4\,\theta + 354°) \\
&+ 10.3 \sin (\;5\,\theta + 330°) + \;\;8.4 \sin (\;6\,\theta + 347°) \\
&+ \;\;6.4 \sin (\;7\,\theta + 354°) + \;\;8.9 \sin (\;8\,\theta + 290°) \\
&+ \;\;4.3 \sin (\;9\,\theta + 252°) + \;\;2.3 \sin (10\,\theta + 252°) \\
&+ \;\;2.2 \sin (11\,\theta + 230°) + \;\;1.5 \sin (12\,\theta + 211°)
\end{aligned}
$$

The principle behind the prediction of tides, for long periods ahead, is quite comparable to the analysis of the pipe organ tone. Called the harmonic method, it was first devised by Sir William Thompson in 1867. The tidal curve is broken down into a number of constituent curves, each of which may be attributed to a periodic cause, mainly astronomical. These constituents are sine or cosine curves. Sine curves derive their name from the fact that, if you take a circle and plot the *sines* of the angles running from 0° to 360° as equally spaced ordinates, having due regard for signs, the resulting points form one complete wave of a sine curve. Repetitive waves found in natural phenomena — such as light and sound waves — are usually represented as sine curves or combinations of them. All sine curves are periodic, repeating themselves indefinitely. But some periodic curves are not sine curves. For an interesting discussion of the subject see the chapter on Cycles in *The Causes of Economic Fluctuations* by Dr. Willford I. King (Ronald Press).

When tidal curves are once analyzed, the constituents may be recombined by synthesis to predict the future tide for any time.

Figure 6 shows some of the constituents in the tide at Los Angeles. Captain Paul C. Whitney, of the U.S. Coast and Geodetic Survey, says of the work of analysis of such constituents:

* Reproduced by permission from Miller, *The Science of Musical Sounds* (The Macmillan Company), p. 124.

The actual computations necessary in making the harmonic analysis are quite laborious, although the work has been reduced by systematic methods. Even so, to determine, say, 24 constituents at a given place from a year's tidal series means computations involving about a million figures.[*]

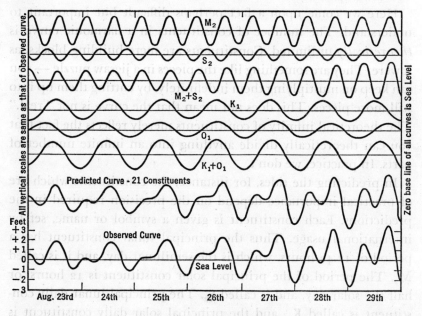

FIG. 6. TIDE PREDICTION

The predicted tide at Los Angeles, California, for August 23–30, 1936; the observed tide; and four (M_2, S_2, K_1, and O_1) of the 21 constituents that went into the prediction (after Whitney).

The two rhythms shown at the bottom of Fig. 6 illustrate the tide as it was predicted from a synthesis of the constituent curves, and the tide as it was actually observed. Very close agreement is indicated. The illustration shows only 4 out of the 21 constituents used for this particular prediction.

The harmonic method of analysis, by which the observed tide

[*] "The Prediction of Tides," *U. S. Naval Institute Proceedings*, December, 1940, pp. 1723–4.

[167]

curve is separated into the cosine curves, which are called constituents, is now used by all leading maritime nations in predicting tides. It is based on the principle that any *periodic* motion or oscillation can always be resolved into the sum of a series of simple harmonic motions.

Here we come upon a fact perhaps difficult but important to understand. The number of constituents in a harmonic curve is *theoretically* unlimited. Constituents are mere building blocks, as it were. They are something like the pieces in a jigsaw puzzle — you can keep on multiplying them indefinitely, by cutting them up into still more pieces. This does not mean that the curve is not " real." The theoretical infinity of constituents merely reflects the fact that you can theoretically divide anything into an infinite number of parts. In practice, we don't.

In predicting the tides, for instance, the constituents which are of practical importance depend on the precision required in the predictions. Each constituent is given a symbol or name, set by international usage. Thus the principal lunar constituent has a period of 12.42 hours, which is the semilunar day, and it is called M_2. The period of the principal solar constituent is 12 hours, or half the solar day, and is called S_2. The principal lunar daily constituent is called K_1, and the principal solar daily constituent is called O_1. The solar annual constituent is called Sa.

In Fig. 6, which we have already observed, the constituents M_2 and S_2 — after being traced separately — are shown combined into a curve. And K_1 and O_1 — pictured separately — are also shown combined. The predicted curve is a synthesis of these and 17 other constituents, or 21 in all.

Because the mathematical computations involved in using harmonic constants for tide predictions are so laborious, Thompson developed practical machines for rapidly analyzing and summing the various constituents. The predictor that has long been used by the U.S. Coast and Geodetic Survey is based on Thompson's original design, now much improved, and is constructed for summing 37 constituents. In about seven hours, it will make daily predictions for a year at a given point.

Prediction of such a curve thus involves two principles: analysis of the known curve to obtain its constituents; and then synthesis of the constituents to permit extending the curve into the future. Synthesis also serves to verify or prove the correctness of the analysis, by reconstructing the original curve — or a close approximation thereof — from the constituents.

The machines used for analysis and synthesis are employed in many fields. Professor A. A. Michelson devised an ingenious harmonic analyzer and synthesizer for 80 components, which has been used to study light waves. Such machines are also employed in electrical engineering for the study of alternating current waves and other periodic curves; they are useful in fields as various as electricity, acoustics, optics, astrophysics, naval architecture, and aerodynamics. The machines accomplish what the mathematicians can perform equally well by rather laborious methods which call for the resolving of involved equations.

Harmonic analysis is based on the mathematical principle called Fourier's Theorem, for which Baron J. B. J. Fourier first published the statement and proof in 1822. The Fourier Equation is not a tool for laymen untrained in mathematics; but it has been stated as follows, in language a layman can grasp, by Dr. Dayton Clarence Miller of the Case School of Applied Science:

If any curve be given, having a wave length l, the same curve can always be reproduced and in one particular way only, by compounding simple harmonic curves of suitable amplitudes and phases, in general infinite in number, having the same axis, and having wave lengths of l, $\frac{1}{2}l$, $\frac{1}{3}l$, and successive aliquot parts of l; the given curve may have any arbitrary form whatever, including any number of straight portions, provided that the ordinate of the curve is always finite and that the projection on the axis of a point describing the curve moves always in the same direction.*

* *The Science of Musical Sounds* (The Macmillan Company), p. 93.

[169]

And Dr. Miller explains the application of the Fourier Equation as follows: " Many of the curves studied by this method can be exactly reproduced by compounding a limited number of the simple curves. For sound waves the number of components required is often more than ten, and rarely as many as thirty. In some arbitrary mathematical curves, a finite number of components gives only a more or less approximate representation, while an exact reproduction requires the infinite series of components." *

In the study of economic rhythms, harmonic analysis is only one of our tools. The method does give an over-all picture useful for preliminary and reference purposes, and also gives to any desired accuracy a mathematical description of the behavior. But harmonic analysis is of use primarily in connection with a wave — such as a sound wave — which is more or less exactly repetitive.

Harmonic analysis fails of itself to give the true length of a rhythm; it ignores individual variation and changes in amplitude and shift of phase. It also fails to unscramble a wave from its own almost-harmonics. Multiple harmonic analysis gives a much closer approximation to the length of the rhythm; but other than this, it has all the limitations of ordinary harmonic analysis.

Some twenty other methods of analysis are available. The periodogram is a method of approach to analysis which we can use when the problem is to determine dominating waves in a series of data the period of which may not belong to the Fourier sequence. This method is also a useful preliminary in determining rhythms.

For the student of economic fluctuations, the Hoskins Time Chart is a tool of great usefulness. It makes possible a rather complete analysis of a series with celerity and ease, and suggests and reveals rhythms that do not appear from the study of an ordinary graph through mere inspection or the use of a graduated rule. The method does have its limitations; it fails, for instance, to give either the shape or the amplitude of the wave, or to give the length as accurately as some of the other methods do. But these shortcomings

* *Ibid*, p. 93.

can be met by supplementary use of the Moving Cycle Average, of the Periodic Table, and by other methods.

Unfortunately, we as yet have no machines generally available for conducting research work in economic rhythms on a scale matching the importance of the subject. The so-called Cyclograph exists in the form of only two machines — one is owned by its inventor in Chicago, and one is the property of Andrew E. Douglass in Tucson, Arizona.

Electrical spectrum analysis, if a machine and the skill to run it were available, would save vast amounts of time that must now be spent in multiple harmonic analysis. Electromechanical machines, if they were refined and made generally available, would save much time in periodogram construction, with the added advantage of finding the values for all positions for each period, as in the periodic table.

Such matters are mentioned here in passing, and only briefly, for the purpose of indicating to the general reader the scope of the problems involved. The problems themselves can safely be left in the hands of those with the technical training for their ultimate mastery. Our own immediate interest is confined, from this point on, to answering the questions with which our study began.

XII

Timing a Business

WHEN WE ASK what time it is on the clock, we are really asking a spatial question. Its fundamental meaning is: "Where is my spot of earth in reference to the earth's course around its axis and around the sun?" One could plot the answer with a graph. A clock is merely a kind of graph in mechanical form.

When we ask whether a business should expand, or whether its stock is a good investment, or whether it can better raise funds by selling stocks or bonds, we are asking a similar sort of question. For the essence of our question is merely: "Where does this business stand in reference to its course of life?" Every business has its rhythms. These rhythms, wrapped around its trend, combine to make a path that can be graphed like an orbit. We can discover these rhythms by analysis, much as we discover the separate rhythms in the tides.

A business is an organ — major or minor — in the whole economy. We should therefore expect to find in it at least one of the major rhythms that we meet in the economy as a whole. We ordinarily do. In addition, we often meet one or more rhythms seemingly unique to that particular business. Why this should be so, we do not yet know.

An illustration of the sales chart for one business is shown in Fig. 1. The business represented is an important public utility company of the United States. The sales from 1883–1939 in physical units are plotted on logarithmic paper to show rate of growth, in the fashion to which the reader was earlier introduced. It is worth noting, at this point, that this entire plotting and analysis was made in 1940, before the United States became involved in war.

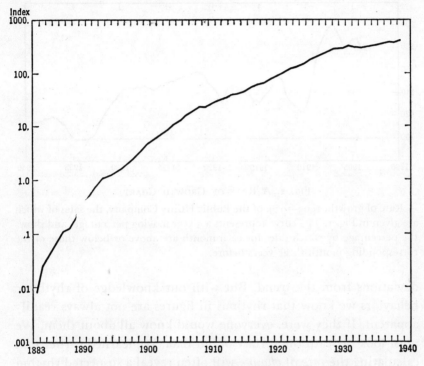

FIG. 1. A SALES CHART

Sales of a Public Utility Company 1883–1939. *Ratio scale.*

Figure 1 shows us a company that has had a strong and healthy growth — one whose growth is continuing in terms of annual increases in dollars of sales. But the fact that the slope of the line is getting flatter shows that the *rate* of growth is now on the downgrade. The company is rapidly becoming mature. A comparison with some of the charts showing the trends for major American industries, as indicated in the early pages of this book, will show

[173]

a marked similarity in the trend line. We are, therefore, dealing with a more or less typical major industry.

Nothing that meets the eye of the reader in Fig. 1 suggests any particular rhythm — there are merely some apparently irregular

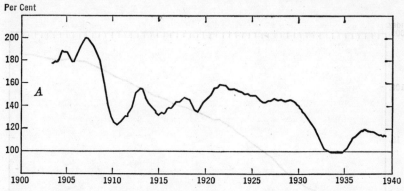

FIG. 2. A RATE OF GROWTH CHART

Rate of growth, 1903–1939, of the Public Utility Company, the sales of which are given in Fig. 1. The curve represents a 3-year moving percentage, and shows the percentage by which sales for each month are above or below those of the corresponding month three years before.

deviations from the trend. But with our knowledge of rhythmic behaviors we know that rhythms in figures are not always readily apparent. If they were, everyone would know all about them. We must look beneath the surface of our data. We learned earlier that calculating the *rate of change* will often reveal a suspected rhythm with great clarity. We therefore calculate the monthly rate of change in this business, using in this instance a 3-year interval.* That is, we use a 3-year moving percentage.

* The possible treatments of figures to reveal rhythm are exceedingly numerous. They include, beside various moving percentages: (1) deviation of the data from various simple moving average trends; (2) deviation of the data from various weighted moving average trends; (3) deviation of the data from various mathematical trends; (4) deviation of various moving averages of the data from various moving average trends; (5) deviation of various moving averages of the data from various mathematical trends; (6) deviation of one mathematical trend from another; (7) various moving section averages. Al-

Figure 2 shows us the result. If we have not yet revealed a rhythm clear to the eye by simple inspection, at least we have before us a chart that shows wide swings in the rate of change.

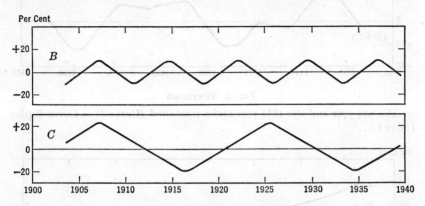

FIG. 3. TWO REGULAR CYCLES

Cycle B has a period (length from high to high or low to low) of 90 months (7½ yrs.). Cycle C has a period of 220 months (18⅓ yrs.).

Our problem now becomes one of analysis. The outcome is the two sets of waves shown in Fig. 3. We have come up with two perfectly regular rhythms — one of 18⅓ years, and the other of 7½ years. They were concealed from us in Fig. 2 because crests and troughs were so combined, at various times, that crests sometimes augmented crests and sometimes tended to wipe out troughs, while troughs sometimes combined to deepen troughs and at other times obscured crests.

But we have not yet finished our task. As one test of our work, we must move from analysis back through synthesis. Figure 4 shows the two rhythms, which were isolated in Fig. 3, recombined into a complex. Figure 4, when compared with Fig. 2, shows a suggestive similarity. Our work, however, is still not finished. We are dealing in this business not only with rhythms, but with a trend. Figure 5

though the methods are various, they all have one basic purpose, namely, to subordinate or minimize the irregularities (including rhythms of other lengths) so that a rhythm, if present, can be observed and studied.

[175]

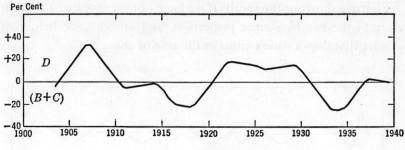

FIG. 4. SYNTHESIS

The 7½-year and the 18⅓-year cycles combined (Curve D = Curve B plus Curve C).

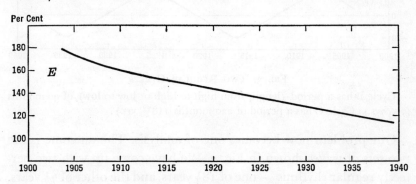

FIG. 5. THE TREND LINE

Trend of the Rate of Growth, as Charted in Fig. 2, of the Public Utility Company, the actual sales of which are charted in Fig. 1. The Company is growing, but at a decreasing *rate*. For a simpler example, refer to the hypothetical company discussed in Chapter 1.

shows this trend — the basic underlying trend in the rate of growth. Here the graph is in terms of per cent. It is decreasing, and our trend line slopes steadily downward to the right.

Now, in Fig. 6, the trend line delineated in Fig. 5 is combined with the complex wave, created by synthesis, shown in Fig. 4. The total synthesis gives us something closely approaching the wave we started out with.

For convenience, Fig. 2 is repeated under the new synthesis in Fig. 6, so that we may make a ready comparison. When the two curves are compared in detail, it is clear that there are certain fluctuations in the true curve of Fig. 2 for which there are no counterparts in Fig. 6. On the whole, however, the comparison is excellent, and conformity is seen to have been especially close in

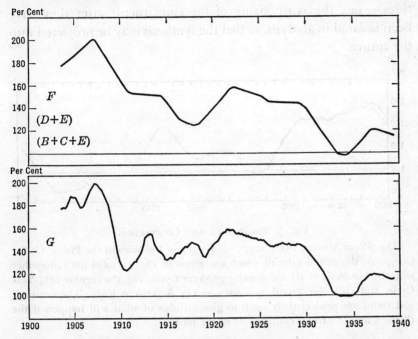

FIG. 6. TREND LINE AND CYCLES

Trend of the Rate of Growth of the Public Utility Company as shown in Fig. 5, plus the combination of the 7½-Year and the 18⅓-Year cycles, as shown in Fig. 4. Curve F = Curve B plus Curve C plus E. For purposes of comparison, curve A is reproduced again and labelled G.

the past twenty years, or since the business has reached maturity. We may therefore assume that we have isolated the *major* rhythms which move along this trend line.

The conformity between our synthesis and the actual curve may be seen better if, for the past twenty years, we draw the derived curve, as shown in Fig. 6, in dotted lines, and place it on the actual curve first shown in Fig. 2. This operation is performed in Fig. 7.

The synthesis of the two waves ($7\frac{1}{2}$ and $18\frac{1}{3}$ years) is projected here for the next twenty years.

Figure 7 shows us, in other words, the application to economic prediction of the same principle that is used in predicting future tides — i.e., the synthesizing of the constituents after they have been isolated in analysis, so that the synthesis may be projected into the future.

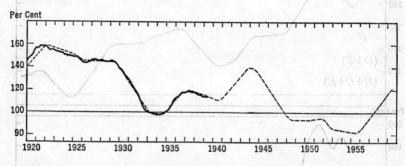

FIG. 7. PROJECTION AND COMPARISON

The 3-Year Moving Percentage, 1920–1939, of the Sales of the Public Utility Company, the actual sales of which are given in Fig. 1 (solid line), together with the Synthesis of (i) the regular $7\frac{1}{2}$-Year Cycle, (ii) the regular $18\frac{1}{3}$-Year Cycle, and (iii) the Trend, as shown in Fig. 6 (broken line). The synthesis and trend are projected to 1959, to give an idea of what will happen if the rhythms and the trend continue as in the past.

For this particular company, the projection has been extremely close to the actual curve, as subsequent experience has drawn that curve from 1939 through 1945. The two rhythms on which the projection is based go back as far as the series — 57 years — and pretty well describe the series' behavior, at least since the company has reached its majority. The probability of their continuing seems high, and the unwisdom of ignoring this probability would seem real.

In Figure 8 the rate-of-change projections have been converted back into an actual physical projection. Figure 8, that is, is the final part of Figure 1, enlarged. This particular chart showed that in 1938 and 1939 the plant facilities could be expanded boldly — in-

[178]

cidentally, at a time of reasonable costs. It showed that between 1939 and 1946 refinancing should be possible on a most favorable basis, presumably because of satisfactory earning statements of a kind that might not be possible in the following decade when earnings would probably be drifting below 1939 averages. The marked downgrade indicated in the chart after 1946 suggested the wisdom of considering whether earnings should be generously distributed

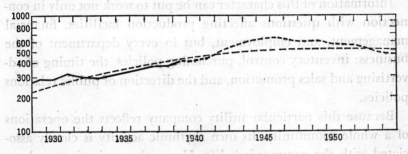

FIG. 8. AN ENLARGEMENT

Sales of the Public Utility, 1930–1939. (The last ten years of the curve in Fig. 1 are here enlarged.) *Ratio scale.* There have been added the trend, and a projection into the future, based on a conversion of the rate of change figures charted in Fig. 7, to give an idea of what will happen if the rhythms and trend continue as in the past. For a simpler example of the same sort, refer to the hypothetical company in Chapter 1.

from 1939 to 1946, or whether surplus should be built up to help maintain dividends after the decline sets in.

Clearly, on the basis of the pattern, 1944–1945 were years when no new vice-presidencies should have been created; 1945–1946 were years when new employees should have been taken on slowly, if at all; and 1947–1948 show as years in which employees may have to be weeded out. Certainly our chart tells us that they should not be retained merely in the hope of a revival in sales two or three years later.

After 1946 the company may begin to find itself with some excess plant facilities; undoubtedly, after 1946 has come and gone, and the downturn has definitely established itself, the company should consider scrapping surplus plant and equipment that will not justify carrying charges during the eighteen years or so that they will not be needed. For our chart shows definitely that, if the underlying growth trend for this particular business continues to flatten at the rate of the past twenty years, and if the cycles continue, more than eighteen years will pass before the company will again reach the levels of 1946.

Information of this character can be put to work not only in connection with questions affecting production facilities, financial management, and employment, but in every department of the business: inventory control, purchasing policies, the timing of advertising and sales promotion, and the direction of public relations policies.

Because this particular utility company reflects the operations of a whole community, its own rhythmic activity is closely associated with the community's life. Hence the projection we have drawn for it will apply with not too great a divergence to the economic activity of the entire city in which it operates.

In 1946 this city was enjoying a great real estate boom. Residential rents were under government control, but rents for commercial properties were soaring. Landlords were demanding rental increases of from 100 to 300 per cent from some business tenants, together with new leases running from five years up. The great business activity reflected in the public utility's sales enabled many landlords to get heavy rentals on the long-term leases they demanded, for tenants were desperate. A shortage of loft buildings and other commercial space left no place to move.

But if our chart correctly portrays the future of this community, there will be a great letdown well before the forties have ended, and those with long-term leases at high rentals may have regrets.

Interestingly enough, the $18\frac{1}{3}$-year rhythm which has been isolated in the life of this utility company is the one that shows up so clearly in real estate activity — the rhythm that Warren and Pearson have declared the next most important in our economy, after price movements. For it is closely associated with the activity of many basic industries. Whether the $7\frac{1}{2}$-year rhythm, which we find operating beside it in this utility company, exists in other activities of the metropolis where the utility is located is a question which only long study and exploration could answer.

This chart indeed raises more questions than the present state of our knowledge permits us to deal with. For instance, when the projection in Fig. 8 was drawn, it was not known that 1941–1945 would be " war years." But notice the large increase in sales projected for those very years, on the basis of the two rhythms isolated in this company's operations. There is much in the analysis of rhythm to indicate that many rises in prices, sales, and other indices of economic activity come on schedule, war or no war. And declines come similarly. As stated before, war may, and usually does, distort the *amplitude* of a wave — just as a strong wind may sweep a high tide higher — but it often seems to interfere with the *timing* of the wave to a very small degree, if at all.

The projection shown in Fig. 8 warrants a word of warning as regards the war question. Some observers, around 1942, put their finger on the 1946 peak and said, in effect, " Ah, that's when the war is going to end! " There is nothing in our knowledge of rhythms that could warrant this kind of interpretation. It can be hazardous to read such " reasons " into these rhythmic patterns.

The pictures seen in the graphs are inevitably very generalized portrayals of the landscape that lies ahead of us. In this method we have a tool for our journey toward the future, but it is not a key which unlocks all mysteries. The further we go in every science, the more profound the chasms in our knowledge can appear. One such gap faces us when we note the projection for the utility company (as shown on page 179) for the years after 1946. The long decline forecast there agrees very well with the decline in America's national economic activity which the four chief economic rhythms are now forecasting after 1946–1947. But only one of the four national rhythms — the $18\frac{1}{3}$-year — is a constituent of the utility company's wave. Why, on the basis of different constituents, the waves for the nation and the one company should be so similar in character is not for answer here.

A similar analysis and synthesis is shown for an industrial company in Figs. 9, 10, and 11. Figure 9 shows adjusted net shipments, 1871–1940; a 3-year moving average has been charted here on ratio ruling, to show change in rate of growth. Figure 10 shows the

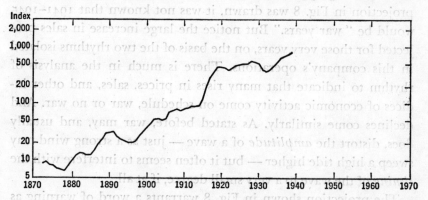

FIG. 9. SALES OF AN INDUSTRIAL COMPANY, 1871–1940
Three-year moving average. *Ratio scale.*

analysis. We see a $9\frac{1}{3}$-year wave (A) ; an $18\frac{1}{3}$-year wave (B) ; and an underlying growth trend (D). The effect of World War I on this company shows in a lift of the growth trend from one level to another. The pattern and the rate of growth were not affected at all. When the company was expanded at this point by the war forces, the trend line merely continued its established course at a somewhat higher level. Figure 11 shows the synthesis of A plus B plus D, projected to 1970, and matches it against the actual data (until 1940) that was first plotted in Fig. 9. It will be noted that the synthesis shows very close correspondence with the actual data, as far as these data go. After 1940 war forces lifted actual shipment figures above the synthesis line, much as in World War I.

The data for another corporation are shown in Figs. 12, 13, 14, 15, 16 and 17. Permission to use the data here has been granted

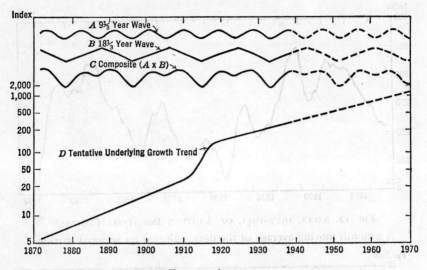

FIG. 10. ANALYSIS

(A) A regular 9⅓-Year Cycle; (B) a regular 18⅓-Year Cycle; (C) the Two Combined; (D) the underlying Growth Trend of the Industrial Company, the actual sales of which are charted in Fig. 9. *Ratio scale*.

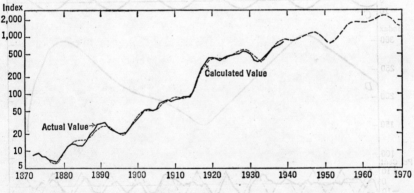

FIG. 11. SYNTHESIS

Sales of an industrial company, 1871–1940 (3-year moving averages), as shown in Fig. 9, together with a synthesis of the regular 9⅓-year cycle, the 18⅓-year cycle, and the underlying growth trend, as shown in Fig. 10. *Ratio scale*. This projection gives an idea of what will happen if the rhythms and the trend continue as in the past.

[183]

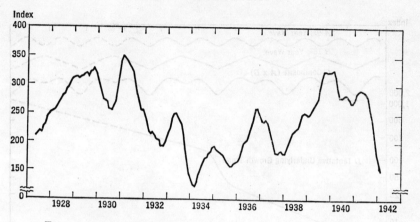

FIG. 12. SALES, 1927–1941, OF ANOTHER INDUSTRIAL COMPANY

A 9-month moving average of the data, adjusted for seasonal rhythm.

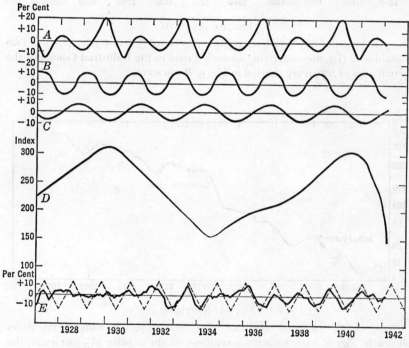

FIG. 13. ANALYSIS

(A) A regular 41-month cycle; (B) a regular 24-month cycle; (C) a regular 33-month cycle: (D) a 10-year wave; (E) residual showing 15-month cycle.

[184]

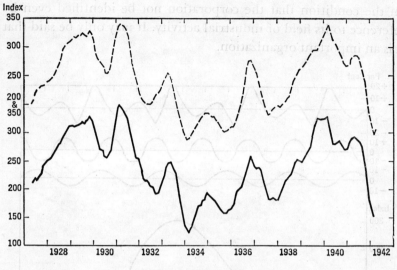

FIG. 14. SYNTHESIS

Above, synthesis of the regular cycles and the 10-year wave, shown in Fig. 13 (dotted line) ; below, actual sales of this company as shown originally in Fig. 11 (solid line) .

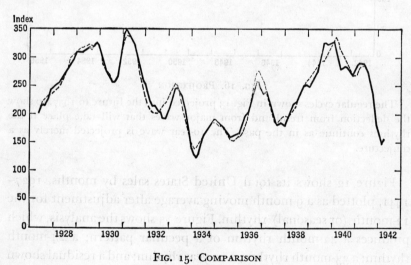

FIG. 15. COMPARISON

The curves shown in Fig. 14 superimposed.

[185]

on the condition that the corporation not be identified even by reference to its field of industrial activity. It may only be said that it is an important organization.

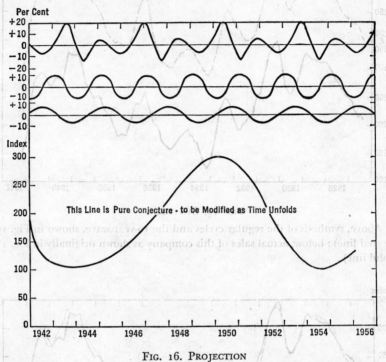

FIG. 16. PROJECTION

The regular cycles shown in Fig. 13 projected into the future to 1957, to show the deflection from trend and from major waves that will take place if the rhythms continue as in the past. The 10-year wave is projected merely as a conjecture.

Figure 12 shows its total United States sales by months, 1927–1941, plotted as a 9-month moving average after adjustment for the 12-month (or seasonal) rhythm. Figure 13 shows the analysis, which produces a 41-month rhythm of a peculiar pattern; a 24-month rhythm; a 33-month rhythm; a 10-year rhythm; and a residual shown at the bottom of the chart as F, where we find strong suggestion of a further rhythm of approximately 15 months.

[186]

Figure 14 shows, at the top, the synthesis of these various rhythms, and at the bottom — for easy comparison — the actual line that was first plotted in Fig. 12. The correspondence is close. In Fig. 15 we

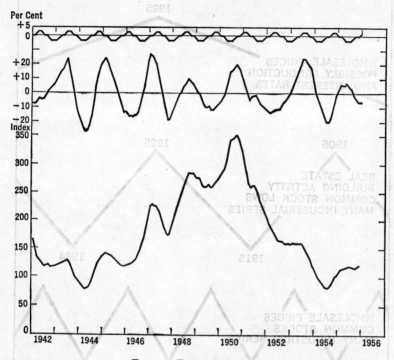

FIG. 17. FINAL SYNTHESIS

Synthesis of the cycles and the wave shown in Fig. 16. Top, the 15-month cycle; middle, the synthesis of the 41-month, 24-month, and 33-month cycles; bottom, synthesis of all four rhythms with the conjectural 10-year wave.

can compare our synthesis and the actual line in another way, since one is superimposed on the other. Here the dotted line represents our synthesis, and the solid line the actual sales figure.

We observe that our synthesis checks very well with the " real " line. Thus we are ready for a further step. In Fig. 16 our various rhythms are projected into 1956. The 10-year wave here is projected as a conjecture, inasmuch as this particular corporation has too short a history (dating back only to 1927) to permit of any opin-

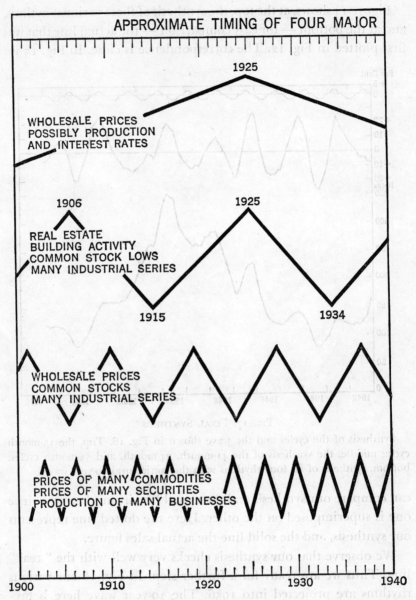

FIG. 18. DIAGRAMMATIC REPRESENTATION OF THE

It should be pointed out again that these rhythms manifest themselves progressively in various sorts of business and prices and that the timing is therefore only approximate. The diagram makes no pretense of showing relative strength

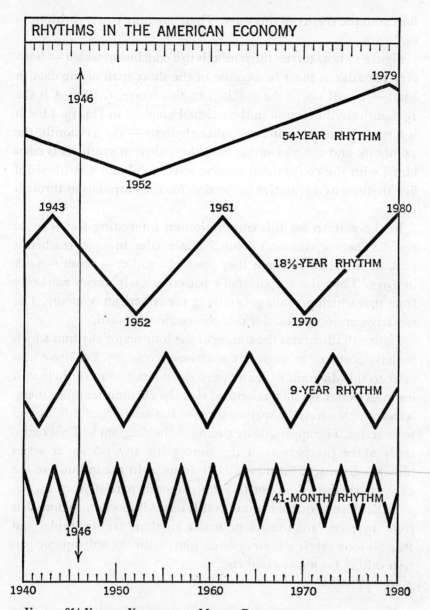

RHYTHMS IN THE AMERICAN ECONOMY

1946

1979

54-YEAR RHYTHM

1952

1943   1961   1980

18⅓-YEAR RHYTHM

1952   1970

9-YEAR RHYTHM

41-MONTH RHYTHM

1946

1940   1950   1960   1970   1980

54-Year, 18⅓-Year, 9-Year and 41-Month Rhythms

of the various waves, which also varies with the series. The projections from 1946 to 1980 show the structure that will prevail if these rhythms continue. A ruler laid up and down the page will show rhythms in any given year.

ions as to the reality of this wave. There are only two repetitions to deal with.

Figure 17 now carries the synthesis to a conclusion which — however tentative it must be because of the short span of the data in hand — is still worth the making. In this figure, rhythm A is the 15-month rhythm found in the residual graphed in Fig. 13. Line B is a synthesis of A with three other rhythms — the 41-month, the 24-month, and the 33-month. In C the 4-rhythm synthesis is combined with the conjectured 10-year wave, to obtain a synthesis of five rhythms as a tentative projection for the corporation through 1955.

In the pattern for this corporation an interesting fact is to be noted. The corporation's United States sales in 1930 reached a peak higher than in 1929; they reached another — lesser — peak in 1932. Thus the corporation's pattern clearly varies markedly from that which prevails generally in the American economy. The tentative projection carries this observation forward.

Figure 18 illustrates the timing of the four major rhythms which we have observed at work in the national economy. For those who refer to this diagram with an eye to the management of their own business affairs, let it be reiterated that the rhythms manifest themselves progressively in various sorts of business organizations and price series. The approximate timing in the diagram will not necessarily agree precisely with the timing for any particular series hitherto discussed. Further, this diagram, as in the instance of the 18⅓-year rhythm, does not take into account partial years.

With all such qualifications, it still seems important to note that from 1947 onward these four major rhythms are declining, and that all four reach a bottom *circa* 1952, with the subsequent pattern calling for a concerted rise.

XIII

Avoiding Some Economic Illusions

MANY BUSINESSMEN (and some economists) find it hard to use the trend and the rhythms in their economic calculations, because of an *a priori* prejudice. That is, they find it hard to believe any kind of human experience can be "determined" by factors outside the control of man's own conscious life. And so they resist recognition of the evidence. They accept the need of adjustment to the weather, knowing it is out of man's control. But they resist passionately any suggestion that changes in the social and economic climate may be beyond the total rule of man's conscious will.

A man accustomed to think that certain "causes" must always have given "results" and that we control results by advance manipulation of causes may feel especially confused. If, for instance, he believes that raising the price of gold will raise the price of commodities, then he thinks he knows the "cause" of the American price rise in 1933. How then, he may ask, could rhythms have had anything to do with it? Isn't it common sense to think that this rhythm business — whatever the evidence — is esoteric nonsense?

The fact is that most of the "causes" we commonly assign to events are the real nonsense. Science knows this. It was one of Freud's great contributions, for instance, that he showed how we do what we feel subconsciously impelled to do, and then satisfy

[191]

our conscious mind by devising adequate "reasons." Most of us talk, think, and plan in the same kinds of patterns our ancestors used in days before science was born. The outcome is illusion. We must free ourselves of many of the old patterns if we are to use the knowledge that is now available.

To that end let us consider in terms of modern psychology and physics a few facts important for our approach to economic science.

P. D. Ouspensky * once asked his readers to make an experiment. Imagine, he said, that you live in two dimensions, instead of three. An easy way to do this is to imagine you are a being like a piece of paper, infinitely thin, living upon a table. You can look neither up nor down, for up and down are in a third dimension. You cannot even *think* up and down, or conceive it. For you have no thickness, and hence cannot even *imagine* thickness.

Now in the center of this tabletop where you live, there is cut a slot. In this slot there revolves a wheel, so hung that half the wheel is always below the table, and half of it above. This wheel is solid and you can see only the edge of it. Let us imagine its edge is painted in four colored segments — black, white, blue, and red. As the wheel revolves, and you observe it end-on, you of course do not know that it is a wheel you see. For you are a two-dimensional being, and therefore see only a *single line of color* along the tabletop. Occasionally, as the wheel slowly revolves, you do see that line change suddenly in color. Red will suddenly change to black, and black to white, white to blue, and blue to red again.

Now, if you observe this phenomenon long enough, you will finally decide that when the red comes up, it will eventually cause black; and when the black appears, it will eventually cause blue. You will think you know the causes of the phenomena you observe.

If a two-dimensional scientist is observing the phenomena, he will eventually discover a " law " in this continuity of event. Using this law, he will be able to predict changes of color accurately. The scientist, by the use of mathematics, might also discover that a third

* See *Tertium Organum* (Alfred A. Knopf, 1922), p. 65.

[192]

dimension was necessary to account for the real phenomenon he saw in two dimensions only. But neither of you could *imagine* this third dimension as a sensory reality. Nor could you know the real nature of the causes operating there. The scientist would admit this frankly, saying his law merely described what happened, without explaining it. But you, untrained in such fine distinctions, would speak boldly of a " cause " being followed by an " effect." And each " effect " would in turn become a new cause (in your way of thinking) resulting in a further effect which followed. If you persisted in this belief, you might eventually resent being told that you knew nothing about the real causality.

This little exercise in make-believe illustrates how our senses, being limited to three-dimensional experience, limit the kind of knowledge which we call " common sense." As human animals, we are three-dimensional beings. But the universe has more than three dimensions; for convenience, and to avoid mathematical talk, let us call it a three-*plus* universe. In such a universe, we shall err seriously if we think perception alone can ever tell us true causes.

When a historical event does occur, we shall probably recognize a " cause." Or rather, we think we can. But before we get to that event, we are never able to recognize in society a present cause A that will inevitably produce a future social effect B. After the stock market has gone up, for instance, almost any commentator can find a sound " reason " for its action. But before it goes up, no one can predict for sure what it will do on any particular day. In short, and to repeat: Our recognition of cause is always associated with past events that we view in retrospect.

This brings us to a vital fact: What we call our recognition of " *cause* " and " *effect* " is *somehow associated with time,* and with our perception in time. This is important to understand, for what we call time is apparently only a mode of perception. Psychology has long suspected as much; physics has laid the essential groundwork of evidence. Following Einstein's original publication of his findings, in 1905, Minkowsky showed that electrical phenomena must be regarded as occurring not in space and time separately, but in space and time welded together so closely that a joint could not be detected. Thus the phenomena of electromagnetism may be thought of as occurring in a continuum of four dimensions — three dimensions of space and one of time. *And it is impossible to separate the space from the time in any absolute manner.* Mathematics today uses a factor representing time interchangeably with factors representing space.

Ouspensky, approaching the problem from a psychological background, goes so far as to suggest that time is the way we experience space in its higher dimensions. That is, the unknown dimensions of space are revealed to us in time. A rough comparison, to illustrate this idea, can be found in the perception of a soldier who stands at the foot of a hill. He will not know what lies on the other side of the hill until he spends the time necessary to walk to the crest. But an aviator, in the sky directly above him, can already perceive what the soldier will not know for another half hour. The aviator sees the soldier's future experience as present, because he occupies a different *spatial* relation to the event awaiting the soldier's perception.

Modern physics tells us that two individuals separated by enough space will not even be able to know what simultaneity means. The event that is still future for one individual may be past for another located in a different frame of reference. Eddington has dramatized this relativity of time with a happy illustration:

Suppose that you are in love with a lady on Neptune, and that she returns the sentiment. It will be some consolation for the melancholy separation if you can say to yourself at some — possibly prearranged — moment, "She is thinking of me now." Unfortunately a difficulty has arisen because we have had to abolish Now. There is no absolute Now, but only the various relative Nows differing according to the reckoning of different observers.*

* *The Nature of the Physical World* (The Macmillan Company and Cambridge University Press), p. 49.

[194]

Obviously, if time is relative, then our perception of cause and effect is equally relative. For cause and effect are ordered in time — cause must precede its effect, by the very definition of the words. If *Now* has no absolute meaning, neither can *Cause*. If time is only a mode of perceiving a three-plus universe, so is our idea of cause and effect.

When we put a pot of water on the hot stove, we tend to think that is what causes it to boil. But we shall do well to recognize the fact that the water boils under what may be called a "law of averages." We may assume it always will. But we know of no absolute law that it must, and the formulation of the Quantum law in physics has shown us how we are limited in our knowledge that it always does. We have no grounds for predicting that any selected, single molecule of the water will boil. We predict on the basis of the group. As Eddington phrases it:

When we ask what is the characteristic of the phenomena that have been successfully predicted, the answer is that they are effects depending on the average configurations of vast numbers of individual entities. . . . The laws governing the microscopic elements of the physical world — individual atoms, electrons, quanta — do not make definite predictions as to what the individual will do next. . . . But short odds on the behavior of individuals combine into very long odds on suitably selected statistics of a number of individuals. . . . *All the successful predictions hitherto attributed to causality are traceable to this.* It is true that the quantum laws for individuals are not incompatible with causality; they merely ignore it.

Human life is proverbially uncertain; few things are more certain than the solvency of a life insurance company. . . . The eclipse in 1999 is as safe as the balance of a life insurance company; the next quantum jump of an atom is as uncertain as your life and mine.*

Having come thus far, it is hoped that the reader now understands we are sailing no esoteric seas, but are cutting away some underbrush to reach firm, sound ground. Here is that ground:

* *Ibid.,* pp. 300–302.

In economics, as in physics, we cannot predict what any given individual will do. But we do have useful methods of predicting what groups will do. And we can succeed within tolerable margins of error. In using our knowledge of rhythms to do exactly this, we rely, just as in physics, on statistics for large numbers of individuals. In using them, we ignore the usual concepts of causality. And we ignore the fact that the future where the predicted action will occur is not yet present to the senses. An equation that will be balanced in the future is just as valid as " $2 + 2 = 4$ " is now.

After an event has happened, the human mind will always seek to associate it with another event which can be thought of as a cause. This is a characteristic mental need of man, who tries to impose his own special kind of order on the whole universe, in the process of trying to understand that universe. But it is not a need of science. Indeed, it merely handicaps scientific inquiry into the real nature of the universe, and of the phenomena of which we are a part. The new economics, having adopted this approach, has made more progress in a few decades than was accomplished during whole generations of economic argument over which came first, the hen or the egg.

Economists who have viewed society as a mere multiplication of individuals, and so tried to describe it in terms of each individual's reason-why, were bound to fail. People banded together in an economic community are more than a simple sum of individual beings. As " members one of another " they form a biological organism whose whole is always greater than the sum of its parts. They are cells subject to the mathematical laws which control aggregates. The scientist who studies them with the techniques of true science is no more concerned with their individual concepts of reason-why than he is interested in the possible thoughts of the yeast cells whose life in a test tube he charts on a graph. His only proper question is not why they act as they do, but how and when. With people en masse, as with yeast cells, his graphs will tell.

The individual need not feel his intellectual dignity hurt by this reserved approach to the affairs in which he plays a part. To the man who quails at this approach we may extend the promise that when prices go down he can always discover what looks like a cause; when they go up, he can also discover a plausible cause; and when they remain stable he will always be able to cite a reasonable reason. We need not argue with him about the reality of the causes he thinks he sees in operation. We have a much briefer way out. We merely show him Fig. 1 and ask him what he sees. Depending on

FIG. 1. ILLUSION

What you see here depends on the focus of your attention. A cave entrance? Glowering Jap wrestlers? (After Ruben and Hartman.)

the focus of his eye, he may see an urn, or two faces, or the entrance to a cave — or what he will. If his focus on a phenomenon in two dimensions will play him such tricks, what may not happen when he views events in three dimensions? And how can he ever hope to know the true nature of an event in a three-plus universe?

This is not nihilism — it is the essence of sound approach to knowledge. For only by knowing the limitations of our working tools can we properly value the results. And only by recognizing the limitation of mind can we think truly.

The outcome is itself sufficient justification of the method — an outcome that permits prediction, which is the goal of every true science. The method has another advantage — it draws economics close to all the other sciences, just as they, too, converge. " The separate sciences — epistemology, physics, chemistry, mathematics, astronomy — are approaching one another with acceleration, converging toward a complete identity of results." Those were the words of Spengler; he could well have added biology, psychology, economics, and sociology to his list.

It is not the business of economics to explain *how* the human mind divides a series of events up into Past, Present, and Future; this is a problem for other sciences. But for progress in the ability to make useful predictions in the economic field we do need all the knowledge that the other sciences have to offer on this subject. And we need a working hypothesis (we may accept it wholly tentatively) which permits us to understand how the future already exists in the present — not as the result of a *cause* now in operation, but as the continuance of a pattern. Sir James Jeans offers us a physicist's hypothesis:

" It may be that time, from its beginning to the end of eternity, is spread before us in the picture, but we are in contact with only one instant, just as the bicycle-wheel is in contact with only one point of the road. Then, as Weyl puts it, events do not happen; we merely come across them." *

Whatever hypothesis we prefer, we must avoid one temptation as we look at our charts that project patterns into the future. We must always regard cause-and-effect thinking as only *partial*. We can even call it three-dimensional thinking applied to a three-plus environment. When we are tempted to use it, in estimating the future, let us recall the two-dimensional being on the table top. Let us imagine that he liked the color red very much, and that he was one of a whole colony of such beings living around the wheel. When red came into view on the tabletop horizon, he and his fel-

* *The Mysterious Universe* (The Macmillan Company and Cambridge University Press), p. 127.

lows felt gay and happy all over. They joined hands — touching two-dimensional finger tips. They spun round and round in dancing. So pleasant was their sensation that they started an inquiry to ascertain what measures could be taken to keep the red always in view.

A group of investigators was appointed, with the object of making an orderly inquiry. It was found that the red always appeared after a period of community malaise during which the color had been blue, for which no one cared. Following a long spell during which various community readjustments to life with the blue had been made (and these were catalogued at length), the community suddenly felt a new access of well-being. Simultaneously the red appeared. The investigators could report that the red was therefore undoubtedly the result of a balanced state in the economy, reached as a result of the readjustments in the blue period. Unfortunately, as the dancing activity mounted during the happy red period, excesses apparently developed, which the investigators saw evidenced in the fact that the tempo of the spinning grew exceedingly rapid. The investigators measured these mounting excesses, and compiled them into voluminous statistical reports. It was their unanimous conclusion that the sudden passing of the red — which had happened so many times in their two-dimensional history — had always been the direct result of such excesses. The investigators ended their report with recommendations for a further study as to legislation that would keep the excesses under control.

Fantasy though that may seem, it has as much sense in it as many of the prevailing economic doctrines which dispute learnedly over the " causes " in the world we live in.

It is not within the province of our charts to tell us about the nature of that world. But it is their virtue that they enable us to avoid, in thinking about it, some of the illusions inherent in cause-and-effect argument.

XIV

War and Its Dislocations

THERE IS some limited evidence that wars and periods of war activity may have a rhythmic periodicity in the affairs of men. Dr. Lin Yutang, in *My Country and My People*, * reproduces three charts prepared by Dr. J. S. Lee for a study, " The Periodic Recurrence of Internecine Wars in China," published in the *China Journal of Sciences and Arts* in 1931. The Chinese people have a continuum of history far exceeding that of any other people with extant records for study. Dr. Lee found two 800-year periods in Chinese history, and the beginning of a third, which when compared show striking parallelism in their periods of peace and disorder. He concluded that the parallelism " far exceeds the limits of probability " and is " perhaps too exact to be expected from the proceedings of human affairs."

Each period began with a short-lived but militarily strong dynasty, which unified the country after centuries of disorganization and civil strife. Then would follow four or five hundred years of peace. Then a change of dynasty would be followed by successive wars. The capital would be moved from the North to the South, secession and rivalry between North and South would create intensified conflicts, subjugation of the dissidents under foreign rule would result, and the cycle would end.

Spengler, who believed that all cultures have a life course in the

* John Day Co. and Reynal & Hitchcock (1935), pp. 30–31.

general order of 1,000 years, and saw comparable phenomena emerging at parallel periods in the life course of each culture, would have found Dr. Lee's data of irresistible interest. Spengler, for instance, saw evidence indicating that in the " springtime " of a culture its life spirit always blooms in great architecture, such as the cathedrals of the Renaissance. Dr. Lee mentions the undertaking of vast architectural projects in the early part of each of the 800-year periods he cites. In the first 800-year period (221 B.C. to A.D. 588) there was the building of the Great Wall under the Ch'in dynasty, and the colossal palaces. In the second period (589–1367 A.D.) the Grand Canal was built under the Sui emperor, and also palaces of great magnificence. In the beginning of the third cycle (the Ming dynasty [1368 A.D.] to the present time, and hence uncompleted) the Great Wall was reconstructed, new canals and dams were laid out, and Peking was built.

The charts which Dr. Lee created, on the basis of the records at his disposal, to picture visually the parallelism of wars in these three Chinese periods, are reproduced in Fig. 1. While we may regard with due reservations the wave lines intended to show the frequency of internecine wars per quinquennium, in view — among other reasons — of the great antiquity of the history involved, no student of the subject can fail to be impressed with the regularity in the parallels, and with the thought that the subject deserves far greater study than it has yet been accorded by scientific research.

Spengler, convinced of the validity of such parallelisms, declared that periods of war and social upheavals show up at corresponding points in the life of every culture. He believed, for example, that the Napoleonic period in our " Western " culture corresponded closely to the Alexandrian period in the classical, and predicted that our present " Caesarian " age would duplicate, with wars of extermination wiping out whole nations, a similar period in the history of classical Rome.

But scientists must still regard these historical parallels as more interesting than scientifically fruitful, in view of our failure to

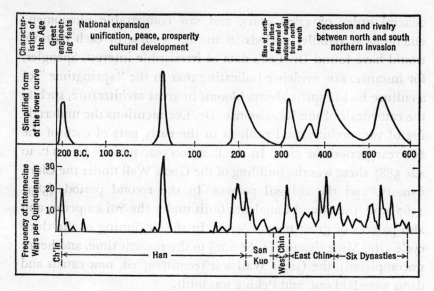

Fig. 1-A. First Chinese Epoch (800 years: 221 B.C.–A.D. 588.

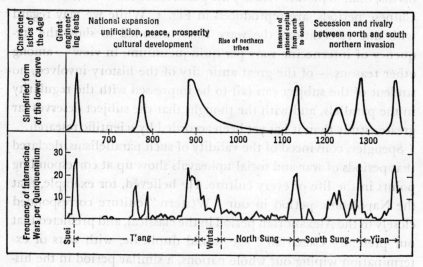

Fig. 1-B. Second Chinese Epoch (780 years: 589–A.D. 1367.

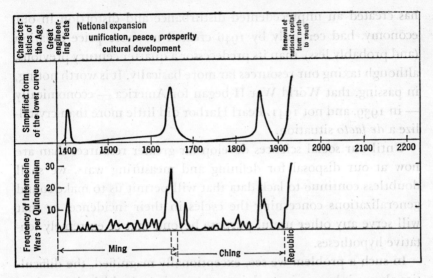

Fig. 1-C. Third Chinese Epoch (A.D. 1368 to present).
All three charts after J. S. Lee and Lin Yutang.

devise ways of *measuring* the phenomena. In the present state of our knowledge, we as yet have no satisfactory statistical approach to wars, for instance, that would guide the undertaking. Hotelling's effort to weigh wars statistically by measuring their impact on prices seems hardly adequate. Our Spanish-American War, for instance, was only a fracas, compared to some of our other conflicts. It had little immediate effect on the economy. And yet, by consensus of the histories, it marked America's emergence as a first-class power.

Conversely, a historian five hundred years hence might possibly find our participation in World War I little more than another border adventure. The soldier deaths that occurred were fewer than our annual civilian toll from automobile traffic a few years later. The privations that were suffered by the American population were considerably less than in the great peace depression of 1930–1932. Statisticians similarly could hardly feel justified in taking price inflation as a guide to measuring the importance of World War I to American life. For World War II, which demonstrably

[203]

has created an unprecedented disturbance and distortion in our economy, had certainly by 1946 created no more price inflation (and probably less) than its predecessor a quarter century previous, although taxing our resources far more basically. It is worth noting, in passing, that World War II began for America — economically — in 1939, and not 1941. Pearl Harbor did little more than crystallize a *de facto* situation.

Until our social sciences develop far greater resources than are now at our disposal for defining and measuring wars, we shall doubtless continue to lack data that will permit us to make sound generalizations concerning the cycles in their incidence, or that will serve any other useful purpose beyond that of extremely tentative hypotheses.

In such a problem we see, exceptionally magnified, the difficulties always inherent in studying an organism of which the student is himself a member. As has already been noted, it is extremely important, for scientific progress, to try to observe as if one were *outside* the frame of the phenomena being studied. What could be learned about man, for instance, by one inquiring cell in a man's body — even granting to this hypothetical cell the highest gift of observation that you please — and giving it, through the blood stream, mobility and power to visit every nook and cranny of the man's physique?

Every person is to be comparably regarded, in one aspect, as a cell in the social entity. In thinking about certain surrounding social phenomena, he must try to detach himself imaginatively from the organism. His measure of success in this is one measure of his scientific progress. It happens that our society has seen little such scientific thinking about war. We cannot yet — by means of a knowledge of cycles — predict the timing of war's arrival. But we have data to make estimates concerning certain associated reactions, in the event that war has come.

First, by knowing the cycles involved we can — ideally at least — determine what would have happened had there been no war. After

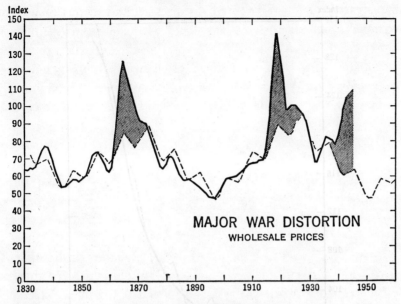

Index

MAJOR WAR DISTORTION
WHOLESALE PRICES

FIG. 2. WAR-TIME DISTORTION

Chart showing distortion in the Wholesale Price Index in time of War. The solid line shows the three year moving average of the Index of Wholesale Prices in the U. S., 1830–1945. The broken line shows the synthesis of the regular 9-year and 54-year cycles. The shaded areas show the difference between the Index and the regular pattern for the periods of the Civil War, World War I, and World War II.

The 3-year moving average has been extrapolated to 1945. The shaded areas begin one year prior to the outbreak of wars, since in a 3-year moving average the effect of the first year of war is extended one year backward.

It is interesting to note that in spite of the magnitude of the distortion, the *timing* of the peaks happens to coincide with the normal timing of the 9-year cycle. It is also interesting to note how nearly equal are the distortions.

any given war we at least know what did happen. The difference can be viewed as the *net* distortion due to war. Thus, in Fig. 2 the dotted line indicates what was due to happen, the solid line what did happen, and the shaded area the action and reaction of the war, in regard to average wholesale prices in the United States.

Second, by knowing our cycles we can have useful advance knowledge about the *timing* of peaks and valleys, even in wartime. Short

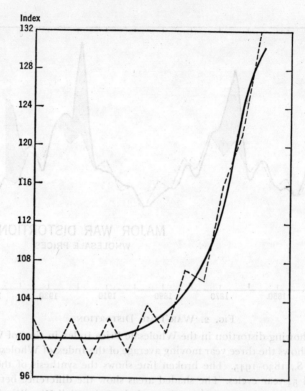

FIG. 3. PERSISTENCE OF WAVE INFLUENCE

Diagram to show how short rhythms often continue to influence a series, despite the impact of a longer wave or some accidental distortion such as a war.

The solid line shows the effect of the longer rhythm or the war. The dotted line shows how a regular 6-month rhythm continues to influence behavior. All waves are exactly 2 per cent in amplitude, but the distortion caused by the rapid rise of the "trend" line obscures this fact. The vertical scale has been greatly exaggerated.

cycles ride on the back of the war disturbance, as well as on the back of longer waves. The war seems to make little or no difference. In Fig. 3 the black line shows long waves and/or war; the dotted line shows, for simplicity, *one* short wave riding the long one.

Third, *only* by knowing the cycles involved, and by adjusting for them, can one know correctly the underlying *trend* in effect at the outbreak of a war. It is necessary to know this, if one is to project —

through the war distortion — the levels to which affairs will normally return after the war is over — unless the long prevailing trend is to be completely overturned.

These charts serve parenthetically to illustrate a fact that has been stated before: The forces represented by our rhythms are quite evidently not the only forces at work in our society. There are doubtless many sporadic ones in addition. But the rhythms we have do show a regularity which persists, and usually dominates, regardless of what other forces are present on the scene.

On many of the economic charts and wave patterns we know about, a period of war registers itself as a sort of volcanic explosion above the level of the prevailing trends. All the waves revolving around the trends are tossed high in the air, as it were. Yet the actual wave patterns — as patterns — are often less disturbed by war than one would expect.

We have already seen, for instance, that it would be logical to suppose the steel industry, required during modern war to work at top capacity, would at least have a steady rate of production in such a period. Nonetheless, in World War I at least, we find evidence that the wave pattern persists; it merely goes on at higher levels. Strikingly enough, the pattern of waves in the stock market undergoes relatively small disturbance, and has *always recovered its periodicity* if that has been disturbed.

Still more: Regardless of the degree of disturbance, once the war " explosion " has subsided and the disturbances recede, the previously prevailing trends and levels have usually been re-established in our economy. *Previous wars did not, in themselves, alter basic underlying trends,* insofar as our statistical data show them.

But wars often do alter certain seemingly established relationships within an economy. It is clear, for instance, that no such fantastic, unprecedented spurt in the volume of United States manufactures, as traced in the pattern on page 25, could occur without vast straining of the social gears.

One of these strains, as we should know, is clearly revealed in

[207]

what happened to wage levels in the United States, as these manufactures were produced. An unprecedented shift in the pattern of U. S. income levels took place. For instance, it has been estimated that in 1939 there were 2 million families with an income of no more than $200 a year, 5 million with an income of not more than $500 a year, 1 million more with an income of not more than $700 — making 8 million families of very low income, relatively speaking. Another 11 million families lived in a slightly higher category, still another 8 million existed in good middle-class comfort, and 2¼ million others were receiving top incomes.

There had been much talk of the redistribution of income started in 1933. But the real redistribution waited for the war era of the forties. Many of the 19 million families at the bottom of the heap moved swiftly, after 1941, into incomes that had previously been enjoyed only by the middle class. It has been pointed out, in this connection, that the greatest increases in currency circulation in this country, where the increase had been phenomenal even during the prewar years, occurred in some of the " poorer " districts of the nation. The increase in just four years, from 1939 to the end of 1943, was 520 per cent in the Federal Reserve District of Atlanta; 450 per cent in Richmond, Virginia. In Boston, on the other hand, it was 192 per cent.

Such increases occurred in a period when the former middle and upper income groups were being stripped of their previous margins of income over expenditures, by income and other taxes never previously even imagined.

In the same four years, income taxes rose from under 1½ billion dollars to almost 20 billion. The vast numbers who had previously been on the income fringes, and were now thrust up into income levels of new importance, contributed to these tax payments. But being without long-term economic commitments — life insurance, long leases, etc. — that are accumulated over the years by people used to enjoying generous incomes, these newcomers to the ranks of prosperity had large sums left them after taxes for use in the merchandise mart. This fact was reflected in government reports that consumer expenditures steadily climbed to all-time highs, with department store sales in early 1946 outranking comparable figures for all previous years. Meanwhile, the Census Bureau could report that 15,000,000 American civilians shifted their homes, in the war-years, to " improve " themselves.

American citizens as a whole have realized vaguely that income distribution is a subject of wide political interest; they have seen it become one of the subjects fought over in major political campaigns following the depression of the 1930's. Few of them, however, seem to know that one school of economists regard income distribution as one key to the outlook on a society's stability. The subject has no light to throw on the analysis of trends and cycles; but it does have possible bearing on interpreting certain data that analysis of rhythms and trends puts in our hands.

The law of income distribution has been stated by Vilfredo Pareto (1848–1923) in a formula that has been rephrased by Davis as follows:

In all places and at all times, the distribution of income in a *stable* economy . . . will be given approximately by the empirical formula
$$y = ax^{-v}$$
where y is the number of people having the income of x or greater, a is a constant, and v is approximately 1.5.

This equation has implications that are basically simple. It means that in every *stable* community there will always be a given percentage of people in the top income bracket, in the bottom bracket, and in the middle. The distribution is a fixed constant, whether the community is rich and prosperous or poor.

Obviously such a law, if true, strikes at the fundamental tenets of many professional world-improvers. Thus, efforts to discover a flaw have naturally not been wanting.

The " reason " for such a law has baffled many. Pareto himself said:

These results are very remarkable. It is absolutely impossible to admit that they are due only to chance. There is most certainly a *cause*, which produces the tendency of incomes to arrange themselves according to a certain curve. The form of this curve seems to depend only tenuously upon different economic conditions of the countries considered, since the effects are very nearly the same for the countries whose economic conditions are as different as those of England, of Ireland, of Germany, of the Italian cities, and even of Peru.*

Carl Snyder, in 1936, advanced an explanation of the law, in the thesis that the observed distribution of incomes is only one example of a more general law of inequality which has been referred to as the law of distribution of special abilities. (Schoolteachers are familiar with one form of this law, in the fact that most grades are "average," while the number of those in the top fourth of the class will be about equaled by those in the bottom fourth.)

However that may be, the Pareto formula for social stability has possible implications for the future of any nation like the United States.† And it offers interesting material for those who wish to speculate about the possibility of new trends in our economy. Either the United States seems due for a great wage deflation, or new trends are in the making.

* *Cours d'économie politique*, Vol. 2, p. 312.

† It should be noted that the Pareto value of 1.5 is given as an approximate. N. O. Johnson, making an elaborate investigation of the law, on the basis of income tax data in the United States from 1914 through 1933, estimated values ranging from 1.34 in 1916 to 1.76 in 1932. It has been pointed out that a fairly wide variation has at times existed without undue social unrest, and it seems agreed that research has as yet produced no way of estimating " critical values." H. T. Davis correctly deduced the coming of serious social disturbance in France, on the basis of the 1935 Pareto index for that nation of 1.85. Figures for Germany, which would offer a good test for the period of 1920 to 1935, seem not to have been compiled. It is perhaps worth remembering that American conditions in 1932, reflected in the figure of 1.76, were such that some of the " best " people speculated on the coming of " the man on horseback." And, in fact, revolutionary political, economic and social changes did spring from that year, to become more or less permanently incorporated in the American scene.

World War II was in one respect like the War of the Revolution. It was fought during a period of decline of the great 54-year price cycle, or groundswell, that has underlain prices in this country as far back as there are figures.

The three wars that created the three great peaks familiar to all observers of wholesale price charts covering the past 150 years were: the War of 1812, which occurred when the 54-year rhythmic pattern was approaching its peak in 1817; the War Between the States, which occurred when this same pattern was approaching its peak in 1871; and World War I, which occurred when the long price wave was climbing to its peak in 1925.

Undoubtedly, these wars added great amplitude to current swings of the price rhythm. We have no way — as previously stated — of forecasting the extent of such a distortion in *advance* of its arrival. But it is significant that during all three wars the distortion exercised on wholesale prices seems more or less comparable, as we note it in retrospect on the price charts. This is the more interesting because World War I exerted in some respects less of a strain on our national resources than the two war periods preceding it.

By sharp contrast, World War II was fought wholly in a period when our 54-year price rhythm was downward in its pattern. Thus any upward distortion this war period exercised on prices may be assumed to have been effected *against* the influence of the 54-year rhythmic tendency, and consequently to have been *less* than it would otherwise have been.

In view of the world situation and the enormous volume of money in circulation, possibility of any real price decline in the late forties seemed incredible to most 1946 observers. But skeptics could declare that price levels are related not only to the volume of money in circulation, but also to the volume of money turnover. And they could also ask pointedly whether world famine and decay could really make for booming markets.

We know, of course, from experience that business can be good and the nation can enjoy prosperity in a period of declining whole-

[211]

sale prices. Price levels are certainly not the only determinants of business prosperity. It is nonetheless apparent that any extended period of declining prices following World War II can result in serious problems for a nation with an unprecedented debt,* and with a debt charge burdensome even at high price levels — a nation whose populace has been geared, by admonitions over a long period, to expect vast inflation as a " result " of this indebtedness. Where the debt is so large (see Fig. 4) , and so many are out on traditional limbs expecting inflation to go on growing up to the sky, national reaction to a deflation might force even more radical changes in our economic system than would have been effected by the inflation millions have feared.

This is not a prediction that it will. We have no scientific data to warrant such a prediction. Our data here deal with price levels alone. But in the face of the data, one would be shortsighted not to consider possible social implications. Great changes in our economic and social organization may be the outcome. Walter Lippmann, for instance, has declared:

If we fix our minds upon the fact that the capacity to produce is the nation's wealth and upon the dislocation of that capacity as the supreme evil to be avoided, we shall, I believe, have hold of the saving truth. This is not the economics we were taught in school. But it is the economics we are going to have to learn in order to live in this century.†

* In early 1946 the Federal Reserve Bank of New York estimated that total indebtedness in the United States, both public and private, amounted to at least 350 billion dollars, or double the prewar peak reached in 1930. In the intervening period most of the debt had been shifted onto the shoulders of the federal government. At the end of 1945 the federal net debt amounted to 65 per cent of the national indebtedness, compared to only 22 per cent at the end of 1940. Meanwhile, private indebtedness fell from 68 per cent of the total in 1940 to around 30 per cent by the end of 1945. Debt of the states and local governments fell in the same period from 10 to under 4 per cent. Average interest rates fell about one-half between 1930 and 1945, so that the interest burden on the economy in 1945 was approximately that in 1930, or a little more, according to the estimate.

† New York *Herald Tribune,* Jan. 18, 1944.

Our three wars previous to that of the forties happened to fall at about the same place in the cycle; the postwar patterns were more or less similar not, presumably, because of the wars, but as

FIG. 4. INTEREST-BEARING DEBT OF THE UNITED STATES

1830–1945. Data decennial 1830–1850; annual thereafter. A trend is shown, projected tentatively to 1960. *Ratio scale.*

It will be noted that the trend is concave *upward,* counter to all laws of growth. One may conclude that this situation cannot continue permanently.

the outcome of the phase of the cycle. This provides us today with opportunity to see whether or not it is the war or the cycle that governs postwar behavior. If war governs, we should expect — following World War II — a slowdown of about a year for industry to readjust, and then an upturn to a normal peak corresponding to that of 1920; then a brief collapse, corresponding to the depression of 1921; then eight years or so of advance; and then a major collapse, to be entitled " The Second Postwar Depression."

If, however, rhythms govern, we should not expect the events that followed World War I to repeat themselves. Rather we should expect the so-called First Postwar Depression to be the major one; we should find that the 8- or 10-year period of crest which came after War I will not be so conveniently available this time to stave off prompt retributions for our trespasses.

Postwar Trends

BEFORE INTERPRETING more specifically the major rhythms we have available for examining postwar probabilities of the near future, we may well review some of the facts we now know about the basic trends around which the rhythms move — trends established in America's economy which in all probability will continue:

1. As the trends in so many instances show, the United States has now achieved what some commentators have called " maturity," and, to a greater or lesser degree, relative stability in fundamental or underlying aspects of life where once there was rapid growth.

2. For many years now the nation's land area has been constant. The area in farms fluctuates, but basically is no longer increasing. Our population is still increasing but at a decreasing rate, and the peak is apparently just ahead of us. Our foreign trade seems to have passed its peak and — except as we give things away — would seem due for the future to maintain no more than the levels reached twenty years ago.

3. Some indices, like railroad mileage, have actually started down.

4. Manufacturing activity is still increasing, but at a decreasing rate. And some basic industries, such as steel, seem to be reaching the summit.

5. Depressions when the national trend shows " maturity " — even depressions that in earlier times would have seemed unimportant — will be felt deeply.

This is a brief statistical picture of the society we live in, of the milieu in which we as individuals must create our life. One could possibly wish something else, as did Oscar Wilde, mourning that he was a Greek born out of his time. On the other hand, it is natural, sound and inevitable that at some point growth of all things slackens and then stops. Every organism — and society *is* an organism in at least one sense, and so is each of its institutions — carries in its very form of life the limitations of its growth.

What we know about the supplies of some of our major mineral resources reinforces what our trend charts tell us. World War II, for instance, reduced our known natural oil supplies to unprecedentedly low levels. Our resources of iron and copper were similarly reduced to the point where we shall soon be competing with other nations for foreign supplies. In many respects, the long-term postwar problem will be not a question of how to maintain wartime levels of income — but rather how to maintain even prewar levels. As Bernard M. Baruch said before the war ended:

In our domestic readjustments alone we face the greatest task in history. Nothing comparable to it has ever been faced before. Few seem to realize how drastically our war is draining our raw material resources — especially American oil and American metals — or what the impact will be from our high debt structure.

After the war the great raw material reservoirs, to say nothing of the great manpower centers, simply will not be within the United States. The principal natural resources of the world will be in other nations. *The bedrock fact is that after this war the United States will face a struggle to remain the first power in the world. It will not be easy for America to hold that place.**

Thus, for the United States the upper limits of growth seem already to press down on us from many and various directions. Until this tendency of our growth to proceed at a decreasing rate is

* Italics supplied. In a copyrighted article by Henry J. Taylor from the New York *World-Telegram,* Feb. 22, 1944.

demonstrably changed, it is sound procedure to expect its continuance.

The patent commissioner who wrote in the 1880's that everything worth while had been invented, and that the Patent Office might as well be closed, made just one mistake. He *reasoned* out what *ought* to happen. He ignored the trends. The reasons he selected as a basis for his conclusions — in a time when the trends were of course the reverse of today's — had a scope exceedingly finite. Reasoning will always be similarly limited in its resources, particularly when applied to phenomena of which we ourselves are a part. To look dispassionately — that is to say, statistically — at what has been happening, what is happening, and what will happen if present trends continue, helps to avoid at least one common pitfall of logic. And to know how fundamental a revolution must be, to permit the establishment of new trends in an environment, should obviate another pitfall in wishful thinking — something to which the American temperament is prone.

It is perhaps typical of our lack of needed progress in the social sciences that even the rate of growth of a nation can still be a matter of opinion subject to political argument and commercial ballyhoo. In the advanced year of 1944 there appeared a laudably cheerful advertisement of a great agency, for instance, telling first how Mr. Clarence Birdseye made himself millions after various shortsighted investors had turned him down, and then went sweeping into a patriotic peroration, criticizing those who see in our fixed land frontiers a limit to our national growth. The advertisement branded such thinking as unworthy of the American tradition, and placed upon American business the burden of disproving this reasoning.

Doubtless this is all noble sentiment, and ideal for after dinner speeches. But those who proceed to plan their business future on the *probability* that our industries generally will continue growing hereafter at the rate pursued in the past, may be due — with their creditors — for a sad awakening. Mr. Birdseye — or others like him — will undoubtedly go on thinking up inventions (though there will probably be relatively fewer inventions, as our text shows) ; and he and some others will undoubtedly make some new millions, and manage to keep a small part of them after the government gets through taking the largest portion in taxes to meet the interest on the national debt. But one swallow, here or there, makes no summer.

Actually, even our rate of growth in *creative* capacity has declined. Dr. Pitirim A. Sorokin, chairman of the Department of Sociology at Harvard, has compiled an effective analysis to demonstrate the decline. He says, with italics that are his own:

We observe, first, that with the end of the nineteenth and the beginning of the twentieth century *the rate of increase of discoveries and inventions definitely slowed down;* second, that between the outbreak of the World War of 1914 and the year 1920 *even the absolute number of discoveries and inventions declined;* third, that *the climax (in number and importance of discoveries) in most of the exact sciences was reached not in the twentieth century, but either in the nineteenth or (for mathematics) the eighteenth century.* The following figures illustrate this movement:

Period	Total Number of Scientific Discoveries	Total Number of Technical Inventions	Total Number of Geographic Discoveries	Grand Total
1791–1800	149	113	7	269
1801–1810	228	128	6	362
1811–1820	286	157	13	456
1821–1830	388	227	16	631
1831–1840	441	313	9	763
1841–1850	534	356	9	899
1851–1860	584	423	13	1020
1861–1870	553	424	15	992
1871–1880	635	490	17	1142
1881–1890	663	477	13	1153
1891–1900	625	482	2	1109
1901–1908	552	309	1	862

Figure 1 shows how Dr. Sorokin's analysis is borne out by the trend in the number of U. S. patents issued.

Dr. Sorokin adds, in his comment on the present state of the science that thus is faltering:

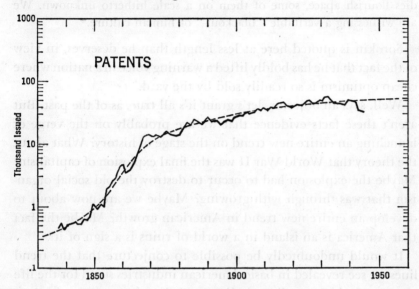

FIG. 1. U. S. PATENTS ISSUED, 1837–1944
A trend is shown, projected tentatively to 1960. *Ratio scale.*

Who, save almighty God, could comprehend its infinite chaos of "facts," especially since we don't know which are relevant and which irrelevant? In the face of this difficulty we elaborate endless mechanical indices and bibliographies, digests and abstracts, indices of indices, bibliographies of bibliographies, digests of digests, and abstracts of abstracts. Human life is too short to master such an overwhelming and indiscriminate agglomeration of facts. . . .

The more economists have tampered with economic conditions, the worse they have become; the more political scientists have reformed governments, the more are governments in need of reform. . . . Despite all the natural and social sciences at our disposal, we are unable either to control the socio-cultural processes or to avoid the historical catastrophes. . . . Neither happiness, nor safety and security, nor even

[219]

material comfort has been realized. In few periods of human history have so many millions of persons been so unhappy, so insecure, so hungry and destitute, as at the present time. . . . Wars and revolutions, crime, mental disease, and other evidences of deep-seated social maladies flourish apace, some of them on a scale hitherto unknown. We are witnessing a veritable " blackout " of human culture.*

Sorokin is quoted here at less length than he deserves, in view of the fact that he has boldly lifted a warning voice in a nation where cheap optimism is so readily sold by the yard.

Well, says an objector, let's grant it's all true, as of the past. But aren't these facts evidence that we are probably on the verge of launching an entire new trend on the stage of history? What about the theory that World War II was the final explosion of capitalism? Maybe the explosion had to occur to destroy the old social organism that was through with growing? Maybe we are now about to develop an entire new trend in American growth? Maybe the fact that America is an island in a world of ruins is a sign of it?

It would undoubtedly be possible to conjecture that the trend lines we see revealed in basic American industries stand for the life pattern of what we call capitalism, and that the explosion of capitalism in our time means that new trends are to be born. A socialist or communist, seizing on such an idea, could then propose the adoption of his own particular economic ism as a method of initiating a new growth pattern, and a new era of industrial expansion.

But the idea is of doubtful validity. True, Professor Schumpeter seems to entertain, on occasion, the hypothesis that the rhythms we can trace in the economic organism are characteristic of capitalism in operation. Kondratieff suggests a similar postulate. The fact is, however, that we can trace the major rhythm — the 54-year wave — far beyond the birth of capitalism, back to the age of feudalism. The life of capitalism, however you define it, has been certainly not more than 150 or 200 years; the persistence of the rhythm has

* From *Crisis of our Age* by P. A. Sorokin published and copyrighted by E. P. Dutton and Co., Inc., New York. Copyright 1941. (pp. 126–131)

been long by comparison. Thus, the waves we see in operation can hardly be merely a characteristic of capitalistic phenomena, however you define them.

Quite similarly — and this may comfort some conservatives — it seems equally doubtful that the trend lines we see in our society are an essence of the capitalistic organization of this society. If they were, then something radical should have happened to those trend lines around 1933, when capitalism *as we had known* it in the United States was transformed into something rather different (much as it underwent transformation in France, Germany, and England).

The conclusion, conversely, can hardly provide fodder for professional reformers. Whatever may be the influence that has slowed down the rate of growth in our society, there is no reason to believe that the *imposition* of any other economic system would of itself suffice to establish a new growth trend there.

Capitalism in its fullest sense has been only a convenient economic word used to describe a whole agglomeration of habits, relationships, thinking patterns, and methods of social procedure. This agglomeration was an organic growth — it was never planned, never imposed by any superminds. No one thought it up, no one sat down to invent it; it sprang from the community spontaneously, as part of a necessary mode of expression at a given point of time.

If a new growth trend is eventually to make its appearance on top of the old one in our society, it may well be *accompanied* by a new kind of economic expression which — when historians survey it in retrospect — they will describe as an economic " system." But this economic system, so called, will hardly be the *cause* of the new trend. Rather, it will be an expression or outcome of it. To understand this, one need only understand man for what he truly is — no mere creature of economics, but one for whom economic activity is only one form of expression among many.

If, with all these reservations, we still cling hopefully to the conviction that a new growth pattern is going to get started in our nation, we are wholly within our rights. Germany seemed to have launched herself on a new trend in the nineteenth century. Russia began one in 1917.

But — we must be warned. We now know enough about trend lines to realize that old ones merge into the take-off of new ones *only* when fundamental, even revolutionary, changes have occurred in the environment and its organization, and perpetuate themselves. Even though our science cannot tell us *when* a new growth pattern will begin — or if the pattern ever will — it does tell us this much. Few really want such a revolution.

Remember Pearl's Drosophila bottle. Imagine for a moment that we Americans are the Drosophila. We are reaching the upper asymptote of our curve. The invention of a few new gadgets by industry — indeed, the invention of a whole new industry itself — is a force in no way adequate to change the relationships in our bottle. We must have a whole new bottle. And if we are among those who call for having the postwar national income maintained at some level around 150 billion dollars — or the equivalent thereof in 1939 values — then we are necessarily demanding some sort of completely new social bottle into which the American nation is going to move.

Now, we can predict that this will happen, if we wish, because science has no evidence with which to gainsay us. It can even offer us a little helpful data, such as the fact that in recent wartime years the birth rate has leaped upward in the United States, as in many other parts of the world. This deviation from one long-established trend line has been assumed by most observers to be merely a temporary phenomenon, a wartime distortion. But it could possibly be something much more significant for the future. We are entitled to our faith and hope. We can believe in the birth of a new world, if we wish.

Only we must be prepared to face the consequences, whether we are right or wrong. If we are right, we still face enormous upheavals (for the ending of the " old " capitalism has as yet not changed our lives much), and some of us are perhaps going to be badly jolted. If we are wrong, we may court serious personal disaster in betting on our judgment in the market place.

If we do *not* expect such a revolution in American relationships of every economic, social, and political variety, then we must assume that the trend lines for our economy will stay flattened out. In this event, we must similarly assume — on the basis of past performance — that four major rhythms declining together can possibly make a very deep economic depression indeed, starting with a crest of " good times " in 1946 or '47, and working downward to the bottom of the trough in perhaps 1951 or 1952.

If we make this assumption, perhaps we should go further, and ask ourselves whether our complex society could withstand another such depression and meanwhile maintain orderly processes in operation. If our answer is a tentative No, then we may expect to get our social upheavals anyway. In which event the old trend lines as we have known them might eventually be superseded by the beginning of new ones, regardless.

These speculations are entered here primarily to demonstrate that our economic charts — however helpful — will by no means suffice to answer all the questions on which judgments of the future must be based. We can synthesize our rhythms to portray the future of a given corporation, without too great a margin of error. But in estimating the future of a nation we are certainly dealing with biological and psychological forces on a scale too great for completely accurate measurement with our still primitive instruments. In reading the instruments we have available, much allowance must be made for error.

Those instruments can neither affirm nor deny — as we have seen — that the trends maturing in the American economy may be in process of being superseded by new ones. Apparently no conscious planning will in itself serve to change whatever trends are now established. Apparently individuals can do little enough to create or hasten developments that must spring from the heart of the whole social organism. We can figure out where we are — mak-

[223]

ing due allowance for a margin of error, but that gives us no recipe for getting elsewhere.

Some economists who do not quite realize this are responsible for much of the literature of recent times which repeats endless exhortations to be up and moving to some place where we aren't. In the words of John Chamberlain, eminent book editor of the *New York Times:*

> There are two kinds of economic piety at large in the world today. The old school piety consists of variations on the refrain, " We must have free enterprise," or " We must preserve the American way of life." The newer piety consists of saying, " We must stabilize the economy at a high level of consumption and employment." In each case the appeal is purely hortatory; it does not tell you how to get from here to there. The more I read, the more I marvel at the reputations that have been made by repeating one or the other of the pious exhortations.*

Mr. Chamberlain is, of course, quite right. But it is possible to go further, and say that the economists of both the hortatory schools which amaze him err not in failing to do the impossible — for they cannot give a practical recipe to achieve the ends they recommend. They err rather in failing to recognize the real limitations of their approach to the problem, and in failing to recognize this problem's real essence. For it is apparently a problem basically biological in its character; and if there is a sound solution to be found in any form of traditional human logic, no expert has as yet produced the key. Churchmen, convinced that the ultimate key will be found in a sweeping religious revival that will spiritually reform the worshipers of today's paganistic materialism, have at least as much logic on their side as those who propose materialistic solutions.

If the interpretations here are correct, then ordinary political and economic tinkerings will not get the problem resolved — as Sorokin says clearly. The community as a whole will ultimately

* *New York Times,* March 11, 1944.

give us the answer, whether in one way or in another. Meanwhile no individual, while he waits to see what that answer will be, is going to effect any " plan " that will really " save " the nation. But he can certainly, with some foreknowledge of what the problem is all about, be in a better position to assay the value of the various plans that will be offered in the future. He will be able better to understand the fallacies inherent in the multitudinous nostrums. He will doubtless be able to help his neighbors more sympathetically, as they find themselves saddled with heavy problems not entirely of their own making, in these times of world-wide misery. And, equally important, he should certainly be able to help himself through understanding some of the limits of the possibilities that surround him.

X V I

Postwar Rhythms

IN ANALYZING and projecting the trends, both for the nation as a whole and for certain basic industries, this study has sought to make clear that a declining rate of growth elevates the " cycle " to greater importance for business and industry than ever before in our history. Limited as our knowledge of such rhythms still is, there are basic data to help us face the problem of the postwar era with more than mere guesswork. We have a tool whereby, for any given series of figures, we can get a fund of additional knowledge for guidance in facing the problems of any specific organization.

Our pattern did *not* serve to show us when World War II would finally end. As previously noted, we do not even know how to define " war." The ending of actual hostilities in 1945 may conceivably prove not even to have been the real end of the war — much as the 1918–1939 period was one in which war merely shifted from the military to the diplomatic level.

But here, in summary, are some findings of which we may be relatively sure:

1. The underlying 54-year rhythm in wholesale prices is on the decline. It turned in 1925; the pattern is due to reach bottom in 1952.
2. The shorter 9-year pattern in wholesale prices — a rhythm that applies also to iron, steel, and stockmarket prices — which had its last high in 1937, reached for another high in 1946. The pattern was due then to turn down until 1951.

[226]

3. Just as the pattern of the 9-year rhythm was due to reach a peak in 1946, or shortly after (it depends on the business in question), so the 3½-year pattern —— almost universal in business —— was forecasting a peak in 1947. Other peaks in the 3½-year rhythm are due in 1950 and 1954. Lows are due in '48 and '51.
4. The 18⅓-year pattern in building activity apparently reached its high about late 1942, the exact date depending on methods of reporting and compiling statistics. In general, building and real estate patterns are due to decline to a low around 1953.
5. The 15-year pattern in the index of the purchasing power of beef cattle prices, an exceedingly interesting index for the farmer, was scheduled for a high around 1944, thereafter declining to a low due in 1951. OPA regulations and wartime black markets veiled the meaning of free market statistics. But declines after 1946 would not be surprising.

It cannot be repeated too often that these findings are *not* offered as unqualified forecasts. The data do not go back far enough to permit unqualified assurance that the observed rhythms are beyond the result of chance. Further, if all the rhythms are real and continue, they might still be so buffeted about by other rhythms and sporadic forces that the *actual* highs and lows would be delayed or accelerated.

Still, with all these qualifications, it is worth noting that the expectancies facing us do not suggest any lengthy postwar boom. On the contrary, the number of important rhythms that come to a low together around 1952 suggest the possibility of a growing postwar crisis. The reader now familiar with this method of analysis will not expect the crisis really to be avoided or halted by any preventive measures which the government might decide to take. In the present limited state of human knowledge as to the ultimate nature of these rhythms and their correlations, we shall suspect that any action adopted by government would be ameliorative in character without being curative. Probably the most we can hope for would be some kind of palliative action if the blows fall.

The individual, on the other hand, can doubtless help himself to some degree in advance — keeping in mind the good example of Joseph in preparing for lean years when fat was still upon the land. To give specific advice is not the purpose of these pages, but a few generalities may be mentioned parenthetically in passing, to indicate recipes that can*not* be relied on.

Obviously no individual, in times like ours, can rely wholly on money saved to carry him through any future periods of social or economic crisis. In other times, if faced by evidence that deflation lay ahead, he could unerringly have put his holdings into money and obligations repayable in money. But since 1929, governments all over the world have learned how to *demonetize* money. Our own government in 1933, for instance, called in all old dollars — just as some European countries have recently done; it can readily call in the current issue when it pleases, and/or make it unspendable. It has learned through experience how to restrict the withdrawals from savings and other accounts. It can delay payments on bonds due. It can, and now does, control the export and import of dollars.

In other words, various monetary controls devised by Dr. Schacht for the mark have already been quietly applied in various ways to the dollar, and no American man planning for the future can safely assume that he will ever again be able to do with dollars exactly what he will. In actual practice (if not in theory!) sovereign states today hold the view that currency and credits are the origination of the state, and thus are the state's property, to be held and used by individuals only so long as that use serves the state's purposes — or, at any rate, does not come in conflict with them.

Nor, for that matter, do present tendencies and trends in the economy suggest future opportunities for freedom that once prevailed in the uninhibited enjoyment of any kind of real property. Metropolitan properties, for instance, will doubtless continue to be milked by high real estate taxes for the support of unemployed city masses. Grim realty taxes, combined with rent controls, could

[228]

ultimately prove almost confiscatory. Thus, income-producing real estate is no longer a perfect hedge for inflation, and in a time of deflation may have questionable merits indeed.

Nor are bonds a perfect refuge for savings any longer. The ultimate value of government bonds is something for conjecture. Of some corporate bonds it is possible to say that in a period of national deflation they have been demonstrated to be as questionable an asset as stocks. And stocks now mean to the investor only the right to participate in what is left after management takes its salaries and expenses and government seizes what it will.

Some of the tax laws that weighed down the American economic outlook during the war years have been changed — but it is probably too much to hope that they will undergo, in any foreseeable future, the wholly drastic change that will restore past relationships.

Thus the man seeking to protect his own future against the turns of the economic wheel must nowadays face difficulties of a rather unexampled kind. He will doubtless wish at least to reduce his dollar indebtedness to the minimum, on the theory that freedom from debt at least means freedom of action in time of emergency. In an era when freedom of choice has been steadily whittled down to the vanishing point for almost every individual in terms of ultimately significant values, freedom from debt is one that can still be chosen. In the era ahead of us it may be valuable to anyone who esteems his freedom dearly.

The foresighted individual will doubtless know that long-term leases, contracted for when properties are at their peak price, are much the same as long-term debt; mortgages inevitably are debt, regardless of terms of payment; and even life insurance policies — unless fully paid up — are a form of debt which, until paid up, can often cost the insured much of his equity in the policy if he fails to continue premium payments and must let the insurance lapse. But these are all details that interested individuals will find more adequately discussed in numerous other quarters. Here it is sufficient to note that hedges to protect principal in periods like the present will continue hard to find, while the returns on capital in general bid fair to continue at around low levels.

In an economy where the rate of growth is rapidly approaching zero, and major underlying rhythms in the expression of energy are also on the decline, what would one expect to meet as a major symp-

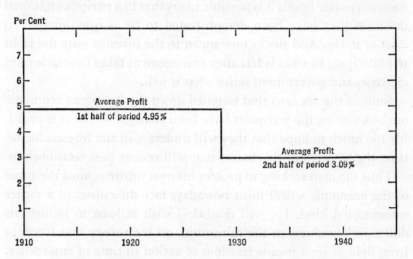

FIG. 1. PROFITS IN THE STEEL INDUSTRY, 1901–1945
(From data furnished by the American Iron & Steel Institute.)

For purposes of comparability the chart shows averages for two 18-year cycles, each containing a war. The situation in steel is representative for many industries.

tom of such lowered vitality? In a profit economy, it could well be a declining rate of profit. And that is exactly what we have met, over a long period of years, in the United States of America. See Fig. 1.

The foregoing is not meant to suggest that our rhythms indicate collapse of our economy. We may only infer, if they continue, that around 1947 a fall-off will start, and our economy will experience rather protracted declines in prices, production, employment, and economic activity generally, reaching a bottom that would presumably be dated sometime in the early fifties.

As has been noted, factors like war — though not (in the past) ultimately changing either trends or rhythm patterns — can for a time emphasize, magnify, or distort a rhythm. There are doubtless, yet unknown, other factors besides those appearing clearly in wartime which may effect the same end. It may be that such a factor will show up in conjunction with the postwar rhythms, to modify their operation. But the data here do not suggest the likelihood of the possibility.

It may also be stressed again that our knowledge of rhythms is still in its infancy. Concerning their reality, some high authorities have testified to conviction; as to the exactness of the timing of the rhythms, some of the greatest authorities still disagree. Nor, of course, can any research assert that a rhythm — however real in the past — will undoubtedly continue. Again, it must be noted that individual industries and companies and commodities have their own patterns, which must be determined one by one. With all these qualifications, the merit of knowing what probabilities the rhythms indicate is obvious.

In studying these rhythms for purposes of postwar guidance, it seems important to note again that for the first time immediately following a major war in over a century, the projected rhythm of building activities will be on the downgrade. As we have already seen, building is closely related to the activity of many basic industries. If building activity does find itself inhibited in the coming years, we could be justified in expecting heightened seriousness in any decline that appeared in other economic activity.

One could have " proved " in advance of the war's ending, with almost irrefutable logic, that after World War II enormous pent-up demand for housing would launch an almost unprecedented building boom, not to say a period of extensive land speculation. But the building cycle is one of the most obvious, evident, and clearly marked. As we have seen, it evidences a simple, not complex rhythm. Its regularity is apparent to the most untrained eye, on almost any charted pattern. If the pattern fails to repeat itself in relative decline following World War II, the failure would be the first to appear since national statistical records have been compiled. Hence we seem to be warranted in taking the post-war implications of a declining rhythm in building activity with some seriousness.

Not the indication of decline in price levels, but the indication of restricted building activity for some years *along with* a decline in price levels of commodities and securities, is a signpost unprecedented for any other immediate postwar era in the past century. Declining price levels would mean, of course, that the dollar would rise in purchasing power. It would indicate, in effect, that the dollar has recently been undervalued in a world where it has survived, under war's various destructive forces, as the strongest, most desirable currency on the globe. From this point of view, price declines could well be viewed as growing recognition of the essential inner strength of the United States of America.

In seeking to time the beginning of the corrective economic downturn following World War II, we may remember, from our various data, that the 1929 stock market panic waited for a turn-down in the 9-year cycle in wholesale and stock prices, and followed the turn in the building activity cycle by some 3 years. A 2- to 4-year lag between the turn in the building rhythm and a panicky fall in stock prices has not been uncommon, as previously noted. Such data from the past suggested to informed observers that the real post-war break in the bull market of the forties could come any time after the middle of 1946 — after the turn-down of the 9-year pattern in June of that year. The break arrived on schedule. After the turn-down in the decisive $3\frac{1}{2}$-year, or 41-month, pattern scheduled for early 1947, the decline could be expected to increase in intensity.

If 1950–1953 looks like a subsequent deep valley on the charts, this much should be noted: It is also the beginning of a long trend upward. Further, it is not the peaks and valleys of the rhythmic patterns, as a rule, that people note so memorably in their experience. The periods prevailing between are often the ones that most affect lives. Thus, the downturn in the 54-year price rhythm was hardly even noted for its significance by most commentators in 1925. Real estate boomed in areas like New York long after the passing of the national activity peak in 1926, and the collapse of the Florida speculation of the period. Not even the stock market panic of 1929 was of paramount significance to more than perhaps a few thousand people who were unhappily too extended in their commitments to meet it. The millions proceeded pleasantly on their way, and many reached 1931 and 1932 before they concluded that things were not normal.

Thus an observer may hazard the guess that the turns in various projected rhythmic patterns, due in 1946 and 1947 if the patterns continue, may at the time hardly be noticed by most of the people.

We could know, as of 1946, that any coming declines would start from such high levels of national income and production that in their early stages of fall most economic indices would still be above all prewar norms. In April of 1946, for instance, production was proceeding at the rate of 150 billion dollars annually — the highest rate of peacetime production in American history. At the same time, the Federal Reserve Board's production index crossed 170, compared to 109 in 1929. The national income, after an insignificant " reconversion " slump, was still almost at its wartime peak. And the Treasury could announce that sales of savings bonds to the people in the first quarter of 1946 amounted to over 2 billion dollars, or three-quarters as much as in the comparable quarter of 1945 when the war was on. We may expect that, by all prevailing definitions, 1947 will be a good business year. Probably many will feel themselves equally as prosperous in 1948 and later.

If, following depression lows, a definite turn upward finally comes around 1952, it should be an important one in many ways, notable particularly because a rise in the rhythm of real estate and building activity will coincide with a rise in the long 54-year price cycle. We do not need to agree entirely with Professor Schumpeter's theories regarding the 54-year cycle to regard his research as of paramount importance, and his ideas as highly significant. It will be remembered that he retraced historical data in the periods covered by three such cycles — following a technique used for rather different purposes by Spengler. Somewhat like Spengler, who identified each one of his cycles with the progress of a particular culture, Professor Schumpeter believes that each 54-year cycle may be identified by its association with some particular economic influence.

Similarly, we need not wholly accept Professor Schumpeter's belief that a new industrial " cause " lies behind each 54-year cycle to agree wholly with his observation that — during the last three cycles, at least — the course of each one has proceeded simultaneously with some particular economic force of a new kind.

It will be recalled that Schumpeter calls the cycle beginning in the late 1700's that of the industrial revolution. The one that followed saw the development of the steam engine and the railroad, to a point where this cycle changed the habits of men everywhere. The latest one, which began around 1898, Schumpeter has associated with electricity and the automobile. This is a striking observation, and one confirmed in the experience of millions who have lived through the period when electricity and personal mobility have changed almost all the living patterns in our nation.

It is at least interesting, and not wholly without possible usefulness, to wonder whether the new 54-year cycle (which, if this hitherto fundamental pattern continues, will begin about 1952) is again to be associated with some great change in our living patterns, stemming from industrial or social developments now hardly visualized.

No such indulgence in pure conjecture is required to note that, for a period of years after 1952, the upward sweep of various major periodicities suggests a time of important constructive accomplishments and prosperity in the general economic life of the nation, regardless of the leveling out of basic trends of growth. Because this is as far ahead as it can serve most readers' purpose to look at the present time, the discussion of the longer term may be dropped

[234]

at this point. The reader wishing to continue the exploration into later years may readily formulate some conclusions of his own by studying and projecting the rhythms grouped for convenience on pages 188–189 and by determining and projecting the rhythms that may be present in the series in which he is particularly interested.

Meanwhile, it is apparent that our nation will have various bridges to cross that do not look wholly easy of negotiation. Some commentators, like the sober Sumner Welles, have indeed hinted at " revolution." Mr. Welles declared, during the war years:

Every great convulsion recorded in history, of which the mightiest will be this global war, has been followed by political and social repercussions which have wholly modified the course of human events.

It is inevitable that after the present war the structure of our modern civilization will be profoundly transformed.*

The data we have for rhythms, with so many declining in concert after 1947, do undeniably suggest a difficult period of adjustment for the short-term future. There is no reason, as we have seen, to assume that the rhythms will act differently just because political government, instead of the business man, now dominates the American economy. There is equally no reason to assume that government planning by government administrators will prevent rhythmic depressions, any more than planning by bankers and businessmen can.†

Our knowledge, however limited, is at least adequate to suggest that American business should not indulge in optimism on this score, and should prepare for distinctly leaner economic pickings in the postwar decade. Even businesses that see every " reason " to expect a boom should be sure of sound grounds for their optimism.

* New York *Herald Tribune*, July 12, 1944.

† It is notable, for instance, that even in a managed economy like Russia there was famine in the twenties, when capitalist nations experienced their own first postwar depression, and famine again in the early thirties, when the second postwar depression arrived. While price statistics for Russia do not lend themselves to tracing rhythms, events of this kind suggest some kind of correlated rhythm that even a statist economy meets in one form if not another.

Countless numbers of American businesses do have rhythms of their own which seem more or less independent of the dominant economic rhythms of the nation. There are many businesses on record, for instance, that made their highs in 1930, and some even in 1931. Similarly, the presidents of large and successful corporations have been heard to say privately that depressions were periods in which their companies had made the greatest relative gains. The depression problem for business management is often only a problem of being prepared.

No general work of this nature can hope to do more than issue a few words of general warning to those who are operating their private and public lives on the supposition that the tide of general postwar " prosperity " will be so great in a world starved for our products that even weak ships will triumphantly ride the waves.

The judgments here, and throughout the text, rest on three assumptions that are basic in this treatise, and are worth emphasizing again:

1. That a rhythm can be considered to be significant only if it has repeated itself so many times and so regularly that it cannot reasonably be the result of chance — and

2. That the rhythms which have evidenced themselves clearly in the past, in our economy, continue to operate repetitively — and

3. That the trends which have been traced in our great basic industries continue on their established courses.

The evidence brought to bear on the problem strongly suggests the probability that at least some of the rhythms are significant, and will continue their patterns as projected. The evidence regarding the trend lines, on the other hand, cannot rule out the possibility that new logistic curves are even now superimposing themselves on American trends that have been long familiar.

The probabilities, of course, are of a different nature. They suggest that every businessman and every responsible head of a family should be looking ahead economically with great caution as the late forties approach. They suggest the rise of problems in govern-

[236]

ment, as well as in business management, which will require the height of wisdom to solve.

The same rhythms that suggest caution in planning for the late forties also foreshadow various new opportunities opening up in the fifties, of a kind such as our nation's youth may hopefully anticipate.

However difficult the interim, it will not be the economic end of our world, as those caught in economic panic are sometimes inclined to think. It will merely be some winter weather. We cannot choose the course of the weather, but we can at least be thoughtful in preparation when we note that the barometer is beginning to fall. If the rhythms are ultimately confirmed by events, in their indications that the immediate postwar era will bring our economy into some economic hard sledding, we can take renewed hope in the very rhythm of the winter's coming. It will help confirm the knowledge we have gained that our economic rhythms do have patterns that can be projected — patterns that assure us that we shall also see, not too long hence, a new economic spring.

Appendices

APPENDIX I

The Ratio Scale

THE SOLID LINE in Fig. 1, on page 3, shows the sales of a hypothetical business that grew 90 per cent in the five-year period
from 1905 to 1910, 80 per cent in the next five-year period, 70 per
cent in the next, and so on. The rate of growth, that is, declines
10 per cent in each five-year period, and falls to a level of 20 per cent
in the five-year period from 1940 to 1945.

The curve in Fig. 1 gives little or no *visual* warning of the drastic
fall-off in sales that lies immediately ahead (as shown by the broken
line in this chart) if the growth pattern continues in the future
as in the past. If this pattern does continue, the sales in 1950 will
be only 10 per cent more than the sales in 1945, and the sales in
1955 will show no growth whatever when compared to 1950.

In order to make this situation visually clear, many businessmen
and students of trends prefer to plot all data pertaining to growth
on what is known as a *ratio* (or *semi-logarithmic*) *scale*. On such a
scale equal vertical distances represent equal *percentage* change.

Let us illustrate by charting the growth of another business using
both the arithmetic and ratio scales.

The business starts at a sales volume of $2,000 a year; the second
year it doubles its sales to $4,000; the next year it doubles again to
$8,000.

On the arithmetic scale these facts would be represented in a
chart laid out as follows:

[241]

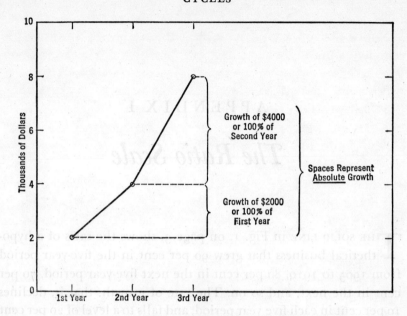

FIG. 1. EQUAL RATE OF GROWTH — ARITHMETIC SCALE

Sales of a hypothetical business organization showing constant *rate* of growth. *Arithmetic scale.*

On a ratio scale, the same facts would be represented on a chart laid out in this fashion:

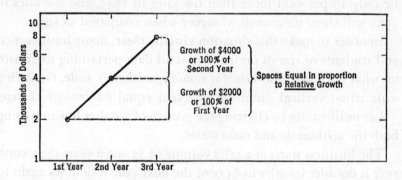

FIG. 2. EQUAL RATE OF GROWTH — RATIO SCALE

Sales of a hypothetical business organization showing constant *rate* of growth. *Ratio scale.*

[242]

Notice that on a ratio scale the numbers on the vertical scale represent equidistant percentage values, and come closer and closer together, in a way that interposes the same vertical distance between 4 and 8 as between 2 and 4 (because 8 bears the same relation to 4 that 4 bears to 2).

A straight line plotted on a ratio scale means that the *rate* of growth is constant. (Such a state of affairs, of course, never exists for long in any real situation.)

When the *rate* of growth declines as the business or the organism gets older, this decline is represented on a ratio scale by a bending-over in the line.

Thus, if the business cited here grew from $2,000 in its first year to $4,000 in its second year, and then grew an equal *amount* — from $4,000 to $6,000 — from its second to third year, these facts would be shown on *ratio* scale as follows:

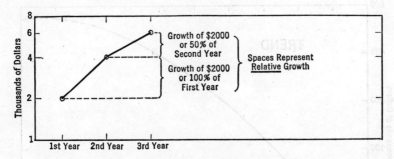

FIG. 3. EQUAL AMOUNT OF GROWTH — RATIO SCALE

Sales of a hypothetical business organization showing constant *amount* of growth. *Ratio scale.*

On the other hand, using the arithmetic scale, the line would continue from the second to the third year at the same slope as from the first year to the second, giving no visual suggestion that the rate of growth was declining. The same figures plotted on the arithmetic scale would look like this:

[243]

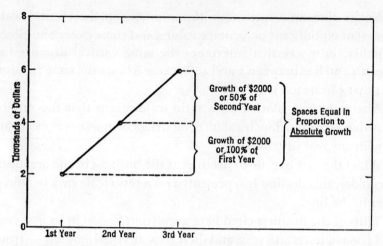

FIG. 4. EQUAL AMOUNTS OF GROWTH — ARITHMETIC SCALE

Sales of a hypothetical business organization showing constant *amount* of growth. *Arithmetic scale.*

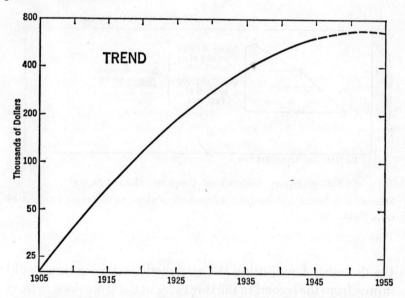

FIG. 5. TREND OF A HYPOTHETICAL BUSINESS ORGANIZATION

Data 1905–1945, with a projection to 1955. The projection is based on the assumption of a continuation in the constant decline of the rate of growth, as discussed in Chapter 1. *Ratio scale.*

[244]

Further to compare the difference between arithmetic and ratio scales, the sales of the hypothetical business discussed in Chapter 1 are plotted on a ratio scale in Fig. 5 on the preceding page.

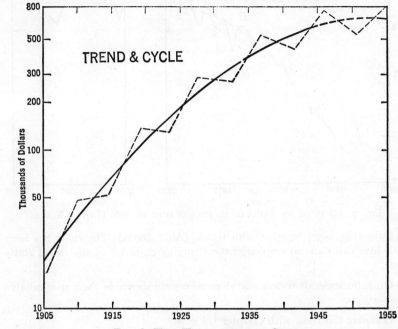

FIG. 6. THE TREND AND THE CYCLE

Trend of a hypothetical business organization, as shown in Fig. 5, with a regular cycle of 20 per cent amplitude superimposed. *Ratio scale.* Note that when one uses ratio scale, the wave has equal absolute magnitude throughout.

One advantage of such a plotting is that it shows directly the falling off in the rate of growth, and permits making a visual or freehand projection into the future that is much more likely to be fulfilled than any similar projecting of a chart on the arithmetic scale.

Ratio scales are usually labeled as such. If not, they can be recognized from the fact that the numbers on the scale come closer and closer together as they grow larger, as in Fig. 2 and Fig. 3 above; or else, for equal intervals, the numbers get proportionately larger and larger, as in Fig. 5.

[245]

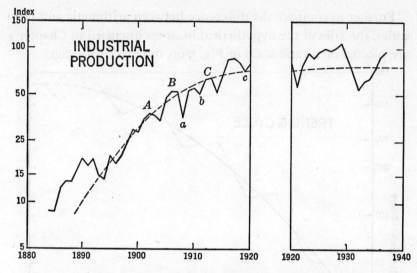

FIG. 7. GROWTH OF INDUSTRIAL PRODUCTION IN THE UNITED STATES

Data 1884–1937, together with trend. (After Davis.) The chart has been split into two parts to emphasize the changing character of the trend. *Ratio scale.*

On ratio scale all booms and depressions are shown in their true relative proportions.

Compare this chart with Chapter 1, Fig. 3.

The interval from one number — let us say 1 — on the vertical scale of a ratio chart to the number ten times higher, in this instance 10, is called a " cycle." The same distance is used to represent the next tenfold growth, from 10 to 100, and so on. In reading a curve plotted on ratio scale, one should always look at the vertical scale to see how many cycles are involved.

So that the reader may make additional comparisons of data charted on ratio and on arithmetic scales, the data of the rest of the charts in Chapter 1 have been plotted on ratio scales, and are given in Figs. 6, 7, and 8.

All the charts in Chapters III and IV and many of the charts in the rest of the book are plotted on ratio scale.

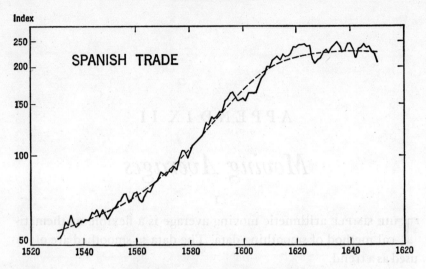

FIG. 8. INDEX OF SPANISH TRADE

Data 1530–1650, (After Davis and Hamilton), together with trend. *Ratio scale.*

Compare this chart with Chapter 1, Fig. 4.

APPENDIX II

Moving Averages

I

THE SIMPLE arithmetic moving average is a flexible mathematical method of smoothing data. The data so smoothed are often used as a trend.

Moving averages may be of any number of terms desired. The process of computing a simple arithmetic moving average is illustrated in the following table:

COMPUTATION OF A 3-YEAR MOVING AVERAGE OF AN INDEX OF
WHOLESALE PRICES, 1931–1939

(A) Year	(B) Index	(C) 3-year moving total of index, centered	(D) 3-year moving average of index, centered. (The data in Col. C ÷ 3)
1931	73		
1932	65	204	68
1933	66	206	69
1934	75	221	74
1935	80	236	79
1936	81	247	82
1937	86	246	82
1938	79	242	81
1939	77		

The first average in Column D is $\dfrac{73 + 65 + 66}{3} = 68$. The sec-

ond average is $\dfrac{65 + 66 + 75}{3} = 69$. And so on.

The moving average figure is posted and plotted against the middle of the group of items being averaged " for the same reason that figures referring to a whole period are customarily plotted on a chart in the middle of the appropriate spaces," as Croxton and Cowden explain.

A 5-year moving average would be computed the same way, using

five terms instead of three. Thus: $\dfrac{73 + 65 + 66 + 75 + 80}{5} = 72$.

And $\dfrac{65 + 66 + 75 + 80 + 81}{5} = 73$.

In using an even number of terms it is impossible to get an exact centering. It is therefore usual to compute, in addition, a 2-year moving average of the result. This procedure is shown in the table on the following page.

COMPUTATION OF A 4-YEAR MOVING AVERAGE OF AN INDEX OF
WHOLESALE PRICES IN THE U. S. A. 1931–1939:

(A)	(B)	(C)	(D)	(E)	(F)
Year	Index	4-year moving total of index, centered	4-year moving average centered. (The data in Col. C ÷ 4)	2-year moving total of the 4-year moving average.	2-year moving average of the 4-year moving average. (The data in Col. E ÷ 2)
1931	73				
1932	65				
		279	70		
1933	66			142	71
		286	72		
1934	75			148	74
		302	76		
1935	80			156	78
		322	80		
1936	81			162	81
		326	82		
1937	86			163	81
		323	81		
1938	79				
1939	77				

This method of computation permits of exact centering.

In practice it is usual to take 2-year moving totals of the 4-year moving totals, center them, and divide by eight.

The following chart tells what happens to a regular cycle when the curve of which it is a component is smoothed by moving averages:

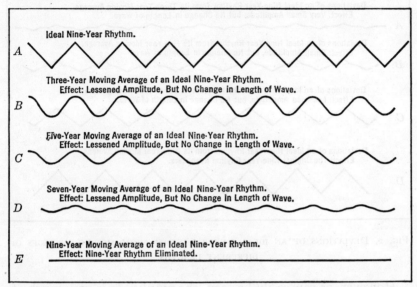

Ideal Nine-Year Rhythm.

A

Three-Year Moving Average of an Ideal Nine-Year Rhythm.
Effect: Lessened Amplitude, But No Change in Length of Wave.

B

Five-Year Moving Average of an Ideal Nine-Year Rhythm.
Effect: Lessened Amplitude, But No Change in Length of Wave.

C

Seven-Year Moving Average of an Ideal Nine-Year Rhythm.
Effect: Lessened Amplitude, But No Change in Length of Wave.

D

Nine-Year Moving Average of an Ideal Nine-Year Rhythm.
Effect: Nine-Year Rhythm Eliminated.

E

Fig. 1. Effect of moving average, of different lengths upon an ideal 9-year rhythm

It is evident that a moving average has no effect on the *period* or length of the rhythm in the series being averaged. But it does have an effect upon the *amplitude* of the waves.

One may generalize by saying that any moving average with a length less than the period of a rhythm diminishes the amplitude of the rhythm. The more nearly the length of the moving average approached the period of the rhythm, the more nearly it removes it. When the length of the moving average equals the period of the rhythm it completely removes it.

On the other hand, when one computes the deviations of a curve evidencing a rhythm from a moving average of that curve, the length of the rhythm is unaffected, regardless of the length of the moving average.

[251]

This fact is illustrated in Fig. 2.

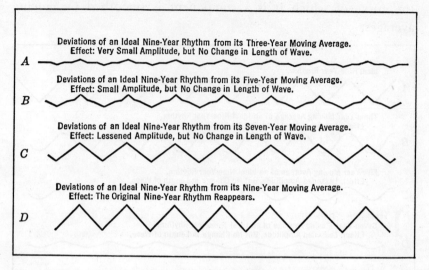

Deviations of an Ideal Nine-Year Rhythm from its Three-Year Moving Average.
Effect: Very Small Amplitude, but No Change in Length of Wave.

A

Deviations of an Ideal Nine-Year Rhythm from its Five-Year Moving Average.
Effect: Small Amplitude, but No Change in Length of Wave.

B

Deviations of an Ideal Nine-Year Rhythm from its Seven-Year Moving Average.
Effect: Lessened Amplitude, but No Change in Length of Wave.

C

Deviations of an Ideal Nine-Year Rhythm from its Nine-Year Moving Average.
Effect: The Original Nine-Year Rhythm Reappears.

D

FIG. 2. DEVIATIONS OF AN IDEAL 9-YEAR RHYTHM FROM MOVING AVERAGES OF
DIFFERENT LENGTHS

However, as can easily be seen, the amplitude is very much affected by the length of the moving average used.

APPENDIX III

The Section Moving Average

THE SECTION moving average, like the simple moving average described in Appendix II, is a mathematical device for removing irregularities in time series.

Unlike the moving average, however, it does not average consecutive terms or figures of a series. What it does do is to average two or more consecutive sections or cycles.

For example, imagine a series of figures representing the monthly sales for ten years of some business with a seasonal pattern (such as the ice-cream business). In the case selected, the cycle, being seasonal, is twelve months in length. The behavior for each year is influenced by its seasonal pattern, plus accidental distortions, cycles of other than 12 months in length, and trend.

Suppose we wish to calculate a three 12-month section moving average of these figures. We take the first, second, and third Januarys and average them; the first, second, and third Februarys and average them; and so on, month by month, until we have averaged all the months of the first three years. This average of the first three 12-month sections is the first section of the three 12-month section moving average. It is plotted in the second year.

Next we average the second, third, and fourth Januarys, the second, third, and fourth Februarys, and so on, until we have averaged the values for all months in the second, third, and fourth years. This gives us our second section of the three 12-month section moving average. We plot these values in the middle of the span being averaged, namely, the third year.

We proceed in this way until each possible consecutive group of three years has been averaged.

The effect of such a series of calculations is to minimize any of the month-to-month irregularities in much the same way that a 3-month moving average would minimize them. That is, from the standpoint of accidental variations from the true cycle, it is unimportant whether or not we smooth the curve by averaging three consecutive numbers or by averaging three numbers twelve figures apart. In either case, minus distortions will tend to offset plus distortions, and accidental variations of one sort or another will tend to be spread over three months rather than be concentrated in the month in which they occur.

This technique is frequently used to reveal and determine a seasonal variation that changes over a course of time. Suppose, for example, that the seasonal variations have decreased percentage-wise with the increased size of the business. Then any average seasonal variation determined for the entire life of the business will fail to express the variation that took place in the earlier years, and will exceed the variation now present in the business figures. A section moving average will enable one to compute it on a varying instead of a fixed basis.

This technique serves also as a powerful tool in connection with cycle analysis.

First it is useful as a smoothing technique.

Second, it is useful because — even if the length chosen for the section moving average is different from the length of the cycle — this fact has no influence upon the length of the cycle disclosed in the resultant. Thus, in the example chosen above, if we had chopped all series of figures into sections thirteen months long, averaging the first January with the second February and the third March, and so on, the cycle disclosed by this three 13-month section

[254]

moving average would still show a 12-month period. Likewise, if we had chopped the curves into 11-month sections, the resultant pattern would not have been eleven months in length, but would have been twelve months as it was in the original series. There would, however, in these instances have been a certain dampening of the amplitude of the cycle.

We may generalize by saying that the length of the section moving average has no effect upon the *length* of any real cycle present in the original data, but that, as the length of the section moving average departs from the true length of the cycle, the *amplitude* of the cycle in the resultant average becomes less, until eventually it disappears entirely.

The third useful characteristic of the section moving average is the fact that when a series is simultaneously influenced by two rhythmic forces, and is long enough, a section moving average will completely eliminate either rhythm, no matter how close the length of rhythms involved, leaving the other rhythm undisturbed.

For example, suppose a series simultaneously influenced by two regular cyclic forces, one of eleven months in length and the other of twelve months. By taking an 11-month section moving average of enough terms, the 12-month wave will vanish, leaving the 11-month wave undisturbed. Similarly, a 12-month section moving average of enough terms will eliminate the 11-month wave.